FAVORITE MOVIES OF THE 90s

Volume 1   Ed. Jürgen Müller

VOLUME 2

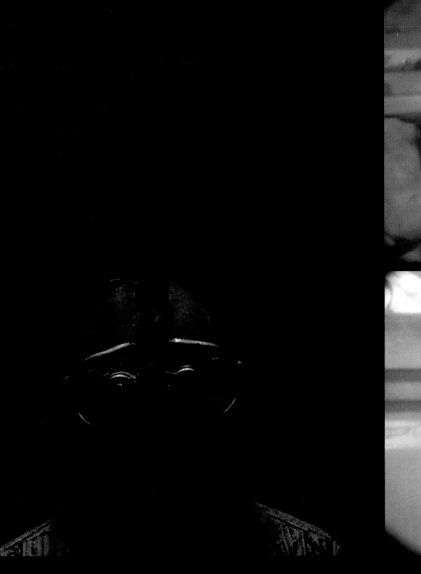

20 CAMERA SHOTS
FOR 6 SECONDS OF FILM
Observations on Cinema of the '90s

Movies of the '90s contain imperceptible images. Shots can be accelerated so that they fall below the perception threshold. An example of such acceleration occurs at the end of Jonathan Demme's *The Silence of the Lambs* (1991, p. 34), in what is perhaps the shortest showdown in cinematic history. The exchange of fire between the FBI agent Clarice Starling and the mass-murderer Buffalo Bill takes no more than six seconds, even though it comprises 20 camera shots. It seems odd to devote only six seconds to the most exciting part of a two-hour movie, but Demme allows the climax to implode in the true sense of the word and uses extremely powerful visual images.

The director skillfully and expertly creates the build-up to the showdown: After a tense parallel montage, at the end of which we expect the murderer to be caught, it is not the FBI task force that is standing at his door

but Clarice on her own. She doesn't know it, but she has found Buffalo Bill. Before she realizes who it is standing in front of her, he is able to take refuge in his cellar, where he is holding his latest victim captive. The murderer switches off the light when the FBI agent follows him into the cellar. While her adversary watches, Clarice gropes uncertainly in the dark. Throughout this scene, the audience sees through Buffalo Bill's eyes, his night-vision device turning everything a ghostly green. During the chase, Clarice's irregular, panic-stricken breathing is all that can be heard. Only when the young agent hears the pistol being cocked behind her is she able to guess the murderer's position. At the speed of light, she spins round and the gunfight begins. In the silence, the cocking of the gun sounds like a thunderclap, as though we are hearing it through Clarice's ears – for in the darkness she has become acutely sensitive to even the tiniest of sounds.

When we in turn find ourselves in absolute darkness, we not only hear through the ears of the FBI agent, but also see through her eyes.

The next shot shows the flash from Bill's revolver, which is reflected in the lenses of his night-vision device. The explosion from the gun looks like an abstract painting, and the fight in fact develops into a symbolic duel. Whereas at first the murderer had the advantage in the darkness, the situation changes when the shooting match begins, as the adversaries dazzle each other when shots are exchanged. The flash from the gunshot allows the camera to show the murderer, who has been hit. This is then followed by a black screen, which lasts longer than the view of the people involved. Again we see a shot being fired, then another black screen. Now the audience can make out Clarice taking aim, but she is blinded by the shot fired from Bill's pistol. A black screen, and renewed gunfire. The FBI agent shoots with her eyes shut. Another gunshot. Again the audience sees Clarice shooting. A black screen. Bill has been hit a second time. A black screen. The murderer is hit again, and we see the look of agony on his face. A black screen. One shot has hit a window blind, loosening it. The daylight penetrating the cellar reveals a steel helmet and an American flag. The camera then cuts back to the cellar and there, lying on the floor, we see the fatally wounded murderer. With his night-vision device covering his eyes, he looks like a dead insect.

Cinema, Television, Video, and DVD

In the cinema, our perception of this sequence is reduced to the knowledge that, after the FBI agent has fired her shots, the murderer lies dead on the floor. It is only in the last few images of this sequence that we return to daylight and viewing at normal speed, whereas what we have just witnessed is for the most part below the perception threshold. It is not until Clarice loads her weapon that it becomes clear what we must have seen: She has actually used up all her ammunition of six cartridges. Although we haven't been able to perceive these six shots consciously, the final images make it possible to come to this conclusion. While the shots are being exchanged, the camera angle changes constantly; we see things alternately through the eyes of the murderer and of the FBI agent. The sequence described here is barely noticeable in the cinema. To see it at all, you really need to be able to break the picture sequence down into stills using new digital playback technologies.

Clearly, technical developments in image production and reproduction during the '90s opened up completely new possibilities. The well-established video recorder, and then DVD, offered the opportunity of a viewing experience

comparable to the CD player before them. These media allowed you to gain expert knowledge, whether you collected the films of a particular director or actor, or were interested in a particular genre.

This new accessibility of the medium has grown exponentially with the possibilities now presented by Internet downloads and streaming. The roots of their aesthetic acceptance, and with it the integration into cinematic discourse, dates back to the '90s.

Martin Scorsese is thoroughly optimistic, seeing in this technology the opportunity for engendering a new enthusiasm for cinema. In a short article called "The Second Screen," he highlighted the advantages of new technology. There is now no problem showing movies that are hardly known anymore but deserve to be studied, and it is finally possible to compare film scenes directly. He also welcomes the wider distribution it has brought for some of his own movies, which now reach a larger audience through DVD.

Digital recording, like the VCR before it, also enables formal and aesthetic analysis by creating stills. You can study the content and composition of a shot or look at a film sequence in the same way as you can listen again and again to a virtuoso performance of a passage of music, just for the sheer pleasure of it. The growth in the numbers of Hong Kong movie fans in the '90s was in no small part due to the fact that video made it possible to appreciate their technical brilliance. Of course, many of these

films were not shown in the cinema; we could view them only on video right from the start.

When a director like David Fincher asked that his movies be watched not once but four or five times, video made this easy for the viewer. Analog video and digital media like DVD can never replace the cinema, of course, but they do now offer us different forms of perception. Lavish Hollywood productions are created with the aim of making them suitable not only for the one-off cinema experience, but also for repeated viewing on DVD. The more details intentionally concealed in a film, the more fun you will have in repeated viewings.

In that respect, most films nowadays have three premieres. First they appear in the cinema, then they are brought out on DVD –possibly after legal or illegal downloading online – and finally they are shown on one of the many television channels. It is doubtful that any development of the last few decades has had a greater influence on filmmaking than DVD and its predecessor, videotape. As their use has become more widespread since the '90s, film and television have come closer together. DVD has become the mediating element between the two – and television is certainly no longer second best. *Star Trek* (from 1979), *The X-Files* (1998), *Mission: Impossible* (1996, p. 344), and *The Fugitive* (1993, p. 188) are all films for the cinema developed from famous television series. The same was true of David Lynch's cult series *Twin Peaks* (1989–91), which

the director subsequently used as the basis for a movie (1992, p. 98). The barriers between the two media are no longer strong. Helen Hunt and George Clooney were popular TV actors long before they became celebrated Hollywood stars, and several of today's prominent directors made music videos or worked for television before they were able to make a full-length feature film.

Seeing and Hearing

Technical developments also show how natural the connection between television and the movies is today. Televisions are now made with a screen format (16:9) that is closer to the wide-screen format of the cinema. Larger and larger televisions are being produced and it is now a long time since the cinema screen was the only way of presenting a film. Dolby surround-sound systems mean that even at home, the sound and music of a film can be experienced spatially. It is remarkable how far watching TV has been transformed through developments in technology. DVD is like a kind of home movie, and even better is the latest innovation: Blu-ray discs.

It must be acknowledged that such technical progress had its beginnings in cinemas. There too it was digital sound quality, particularly in the multiplex cinemas, that opened up a new cinematic age. You need think only

of Steven Spielberg's war movie *Saving Private Ryan* (1998, p. 588), winner of so many Oscars, which in the first 15 minutes gave us a sort of phenomenology of the sounds of war. We can hear how the bullets ricochet off metal, how they hiss into the water or whistle past the soldiers' ears. While the film material at the beginning of *Saving Private Ryan* looks grainy and is reminiscent of the newsreels of the 1940s, the sound is extremely varied. It is as though the images portraying historical events gain authenticity through the soundtrack. We even experience Captain Miller's deafness, when, overcome with horror at the many dead, for a moment he no longer hears any external noises. It has long been natural for the audience to see through the eyes of one of the characters in a movie and to interpret a panning shot as the subjective view of a person. But since the '90s, we can even hear through the ears of a character in a film. The great success Spielberg enjoyed with *Jurassic Park* (1993, p. 132) was also due to the convincing use of sound, as we stand in the middle of a stampeding herd of small dinosaurs, or in the unforgettable scene in which a jeep is pursued by a Tyrannosaurus Rex whose powerful steps seem to make the whole cinema shake.

In the movies of the '90s, it is impossible to overestimate the importance of sound in making the images so convincing. David Fincher produced a winner in this regard with *Alien³* (1992). In the most gruesome scene of the film, a postmortem has to be carried out on a young girl, as no one knows whether there is an alien in her body. We see the instruments that are

needed to carry out the procedure. We don't see the actual postmortem itself, but we do hear the child's rib cage being opened up. The scene is almost unbearable and is one of the coldest "images" that modern cinema has produced. Movie scenes of this sort illustrate the power sound can exert and that it can be just as effective in its own right as the actual images of a film.

All the examples mentioned concern the reproduction technique of cinema and television as creators of illusion. But to what extent did video and then DVD also change the aesthetics of film in the '90s? The example cited above from *The Silence of the Lambs* shows the extreme extent to which images can be accelerated. This becomes clearer when we think, for example, of the influence of music videos, which are largely characterized by brief shots and frequent cuts. Pictures are shown for only fractions of seconds, so that they are barely perceptible. Similarly, in the battle scene at the beginning of Ridley Scott's *Gladiator* (2000, p. 702), the cuts come so quickly that we get no intimation of the significance of a fragment of a second that decides between life and death. At the same time, we are aware of the sudden burst of speed in the sequence. First the legionaries are making meticulous preparations for the battle. Then on the command to attack, the movie speeds up and takes us to the heart of the battle, where nothing is thought out in advance, and everything happens intuitively. Such scenes are an assault and a strain on the senses in equal measure. The viewer is all eyes, his intellect suspended.

Remake?

Reproduction on video or DVD has long been viewed as the enemy of the cinema, as though it would corrupt the pure science of film. In an ironic twist, there is an echo of this criticism even in a successful 1990s film. Nora Ephron's *You've Got Mail* (1998, p. 554) contains the caricature of an art critic who claims in a TV interview that, from a technological point of view, our world is out of kilter. Just think of the video recorder, he says: The idea of a video recorder is that you can record a TV program if you're going out, but to his mind, the fact that you're going out shows that you don't want to watch the TV program. As far as he is concerned, the only medium that can be justified is the radio. With his self-absorbed monologue, the critic tries to convince us that television and video are equally absurd. He maintains that both should be abolished. It becomes clear how serious his assessment is, however, when he casually asks his girlfriend whether she is actually recording the interview. Ephron's film – an updated version of Ernst Lubitsch's classic *The Shop Around the Corner* (1940) – may be dismissed as a romantic comedy, but even so the film poses the important question of the authenticity of the media. Can a love letter be taken seriously when it is sent as an e-mail? Do new technological means of communication make us lose our true personality? Are the contents only credible when they are written on paper?

In a crucial scene, the heroine of the film clutches her copy of Jane Austen's *Pride and Prejudice*, as though her identity might be concealed in this book. Thus the film not only tells a love story, but also constantly questions our relationship with the media. These are not just electronic devices that transmit or record specific information, and they are not neutral records of a technical nature. Rather, they are part of our identity, because we are not just what we stand for, but also what we like, read, listen to, and watch.

Quotation and Hollywood Films

It's often said that the cinema of the 1990s is allusive. DVDs are clearly important here too, as they support this trend. But others feel that the idea of allusive cinema is a figment of some critics' imagination. These critics are selective when choosing movies to prove their hypothesis. People who claim that the cinema of the 1990s is postmodern and allusive cite Francis Ford Coppola's *Dracula* (1992), but not Steven Spielberg's *Schindler's List* (1993, p. 162). Whereas the first movie can be related to many precursors and does actually represent a museum of film history, the second has to be seen in relation to real events of the past. We can also argue against the hypothesis of allusive cinema by saying that there have always been directors who have frequently exhibited their knowledge of cinematic history. It was not only in the 1990s that Brian De Palma's works made reference to earlier films; they had been doing so for years. We need think only of the end of *The Untouchables* (1987), when the American director alludes to the famous scene from Eisenstein's *Battleship Potemkin* (1925), in which a baby carriage clatters down a steep flight of steps. He quotes again, but less obviously, in *Mission: Impossible* (1995, p. 344), a film which makes reference to *The Lady From Shanghai* (1948) and represents a homage to its creator, Orson Welles. De Palma's work shows that the desire to quote is in no way the exclusive preserve of this decade.

Whatever the objections to this idea of the cinema of quotation, it is true that the audience changed in the 1990s. The constant mass-media distribution of films means that there are more viewers who can recognize quotes and therefore know how to appreciate films. It is now much more a matter of course for films to be part of the cultural common knowledge. Without any jury having to rule on it, everybody knows today that *Psycho* (1960), *Ben Hur* (1959), and *Casablanca* (1942) belong to the canon of classic films on which film history is based and from which it continues to develop. In other words, for particular genres, these films set standards that demand quality and originality. Anyone who emphasizes the desire to quote in present-day cinema is really only saying that the history of film is not over, but has always represented a starting point and point of reference for filmmakers.

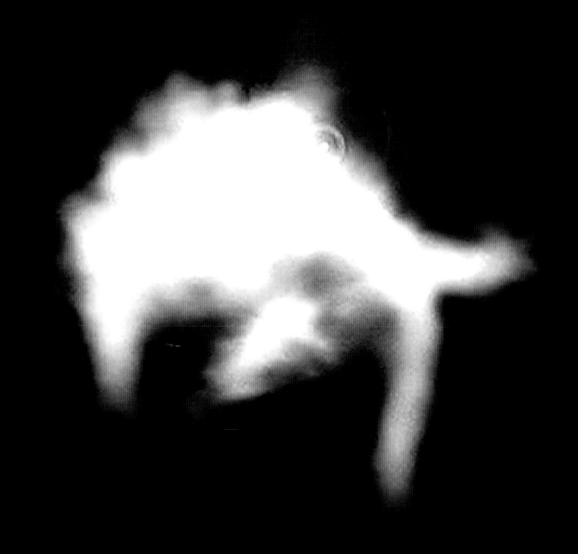

Film and Personal Reflection

Allusive cinema is a rather vague, general term for a highly creative association with originals, because quotes come in various forms: as remakes, as parodies, or as homage. Usually they are allusions used by a director to express his admiration for a particular earlier film or film sequence. Such allusions can be clear, or less obvious. A master of the subtle allusion is the American director Tim Burton. His movie *Edward Scissorhands* (1990) begins with a young girl asking her grandmother where snow comes from. This paves the way for an allegorical trip through the history of film. When the camera leaves the room, we are led over the snow-covered houses of a suburb, until the view rises to a dark castle, in which a light burns. This is an allusion to Orson Welles's *Citizen Kane* (1941): the castle with the lit window recalls Charles Foster Kane's huge mansion, Xanadu, and the snow that falls over the artificial-looking suburb harks back to the glass snow globe that falls from the hand of the dying tycoon. Burton's film quotations attest to his admiration for Welles, who even appears as a character in his film *Ed Wood* (1994, p. 214). With his reference to the snow globe, he is also using one of the best cinematic metaphors: expressing in equal measure both childlike

innocence and astonishment at the magic of the miniature world. Beyond the glass globe, you look toward a world of your own, dappled with dancing snowflakes, which comes to life in your imagination.

Burton's allusions underline the quality of Orson Welles's classics and make it possible to experience film history visually. The quotes in *Edward Scissorhands* are difficult to recognize precisely because they fit the new context so well. The better a quote is adapted to the new context, the more likely that it will be noticed only by a devotee of the original movie.

Danny Boyle is much more direct with his quotes in his film *Trainspotting* (1996, p. 372). At an important point in the action, he refers to a famous earlier film. At a weekend disco, two boys are talking about their girlfriends. The music is so loud that we cannot hear what they are saying, but have to read subtitles, as in a silent film. The camera approaches the two in a single movement and, in the style of Pop Art, we recognize words such as "Vellozet" or "Synthomon" written on the walls, words which refer back to drinks from the Korova milk bar in Stanley Kubrick's *A Clockwork Orange* (1971). Whereas in his movie Kubrick lets his camera focus on the face of the principal actor and then pans out, in Doyle's *Trainspotting* the camera gradually zooms in on the two people – an almost direct quote, in which only one element is reversed. This English director's film continues to allude to famous earlier films. The following sequence shows the principal actor of *Trainspotting*, arms folded, standing in front of a poster portraying Robert De Niro as Travis Bickle in the

film *Taxi Driver* (1976), shooting with two pistols at once. It is not only the poster, but also even the defiant pose with the folded arms that recall Robert De Niro's interpretation of the role. A great many more allusions could be mentioned. In retrospect, the off-screen monologue at the start of the film seems to be a clear parallel with the opening monologue from *A Clockwork Orange*. The film also alludes to the record cover of the Beatles' *Abbey Road* LP, and there are shots that bring to mind Richard Lester's Beatles films. This is not merely an expression of Doyle's admiration for the films in question, for these references to Swinging London give added meaning to the film. They tell of the end of a particular form of pop culture that is being replaced by techno. What has changed is youth culture, which is defined by saying no. Unlike Tim Burton, the English director produces his allusions so that they are clearly recognizable, almost to the point of being literal re-enactments.

Quotations do not, however, necessarily have to refer to what are regarded as great film classics. Take the *Scream* tetralogy (1996, 1997, 1999, 2011), which contains constant allusions to successful horror films such as *Nightmare on Elm Street* (from 1984) or *Halloween* (from 1978). What links the audience and the film characters in this way is detailed knowledge, facilitated in the first place by video, of these horror thrillers. The attraction of *Scream* (1996, p. 394) and its sequels lies precisely in the fact that games are constantly being played with the audience's sense of anticipation. We think we know how the plot will develop, and, as a result, we are fooled time and again, because nothing turns out quite as expected. In the 1990s, cinematic self-reflection is no longer the exclusive prerogative of the *auteur* film, but a component part of mainstream cinema.

Non-linear Narration

Along with speeding up pictures and the desire to quote, the third formal feature of '90s movies was the exploration of non-linear narrative. Now practically a given of mainstream cinema, the radical break with traditional narrative forms in film was seen as sensational. The directors happiest to experiment in this respect were Quentin Tarantino and Steven Soderbergh. But while Tarantino was more interested in the unexpected features of episodic narrative and the resultant relationship of the contents, Soderbergh used this narrative device to develop a particularly eloquent movie slang. What links both directors is that in their films they used ambitious sets with front and back lighting that could not be understood immediately, but became comprehensible only during the course of the movie. The significance of the individual film image no longer arose, as in linear narrative, from any direct connection, but became apparent only when all the elements were brought together. The viewer was left with the task of reconstructing the story.

When, in Soderbergh's *The Limey* (1999, p. 648), one of the first shots in the film shows the principal actor flying from England to America, we initially believe he is on his way to investigate the death of his daughter. By the end of the movie, when we see the same picture again, it has become clear that the story has for the most part taken place in the memory of the protagonist. In fact, the first picture was the last, but this in no way detracts from the suspense of the film. It is more the case that it is extremely logical, because, as a result of this narrative device, the theme now becomes the loneliness of this man who is left with only the images in his memory to cherish. *Out of Sight* (1998, p. 542) by the same director and David Fincher's *Fight Club* (1999, p. 612) are structured in a similarly artificial way.

There is no doubt that the most famous example from the 1990s in the art of non-linear narrative is Quentin Tarantino's *Pulp Fiction* (1994, p. 234), the movie that many saw as the greatest cult film of that decade. It is remarkable in many respects, the first being its narrative form. The episodic representation method makes it difficult for the audience to differentiate between principal and secondary characters in any traditional sense. All the stories revolve around the gangster boss, Marsellus Wallace. So the film starts with the two killers, Jules and Vincent, who are doing a job for Marsellus, dealing with cheating business partners. An unpredictable story now develops, full of suspicion, that will ultimately cost one of the two killers his life. Pulp Fiction, which one critic described as "a joy-

ride through film history," contains numerous cinematic allusions, and its director may regard it as a virtuoso example of such allusive cinema, but it is not really the exceptional feature of the movie. It is much more as though Tarantino wanted to make his films like a treacherous labyrinth, a place with no way out. Even his use of allusion serves more to confuse than to elucidate. Every conceivable form of allusion is used in his film. An obvious example is the ominous briefcase that glows when opened. This prop recalls Robert Aldrich's film *Kiss Me Deadly* (1955), which used the same motif as early as 1955. We never discover what is actually in the case, but know only what we hear when it is talked about, or see the ominous light shining from inside it.

Even the casting of the parts seems to have been inspired by cinematic history. In a dance scene with Uma Thurman, John Travolta recalls his past roles, reminding us of his success with *Saturday Night Fever* (1977); Christopher Walken plays a Vietnam War veteran when he gives the young Butch his father's watch, thereby alluding to his role in the *The Deer Hunter* (1978); and Bruce Willis, familiar to many as the amoral hero of numerous action movies, plays a boxer with character who ultimately remains incorruptible. Such allusions and identification of the actors with their roles make any reality outside of the film disappear.

In the Labyrinth of Images

The time structure of the movie is even more radical. After Vincent Vega has been shot dead, he reappears in a subsequent scene. Of course, this is only possible because Tarantino muddies the chronology of his story. The film does not begin with the earliest scene chronologically, but jumps ahead, without the viewer being aware. This move is a stroke of genius, because it can highlight something that is a matter of principle. Movies do not take place as a sequence starting from the present. They have a different sense of time, operating in a "future perfect" tense. With Pulp Fiction, we find ourselves in a time warp that we can no longer leave. The killer, Vincent Vega, is shot dead when he is guarding the apartment of the boxer, Butch, who has betrayed their joint boss, Marsellus. When Vega reappears in the next but one scene, it can only be a flashback. The story has gone back to the beginning and we find out the macabre events that happened at the end of Jules and Vincent's first job. Even if the audience can make out a logical connection between the individual episodes, it becomes clear during the film that even more things could have happened in the course of events that are initially assumed to represent the time line. Time seems infinitely divisible and another incident can always be revealed as having taken place between the episodes already known to the audience. It is like a person who rambles on in conversation, and always finds new pegs for more stories. In this anecdotal narrative device, the chronology of the episodes, which can be reconstructed only in retrospect, occurs in the background. Instead, events both comical and macabre keep the viewer in suspense and make any questions about a narrative logic subordinate. The attraction of such a narrative device lies in solving the riddle, which impels the viewer into a pictorial labyrinth. We have the impression of being led through different genres, almost like an ironic allusion to channel surfing on evening television.

Dangerous Fictions

There are many more buzz words that we could have chosen apart from those discussed, and the idea of "genre" is a case in point. Whereas at the beginning of the decade you might have had the impression that more and more films were mixing the genres in a new and interesting way, at the end of the decade, with the disaster movie *Titanic* (1997, p. 482) and war movie *Saving Private Ryan* (1998, p. 588), single-varietal genre films of apparently long-outmoded types came back into being.

Another important trend, which became increasingly apparent over the decade, was the growth in the use of digital images. *Toy Story* (1995, p. 296)

was the first totally computer-generated full-length feature film. Whole lavish historic sets are now simulated using computers, like the Colosseum in Ridley Scott's *Gladiator* or the luxury liner surging through the sea in James Cameron's *Titanic*. The prime example of this was George Lucas's *Star Wars: Episode 1 – The Phantom Menace* (1999, p. 672), with its sensational stunts. As predicted at the time, these techniques came to predominate in the action film.

The buzz words of acceleration, allusive cinema, and non-linear narrative represent three paradigms that characterize, not cinema as a whole admittedly, but the important films of the 1990s. These are linked with the assertion that video or DVD is a prerequisite for all three phenomena. Acceleration throws up the question of the relationship between time and perception; allusions link the past with the present; and finally, non-linear narrative is a sort of mind game, which makes it clear that television and cinema do not portray an image of reality, but have been re-creating it for years. Thus some films explained this epistemological question at the end of the 1990s by means of a pessimistic perspective. Consider Peter Weir's media satire *The Truman Show* (1998, p. 526), or Terry Gilliam's *Twelve Monkeys* (1995, p. 304), David Cronenberg's *eXistenZ* (1999), and Larry and Andy Wachowski's *The Matrix* (1999, p. 594). All these films unsettle the viewer and ask whether people are in fact deceived about the real character of the world. The relativity of perception, the reporting of events through the media, and the displacement of the reality of this world com-

bine to become the theme. It may be that the media give us the illusion of reality, that we only ever encounter it vicariously through duplicates, or a gigantic conspiracy is in progress. Such movies bear witness to the uneasiness with which we left one millennium and entered the next. The extent to which such a feeling of unease and the concomitant apocalyptic ideas were due to the pessimism typical of the end of an era remains to be seen. It should be stressed however, that '90s cinema itself expressed this malaise. Film, television, and video are everywhere in the modern world. The more time we spend in front of movie theater and television screens, the more critically we must examine the possibilities and limits of these media. In so doing, we will be forced to the conclusion that there will probably never be a natural or appropriate use of media, even if we knew what such a thing was. Voluntarily limiting oneself, say to only one movie a week? One movie a day might be more realistic. Everyone knows that good films are addictive. In this respect, the situation is no better for cinema than it is for the older media like the radio or the book. Criticism of the media has been around since before the advent of television. Centuries ago, reading too many novels led a Spaniard by the name of Don Quixote to do battle with windmills and think that he was a knight. A classic case of losing your grip on reality because of media consumption. In spite of any illusions, we can certainly neither dispute the good intentions of this sad-faced knight nor fail to admit that he experienced a thing or two.   Jürgen Müller

CAPE FEAR

1991 – USA – 128 MIN. – THRILLER, REMAKE
DIRECTOR MARTIN SCORSESE (*1942)
SCREENPLAY WESLEY STRICK, based on the script of the same name by JAMES R. WEBB
and the novel THE EXECUTIONERS by JOHN D. MACDONALD
DIRECTOR OF PHOTOGRAPHY FREDDIE FRANCIS EDITING THELMA SCHOONMAKER
MUSIC BERNARD HERRMANN, adapted and arranged by ELMER BERNSTEIN
PRODUCTION BARBARA DE FINA FOR AMBLIN ENTERTAINMENT, CAPPA FILMS,
TRIBECA PRODUCTIONS (for UNIVERSAL, GEFFEN)
STARRING ROBERT DE NIRO (Max Cady), NICK NOLTE (Sam Bowden), JESSICA LANGE
(Leigh Bowden), JULIETTE LEWIS (Danielle Bowden), JOE DON BAKER (Claude Kersek),
ROBERT MITCHUM (Lt. Elgart), GREGORY PECK (Lee Heller), MARTIN BALSAM (Judge),
ILLEANA DOUGLAS (Lori Davis), FRED DALTON THOMPSON (Tom Broadbent),
ZULLY MONTERO (Graciella)

"Justice is mine!"

Rapist Max Cady (Robert De Niro) has been waiting 14 years for this moment: after his release from prison, he can finally take revenge on his
lawyer. During his trial, his defense attorney Sam Bowden (Nick Nolte) was
so revolted by his crimes that he held back evidence that could have meant
a more lenient sentence for the brutal criminal. During his time in prison,
Cady has not only learned to read and write and studied American law, but
has also created for himself a bizarre fantasy world to which his tattooed
body bears witness. One of the many tattoos reads "The Lord shall revenge
me" and his back is emblazoned with a gigantic cross on which the scales
of "Truth" and "Justice" hang. Until now, the Bowdens, a small family on the
verge of breaking up, have managed to create their own hell, but now they
are threatened and tyrannized by Cady as well. Cady is particularly interested in Bowden's wife Leigh (Jessica Lange) and his underage daughter
Danielle (Juliette Lewis). In desperation, Bowden turns to smarmy private
detective Claude Kersek (Joe Don Baker) but rather than improving the
situation, this merely puts the lawyer himself beyond the law. Bowden realizes that he alone can save his family from a terrible fate. Martin Scorsese's
movie is a remake of J. Lee Thompson's thriller *Cape Fear* (1962), in which

Robert Mitchum played the part of Max Cady and Gregory Peck played the
panic-stricken lawyer. In the Scorsese version, both of these actors appear
in supporting roles.

The basic plot follows a Spielberg theme: as in *Jaws* (1974), a small
town idyll is suddenly destroyed with horrific violence for no apparent reason.
Unsurprisingly, Spielberg himself originally wanted to film *Cape Fear*.
Scorsese was working on the screenplay for *Schindler's List* (1993) at the
time, which was also originally an idea of Spielberg's. Eventually the directors decided to swap projects.

Early drafts of the screenplay ran into problems as the element that had
attracted Spielberg most wasn't right for Scorsese. Rather than taking an
innocent American family struck down out of the blue, Scorsese and scriptwriter Wesley Strick wrote and rewrote the screenplay, so that the faithful
husband became a notorious serial adulterer with an argumentative wife and
a rebellious daughter going through a difficult puberty.

From a moral point of view, the Bowdens' dishonesty gives Cady yet
another motive for his crazy revenge campaign. Some critics disapproved
of this and Scorsese's *Cape Fear* was even compared to Adrian Lyne's

"*Cape Fear* is the most story-driven film he (Scorsese) has ever made, as well as the one most rooted in genre." *Variety*

"It is De Niro – his body covered with tattoos and the tackiest wardrobe in the New South – who dominates the film with his lip-smacking, blackly comic, and terrifying portrayal of psychopathic self-righteousness."

Newsweek

Fatal Attraction (1988), a movie which illustrates the dire consequences of immorality in the family.

Cape Fear, however, is most definitely not an appeal for marital faithfulness. It is much closer to *Taxi Driver* (1975), Scorsese's early masterpiece, especially in its portrayal of extreme violence: like Cady, Travis Bickle (also played by Robert De Niro) sets off on a righteous crusade and the bigotry of those around him seems to justify his actions. However, whereas Travis gradually becomes divorced from reality, Max Cady is already living in his own world at the very beginning of the film. His Old Testament wrath gives him an almost supernatural strength, and transforms him into a figure like the angel of death. This exaggeration has an almost surreal effect and makes Cady a symbol of the repressed fears and unconscious desires of the average American family – a demon which the head of the family, the father, must exorcise in the dramatic finale.

This earthly purgatory, which Scorsese later laconically described as "a concession to the genre," is reminiscent of the dramatic showdowns of several Hitchcock films. Hitchcock's influence also shows in the atmosphere of panic and the victims' feelings of guilt which make them more vulnerable to their attacker. There's another good reason why Hitchcock seems ubiquitous in *Cape Fear*: the original screenplay from the 1960s was initially supposed to have been filmed by him.

SH

1   The time for revenge has come: Max Cady (Robert De Niro), disfigured by the symbols of his hatred.

2   The wolf has cast off his sheep's clothing: Danielle Bowden (Juliette Lewis) realizes, far too late, that what she thought was a game has become deadly serious.

3   A sick mind in a sound body: Cady's cynicism is surpassed only by his brutality.

4   Even Leigh Bowden (Jessica Lange) is no longer able to keep up the façade of happy families.

5   Modeled on Hitchcock: in the spectacular showdown, Sam Bowden (Nick Nolte) has to face up to his past.

ALFRED HITCHCOCK   Director (London 1899 – Los Angeles 1980). No other director has had such a lasting influence on the thriller genre as Alfred Hitchcock. Nothing happened to change this in the '90s. His powerful style influenced numerous successors and imitators, as did his pessimistic view of the world and the often extreme representation of violence in his movies. This is particularly true for Scorsese's generation, and directors like Brian De Palma, who can be considered the most consistent Hitchcock admirer, true to his role model throughout the last decade, as in *Raising Cain* (1991). Younger filmmakers like Quentin Tarantino (*Reservoir Dogs*, 1991, *Pulp Fiction*, 1994), who were in revolt against the conventional narrative modes of the '90s, were also unthinkable without Hitchcock.

JFK 🏆🏆

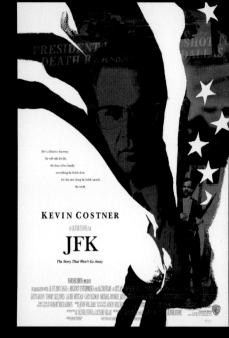

1991 – USA – 187 MIN. – POLITICAL THRILLER, DRAMA

DIRECTOR OLIVER STONE (*1946)

SCREENPLAY OLIVER STONE, ZACHARY SKLAR, based on the books *ON THE TRAIL OF THE ASSASSINS* by JIM GARRISON and *CROSSFIRE: THE PLOT THAT KILLED KENNEDY* by JIM MARS DIRECTOR OF PHOTOGRAPHY ROBERT RICHARDSON EDITING JOE HUTSHING, PIETRO SCALIA MUSIC JOHN WILLIAMS PRODUCTION A. KITMAN HO, OLIVER STONE for IXTLAN CORPORATION, KITMAN HO PRODUCTIONS

STARRING KEVIN COSTNER (Jim Garrison), TOMMY LEE JONES (Clay Shaw), GARY OLDMAN (Lee Harvey Oswald), JAY O. SANDERS (Lou Ivon), SISSY SPACEK (Liz Garrison), JOE PESCI (David Ferrie), MICHAEL ROOKER (Bill Broussard), LAURIE METCALF (Susie Cox), JOHN CANDY (Dean Andrews), WALTER MATTHAU (Senator Long), DONALD SUTHERLAND (Colonel X), JIM GARRISON (Earl Warren)

ACADEMY AWARDS 1992 OSCARS for BEST CINEMATOGRAPHY (Robert Richardson) and BEST FILM EDITING (Joe Hutshing, Pietro Scalia)

"Just because you're paranoid, that doesn't mean that they're not out to get you."

Can two men be hit by the same bullet several times in a row? Can one man, an average shot to boot, fatally wound a man in a moving car with a low quality gun from a great distance and in bad visibility? Jim Garrison (Kevin Costner), state attorney of New Orleans, is convinced that all of that is impossible. That means however that Lee Harvey Oswald (Gary Oldman), the solitary assassin of American president John F. Kennedy, could not have committed the crime alone. "I'm just the scapegoat," Oswald asserted before he fell victim to an assassin's bullet in his turn. Three years after the fatal shots were fired at the President on November 22, 1963, in Dallas, Garrison decides to start searching for the real killers. By chance, the assassination does come under his jurisdiction, as it was suspected that Oswald had spent some time in New Orleans. After an initial investigation, Garrison finds so many inconsistencies and contradictions in the Warren Report, the official version of the murder as represented in the US government's enquiry, that he reopens the whole case. The conclusions reached by the incorruptible state attorney seem even

less credible than the "magic bullet" thesis in the Warren report itself. Could it really be the case that the military, the CIA, and high-ranking government officials including Vice President Lyndon B. Johnson himself were involved in a vast conspiracy to get rid of a president considered too much of a peace-monger by the mighty arms industry?

Director Oliver Stone obviously has no doubts. The masters of war conspiracy theory is based on two accounts of the event: Jim Mars' *Crossfire: The Plot That Killed Kennedy* (1989) and Jim Garrison's *On the Trail of the Assassins*, written a year earlier by the real-life model for Stone's main character. Although it is suspected that in reality the controversial attorney entertained Mafia contacts, Stone transforms him into a shining example of American justice to make his retelling of the case into a general appeal for unreserved critical reappraisal of the past.

When *JFK* was released it became clear that many Americans simply didn't care: "There are conspiracy theories about all sorts of things. There

1 A day that shook America. The assassination of John F. Kennedy on November, 22, 1963, in Dallas ranks among the nation's greatest traumas.

3 Garrison meticulously pieces the clues together. Finally one thing is clear: the American president was the victim of a conspiracy.

5 To track down the truth, director Oliver Stone mixes fact and rumor, footage from historic archives, and reconstructed scenes.

2 District Attorney Jim Garrison (Kevin Costner) is becoming increasingly estranged from his wife Liz (Sissy Spacek).

4 The president in the assassin's sights. It is still a mystery how many weapons were fired at Kennedy.

"I don't know much about the film. I haven't seen it and at the end of the day there are conspiracy theories circulating about all sorts of things. Hey, there are some people who think Elvis is still alive ..."

George Bush, Head of the CIA 1976–1977, US President 1989–1993

... are even rumors that Elvis Presley is still alive ..." So spoke the then US President George Bush Sr., and statements like that were all grist to Stone's mill. The real strength of the film is the meticulous presentation of the evidence showing that the idea of Oswald as solitary killer is no longer tenable. One of his most effective weapons is to ask why the results of the investigation on President John F. Kennedy's murder must remain secret until 2029 if there is really nothing to hide.

Stone is less interested in the psychology of his characters, and some areas are thinly sketched, like the marital problems of Garrison and his wife Liz (Sissy Spacek). An excellent cast ensures that the characters nonetheless manage to remain convincing and the plot never becomes boring. Joe Pesci

plays a manic Communist-hater and Tommy Lee Jones a smooth conspirator – political explosiveness aside, it is the supporting actors rather than the stars which make *JFK* a cinematic event.

Stone finds no definitive proof for his version of the Kennedy murder. The audience are overwhelmed rather than persuaded by the swift succession of staccato scenes and flashbacks, and by the montage of authentic material and staged sequences. Techniques like that moved some critics to describe the film as propaganda. Stone and his supporters do not dispute this charge: *JFK* is propaganda, but above all it is an important lesson in history justified by a universal lack of critical historical awareness – a problem not limited to America alone. SH

FACTION Faction combines facts and fiction without claiming to be historical truth. In this very American way of reappraising the past, people, and events are mostly presented as symbolic figures or as key happenings in American history. The faction phenomenon is not limited to film, but is also found in literature like Norman Mailer's fictional autobiography of Marilyn Monroe (*Marilyn, a Biography*, 1973). The foremost factional filmmaker is Oliver Stone, whose numerous films develop a historical panorama of the USA: movies such as *Salvador* (1985), *Platoon* (1986), and *The Doors* (1991) appeal to the historical consciousness of his people and show the USA as a land divided within itself. *JFK* triggered off a whole series of documentary-style biographies in the USA, many of which were also about conspiracy theories.

RAISE THE RED LANTERN
DAHONG DENGLONG GAOGAO GUA

CHINA.1920. ONE MASTER. FOUR WIVES.

RAISE THE RED LANTERN
A FILM BY ZHANG YIMOU

1991 – HONG KONG / PEOPLE'S REPUBLIC OF CHINA – 125 MIN. – LITERATURE ADAPTATION, DRAMA

DIRECTOR ZHANG YIMOU (*1950)

SCREENPLAY ZHEN NI, based on a novel by SU TONG **DIRECTOR OF PHOTOGRAPHY** ZHAO FEI

EDITING DU YUAN **MUSIC** ZHAO JIPING **PRODUCTION** CHIU FU–SHENG for ERA INTERNATIONAL, CHINA FILM

STARRING GONG LI (Songlian), MA JINGWU (The Master), HE CAIFEI (Meishan), CAO CUIFENG (Zhuoyun), KONG LIN (Yan'er), JIN SHUYUAN (Yuru), DING WEIMIN (Mother Song), CUI ZHIHGANG (Doctor Gao), XIAO CHU (Feipu), CAO ZHENGYIN (Old servant woman)

IFF VENICE 1991 SILVER LION for BEST DIRECTOR (Zhang Yimou)

"People are spirits, spirits are people: breath is the only difference."

"What else is there for women to do?" After the death of her father, Songlian (Gong Li), a young Chinese woman, is married off by her stepmother. Rather than becoming the only wife of a poor man, Songlian chooses to live as one of the many wives of a rich man. As "fourth mistress" in the house of her husband (Ma Jingwu), she is subject to a strict regime. Cared for and guarded by servants and housekeepers round the clock, Songlian and her three "sisters" are condemned to complete inactivity, and the age-old family traditions weigh on them like a curse. It soon becomes clear that the strict morals and tradition are nothing but a façade that conceals suffering and decadence. The "first sister," an older woman who is merely tolerated, finds the arrival of the new, girlish wife disgraceful. Songlian is shocked to learn that her lord and master regularly abuses the underage maidservant. It doesn't take

Songlian long to realize that the real mistress of the house is the wife with red lanterns in her courtyard in the evening, a sign that the master will visit her that night. At first she tries to build up a relationship with her "sisters," but she soon abandons her efforts. Competitiveness, envy, and intrigue rule their day-to-day life. Songlian initially attempts to fight against the ossified family rituals, but she gradually learns to use them as a weapon against her rivals. She joins in the power games of the wives that nip any feelings of solidarity in the bud. The chosen wife enjoys certain privileges, but these are not as important as the favor of the master, the only possible form of self-assertion and human contact that remains in their introverted and isolated world. Instead of joining forces against the inhuman system, the wives begin a merciless war against each other.

1 A bird in a gilded cage. The "Fourth Wife," Songlian (Gong Li), is a captive in her husband's house. It's not long before the rival wives start messing each other around.

2 Songlian is married off to a wealthy Chinese man. She has to give up her university course after her father dies.

3 "What else can you do as a woman?" Isolated and forced into a totally regimented daily routine, Songlian doesn't recognize herself anymore.

4 "You rub my back..." – whoever is the "master's" current favorite is granted certain privileges.

Although the movie is sober and uncompromising, Zhang Yimou's images of 1920s China are breathtakingly beautiful. They can be interpreted both as a psychological study and as a social parable of China oppressed by its communist rulers. The director himself described the movie as a "microcosm of human existence."

Raise the Red Lantern impresses not just with the nuances of its acting, but above all through its highly effective use of cinematic stylistic devices. The camera concentrates on the wives and the servants and never focuses directly on the master of the house, making him seem both unapproachable and threatening. The plot takes an almost mechanical course that follows the cycle of the seasons and reflects the way in which the wives' lives are ruled by others. Visually the film is dominated by repeated takes of the estate's rigorously symmetrical architecture. This gives an impression of the inevitable,

the inescapable, strengthened by the fact that the camera never leaves the compound where the wives' houses are grouped around the main house. Even the "nights of love" are announced with a military shout: "lanterns in courtyard number four!"

Towards the end of the film, the whole compound is covered in snow and the material world seems almost to dissolve into a timeless, abstract sphere. The architecture becomes a compact and oppressive embodiment of life in captivity, devoid of human warmth, amounting to nothing more than a foreshadowing of inevitable death. Sadly, even the final victory over a competitor cannot put an end to the self-destructive rivalry between the oppressed women: the following summer, a new wife, "sister number five," moves into the vacant house.

SF

CINEMATIC ARCHITECTURE Architecture provides both stage and scenery for a movie plot, and makes a major contribution to its atmospheric texture and believability. It is one of the cinema's main means of expression. This is particularly true for genres such as Horror and Science Fiction. Buildings can also be used to structure a plot (*Raise the Red Lantern*) and to generate symbolic meaning, as for example in the some of the films of the British director Peter Greenaway (*The Baby of Mâcon*, 1993). Architecture is the

"In China, *Raise the Red Lantern* is regarded as a symbol of the present situation; the fact that the film has so far not been allowed to be shown in Chinese cinemas is evidence of this." *epd Film*

MY OWN PRIVATE IDAHO

1991 – USA – 104 MIN. – ROAD MOVIE, DRAMA
DIRECTOR GUS VAN SANT (*1952)
SCREENPLAY GUS VAN SANT **DIRECTOR OF PHOTOGRAPHY** ERIC ALAN EDWARDS, JOHN CAMPBELL
EDITING CURTISS CLAYTON **MUSIC** BILL STAFFORD **PRODUCTION** LAURIE PARKER for NEW LINE CINEMA
STARRING RIVER PHOENIX (Mike Waters), KEANU REEVES (Scott Favor), WILLIAM RICHERT (Bob Pigeon), JAMES RUSSO (Richard Waters), RODNEY HARVEY (Gary), UDO KIER (Hans), CHIARA CASELLI (Carmella), MICHAEL PARKER (Digger), JESSIE THOMAS (Denise), FLEA (Budd), GRACE ZABRISKIE (Alena)

"Have a nice day!"

A young man stands on a road that cuts through a monotonous hill landscape as straight as an arrow, disappearing into the distance without interruption. The image imprints itself on our memories. We are in Idaho, the Pacific Northwest of the USA. Mike Waters (River Phoenix), a homeless vagabond, moves slowly away from his duffle bag, counts how long it takes to fall over and cries "I just know that I been stuck here like this one fuckin' time before… the road looks like… a fucked-up face." He holds a hand over his eyes to stare into the distance. The camera follows his gaze, the picture comes into focus, and we see how the road, hills, and bushes form a phantom face like nature looking back at him. Suddenly Mike staggers and drops to the ground like his duffle bag. While he lies on his back on the road, time-lapse pictures show clouds passing over in a stormy sky. In front of an old wooden hut, a woman – we later learn that she is Mike's mother – nurses a child's head in her lap and hums tenderly. Salmon struggle against the current to get back to their spawning ground. Then a wooden hut crashes on to the road, this time in slow motion. Mike is still lying on his back, but not on the road anymore, on a ta-

ble: he's enjoying an orgasm, which allows him to forget his search for his mother for a moment. We do not see his "client." Mike is now part of the gay scene in the metropolis of Portland, where he meets Scott Favor (Keanu Reeves), who is the son of the city's wealthy and powerful mayor. Mike thinks he has finally found the love of his life in Scott. They go off together to find Mike's mother and the search takes them as far as Ostia at the gates of Rome. But wherever he starts out from, Mike never really gets anywhere. An Italian girl wins Scott's heart and Mike is distraught. Scott returns to normal life, but Mike's life remains suspended: he is a streetwalker in Rome, a streetwalker in Portland, on the street in Idaho. He finds neither his mother nor his place in society, and unlike Odysseus, his wanderings are a continuous cycle with no end.

What is it that makes this tale of foolish dreams, this failed search for happiness and this strange, disjointed life such an extraordinary film? Van Sant does far more than tell a story. He combines Mike's fragmentary life with fragments of other classical narratives. Scott, the son of a millionaire,

2

1   In 1993, at the age of 23, River Phoenix died on
Sunset Boulevard in Hollywood – all alone outside a
nightclub. A death fit for a movie.

2   While Mike Waters (River Phoenix) hangs on to his
supposed boyfriend, Scott Favor (Keanu Reeves) is
already envisaging his future – without a boyfriend.

3   Even in the mirror Mike sees somebody else.

4   When people's eyes don't meet in cinema, that's
the end of companionship.

5   A prostitute's love affair that sweeps as far as Italy:
the "Pillars of the Roman Empire" have fallen into
ruins.

INDEPENDENTS   Movies made outside the dominant organizations of the American film industry are known as independents. Independent productions aim to outweigh their financial disadvantages with their creativity and sensitivity to niche markets. Rather than a studio being in charge, those who make the film are in control of its production; they do their own casting, editing, etc. The term independents was coined in the late '50s. In 1959 John Cassavetes's *Shadows* won the first Independent Film Award of the magazine *Film Culture* (editor: Jonas Mekas). The definitions of underground, experimental, and avant-garde movies were still fluid at the time, as was that of the European auteur film. Today, the main division is between the film industry as commercial production ("Hollywood" is considered an insult in certain circles) and as art: along with auteur films, independents are expected to play a role in reestablishing cinema as an art form. The "godfathers" of independent film in the USA are the legendary producer and director Roger Corman, director and scriptwriter John Sayles, and the actor and director Robert Redford.

only sleeps with men for money. He tells Mike that his life on the streets is merely a mask which will increase the effect of his eventual return to normality: "It will impress them more when a fuck up like me turns good than if I had been a good son all along." With this comment, Van Sant translates Shakespeare's Prince Hal from the historical play *Henry IV* into modern American speech. The figure of the errant Prince of Wales who becomes Henry V lives on in Scott. Shakespeare's prince finds a mentor for his journey to the underworld in Falstaff, who initiates him in the ways of depravity. In *My Own Private Idaho* the Falstaff figure is Bob Pigeon (William Richert), a boast-

ful, braggart hedonist like the Shakespearean original, complete with huge belly, and it is he who initiates Scott into the life of the lowest of the low. But the movie is not just an extravagant remake of a literary model. It was Orson Welles's Falstaff movie *Chimes at Midnight* (1966) which really gave Van Sant the idea that the historical drama "plays on the streets," as the director himself said. Welles's Falstaff film is a misunderstood work of genius, the work of a director who began at the top and worked his way down to the bottom. *My Own Private Idaho* has many layers of stories from literature and film; unravelling them helps us forget the missing happy end.   RV

> ## "The world is a street."
> *Cahiers du cinéma*

THE SILENCE OF THE LAMBS ♟♟♟♟♟

1991 – USA – 118 MIN. – THRILLER

DIRECTOR JONATHAN DEMME (*1944)

SCREENPLAY TED TALLY, based on the novel of the same name by THOMAS HARRIS **DIRECTOR OF PHOTOGRAPHY** TAK FUJIMOTO

EDITING CRAIG MCKAY **MUSIC** HOWARD SHORE

PRODUCTION GARY GOETZMAN, EDWARD SAXON, KENNETH UTT, RON BOZMAN for STRONG HEART PRODUCTIONS (for ORION)

STARRING JODIE FOSTER (Clarice Starling), ANTHONY HOPKINS (Dr. Hannibal Lecter), SCOTT GLENN (Jack Crawford), TED LEVINE (Jame Gumb), ANTHONY HEALD (Dr. Frederick Chilton), BROOKE SMITH (Catherine Martin), DIANE BAKER (Senator Ruth Martin), KASI LEMMONS (Ardelia Mapp), ROGER CORMAN (FBI Director Hayden Burke), GEORGE A. ROMERO (FBI Agent in Memphis)

ACADEMY AWARDS 1992 OSCARS for BEST PICTURE, BEST SCREENPLAY based on material previously produced or published (Ted Tally), BEST DIRECTOR (Jonathan Demme), BEST ACTOR (Anthony Hopkins), and BEST ACTRESS (Jodie Foster)

"I'm having a friend for dinner."

Clarice Starling (Jodie Foster), daughter of a policeman shot in the line of duty, wants to join the FBI. At the FBI Academy in Woods, Virginia, she races over training courses, pushing herself to the limit. Wooden signs bear the legend "HURT-AGONY-PAIN: LOVE IT" – they're not just there to exhort the rookies to excel, they also reveal the masochism involved. The movie goes through the whole range of this theme, from heroic selflessness to destructive self-hate. Jack Crawford (Scott Glenn), who is Starling's boss and the head of the FBI's psychiatric department, sends her to Baltimore to carry out a routine interview with an imprisoned murderer who is resisting questioning. As well as being a psychiatrist, the prisoner is also an extreme pathological case who attacked people and ate their organs. For eight years Dr. Hannibal

"The Cannibal" Lecter (Anthony Hopkins) has lived in the windowless cellar of a high security mental hospital. Crawford hopes the interview will provide clues to the behavior of a second monster, a killer known as "Buffalo Bill" who skins his female victims and has so far skillfully evaded the FBI. Crawford's plan works, and the professorial cannibal agrees to discuss the pathology of mass murderers with his visitor Clarice – on one condition. Lecter will give her expert advice on Buffalo Bill in exchange for the tale of her childhood trauma. "Quid pro quo" – she lays bare her psyche, he gives her a psychological profile of her suspect. The gripping dialogue that develops between the ill-matched couple can be understood on many levels. On one hand, we see a psychoanalyst talking to his patient, on the other, a young detective

"It has been a good long while since I have felt the presence of Evil so manifestly demonstrated ..."

Chicago Sun-Times

2

3

1 The naked man and the dead: Buffalo Bill (Ted Levine) uses a sewing machine to make himself a new identity from the skin of his victims; above him are butterflies, a symbol of that metamorphosis.

2 The staring matches between Starling (Jodie Foster) and Lecter (Anthony Hopkins) are a battle for knowledge: Lecter is to help the FBI build a profile of the killer; Starling is to surrender the secret of her childhood.

3 The pair meet in the lowest part of the prison system, a basement dungeon from the underworld.

4 The eyes have it: in the serial killer genre, eyes become a tool for appropriation, destruction, and penetration.

interrogating an unpredictable serial killer, and that ambiguity is the determining quality in Lecter and Starling's relationship. Both follow their own aims unerringly, refusing to give way, and the struggle that results is one of the most brilliant and sophisticated duels in cinema history. The daughter of a US senator falls into the hands of Buffalo Bill, and suddenly the FBI is under increasing pressure to find the murderer. Lecter's chance has come. In return for his help in capturing Jame Gumb alias Buffalo Bill (Ted Levine), he asks for better conditions and is transferred to a temporary prison in Memphis. He kills the warders and escapes in the uniform of a policeman, whose face he has also removed and placed over his own. His last exchange with Starling takes place over the telephone, when he rings from a Caribbean island to congratulate her on her promotion to FBI agent and bids her farewell with the words: "I'm having a friend for dinner." After hanging up, Lecter follows a group of tourists in which the audience recognize the hated Dr. Chilton (Anthony Heald), director of the secure mental hospital in Baltimore, who clearly will be Lecter's unsuspecting dinner "guest."

The Silence of the Lambs marked a cinematic high point at the beginning of the '90s. It is impossible to categorize in any one genre as it combines several. There are elements from police movies (where crime does not pay),

but it's also a thriller that borrows much from real historical figures: the model for both Gumb and Lecter is Edward Gein (1906–1984), who was wearing suspenders made from his victims' skin when arrested in 1957.

But *The Silence of the Lambs* is also a movie about psychiatry. Both murderers are presented as psychopaths whose "relation" to one another forms the basis for criminological research, even though their cases are not strictly comparable. The movie was so successful that it became one of the most influential models for the decade that followed, enriching cinema history to the point of plot plagiarism and quotation.

Suspense and Deception

Hannibal Lecter had already appeared on the silver screen before *The Silence of the Lambs*. In 1986, Michael Mann filmed Thomas Harris's 1981 novel *Red Dragon* under the title *Manhunter*. Five years later, Jonathan Demme refined the material, and the changing perspectives of his camera work give what is fundamentally a cinematic retelling of *Beauty and the Beast* a new twist. Demme films his characters from both within and without.

4

"*The Silence of the Lambs* is just plain scary – from its doomed and woozy camera angles to its creepy Freudian context."

The Wahington Post

The director plays with the fluid border between external and internal reality, between memory and the present, as when we see Clarice's childhood in two flashbacks for which we are completely unprepared. Jodie Foster's eyes remain fixed on the here and now while the camera zooms beyond her into the past, probing her psychological wounds. During the final confrontation between Clarice and Jame Gumb, the perspective changes repeatedly. We see the murderer through Clarice's eyes but we also see the young FBI agent through the eyes of Jame, who seeks out his victims in the dark using infrared glasses.

This changing perspective in the movie's final scenes emphasizes the extreme danger that Clarice is in. Other sequences are straightforward trick-

ery, like the changing perspectives in the sequence which builds up to the finale. A police contingent has surrounded the house where they expect to find Jame Gumb, and a black police officer disguised as a deliveryman rings the bell. On the other side of the door, we hear the bell ring. Jame dresses and answers the door.

The police break into the house, while we see the murderer open the door to find Clarice standing before him – alone. In the next take, the police storm an empty house. This parallel montage combines two places that are far apart, two actions with the same aim, two houses, of which one is only seen from outside, the other from inside. We are made to think that both actions are happening in the same place. The parallel montage is revealed as

5 6

5   The cannibal clasps his hands. Cage and pose
are reminiscent of Francis Bacon's portraits of
the pope.

6   Lecter overpowers the guards with their own
weapons: one policeman is given a taste of his own
pepper spray.

7   The monster is restrained with straitjacket
and muzzle; the powers of the state have the
monopoly on violence for the time being.

8   A policeman is disemboweled and crucified on the
cage. With his outstretched arms, he looks like a
butterfly.

7

a trick and increases the tension: we suddenly realize that Clarice must face the murderer alone.

More than one film critic assumed that this ploy meant that even Hollywood films had moved into an era of self-reflexivity. Instead of consciously revealing a cinematic device, however, the parallel montage serves primarily to heighten the movie's atmosphere of danger and uncertainty. Nevertheless, *The Silence of the Lambs* works on both levels, both as exciting entertainment and as a virtuoso game with key cultural figures and situations. Some critics went so far as to interpret the perverted killer Buffalo Bill as Hades, god of the underworld, and although analyses like that may be interesting, they are not essential to an understanding of the film or its success.

At the 1992 Academy Awards, *The Silence of the Lambs* carried off the so-called Big Five in the five main categories, something which only two films (*It Happened One Night* [1934] and *One Flew Over the Cuckoo's Nest* [1975] had managed previously. Ten years after his escape, Hannibal Lecter appeared again on the silver screen (*Hannibal*, 2001). Jodie Foster refused to play the role of Clarice for a second time and was replaced by Julianne Moore (*Magnolia*) and Ridley Scott took over from Jonathan Demme as director.

R\

8

"I go to the cinema because I feel like being shocked." Jonathan Demme

9   In Buffalo Bill's basement lair, Starling is just about to be plunged into total darkness ...

1◊   ... where she has to feel her way blindly, straining to hear, while Buffalo Bill watches her through infrared goggles.

PARALLEL MONTAGE A process developed early in the history of cinema. Editing enables two or more events happening in different places to be told and experienced at the same time. The best-known kind of parallel montage in movies is the "last-minute rescue," where images of an endangered or besieged character are juxtaposed in rapid succession with those of the rescuers who are on their way. Action movies use such sequences over and over as a means of increasing the tension, and the device has remained basically the same from David Griffith's 1916 film *Intolerance* to today's thrillers. Parallel montage allows us to be a step ahead of the figures in a film. We are allowed to know things that the characters do not themselves realize, and we are also in several places at the same time, an experience which is only possible in fiction.

BOYZ N THE HOOD

1991 – USA – 112 MIN. – DRAMA
DIRECTOR JOHN SINGLETON (*1967)
SCREENPLAY JOHN SINGLETON DIRECTOR OF PHOTOGRAPHY CHARLES MILLS EDITING BRUCE CANNON
MUSIC STANLEY CLARKE PRODUCTION STEVE NICOLAIDES for NEW DEAL (for COLUMBIA)
STARRING CUBA GOODING JR. (Tre Styles), ICE CUBE (Dough Boy Baker), NIA LONG
(Brandi), MORRIS CHESTNUT (Ricky Baker), LAURENCE FISHBURNE (Furious Styles,
Tre's father), TYRA FERRELL (Mrs. Baker), ANGELA BASSETT (Reva Styles), META KING
(Brandi's mother), WHITMAN MAYO (Old Man), DESI ARNEZ HINES (Tre as a 10-year-old)

"Increase the peace."

One in every 21 black Americans is murdered – almost always by another black American. Tre Styles (Cuba Gooding Jr.) is a black American, but
he is lucky. Growing up in a ghetto in south Los Angeles, he becomes ac-
quainted with the daily violence of the lower-class African American neighborhoods at an early age. However, in contrast to his friends, most of whom
are brought up by drug-addicted or alcoholic single mothers, Tre's father pre-
pares him for life in a hostile and violent society. After one of many fights at
school, Tre's mother admits she no longer knows what to do with him and
hands over his upbringing to Father Furious (Laurence Fishburne) who drums
three basic values into the boy: "Always look people in the eye, then they'll
respect you more. Never be frightened to ask for something then you'll never
have to steal. Never respect anyone who doesn't respect you." He teaches

the boy to take responsibility: while the father makes sure that the bills are
paid and that there is something to eat on the table, the son takes care of the
housework. The difference between Tre and his peers is the self-esteem that
this responsibility gives him.

Furious, who according to Tre's friend Dough Boy (Ice Cube) is "some
kind of fucking Malcolm-X-King," has his own explanation for why most
murdered African Americans are killed by their own people: nowhere in
the world are there more drugs, more bars, and weapon stores than in the
black neighborhoods – according to Furious's theory, this is part of the
whites' strategy to force down the prices of real estate in the ghettos so
they can sell it again for a profit. For this reason, the blacks' property has
to be defended.

NEW BLACK CINEMA In 1991, 19 films by black directors were released, marking the breakthrough of "New Black Cinema." African American reality as portrayed in the fresh film idiom of young directors such as John Singleton, Bill Duke (*Rage in Harlem*, 1991), and Mario van Peebles (*New Jack City*, 1991) doesn't just hit a nerve with black audiences. The world is full of troubled areas where it is necessary to take a stand against racism, which is one reason for the international success of black filmmakers. One of the greatest pioneers of New Black Cinema was Spike Lee. Movies like *Do the Right Thing* (1989), *Mo' Better Blues* (1990), or *Jungle Fever* (1991) portray a section of American society which the film industry has largely ignored except in crime movies and the Blaxploitation movies of the 1970s.

Tre's aims are of a more private nature: he mostly thinks about the girlfriend he longs for and his college entrance exam. But one night, while a constant stream of police helicopters thunder over the neighborhood and searchlights flash down into the streets, violence breaks directly into his life: Ricky (Morris Chestnut), Dough Boy's brother, is murdered by members of a street gang over a trifle. A talented football player, Ricky was one of the few who would have had a chance of getting out of the ghetto, and he had taken the college entrance exam along with Tre. In a poignant moment, his mother discovers after his death that he would have just scraped into college. Tre is faced with a terrible dilemma: should he avenge his friend and perpetuate the spiral of violence, or should he find a way to break out of the deadly cycle?

Singleton's drama about violence, responsibility, and life in the ghetto is a political lesson about America at the end of the 20th century. The tranquil, almost lethargic rhythm of the tale reflects the agony of a world where unemployed black youths drink beer on the veranda all day or sit around on the plastic covers of living-room couches and have nothing but cynical comments to make about life. With its clear dialogues and realistic observations, the movie is addressed above all to the people it portrays. When the movie opened in Los Angeles, it sparked off riots among black youths that left two dead and 35 wounded, but the movie can hardly be blamed for that. Its appeal for peace, brotherhood, and responsibility is absolutely unmistakable. Some critics considered its "intellectual simplicity" a weakness, but that simplicity is more like the film's main strength. SH

"Singleton dispenses with explanations. He shows people as they are, bluntly and brutally; he shows what they have become, but not what made them that way." *epd Film*

1 Survival of the fittest is all that counts, even for a simple meeting on Saturday night.

2 Blacks shooting blacks. A human life isn't worth much in the ghetto.

3 Local lads. Dough Boy (Ice Cube, right) and his mates cannot escape the spiral of violence.

4 Furious Styles (Laurence Fishburne) reaches for his weapon only in extreme emergencies. He faces the daily misery of the ghetto with a radical social philosophy and iron principles.

POINT BREAK

1991 – USA – 122 MIN. – ACTION FILM, DRAMA
DIRECTOR KATHRYN BIGELOW (*1953)
SCREENPLAY W. PETER ILIFF, based on a story by RICK KING, W. PETER ILIFF
DIRECTOR OF PHOTOGRAPHY DONALD PETERMAN EDITING HOWARD L. SMITH MUSIC SHARON BOYLE,
MARK ISHAM PRODUCTION PETER ABRAMS, ROBERT L. LEVY for 20TH CENTURY FOX
STARRING PATRICK SWAYZE (Bodhi), KEANU REEVES (Johnny Utah), GARY BUSEY
(Angelo Pappas), LORI PETTY (Tyler Ann Endicott), JOHN C. MCGINLEY (Ben Harp),
JAMES LEGROS (Roach), JOHN PHILBIN (Nathanial), BOJESSE CHRISTOPHER (Grommet),
JULIAN REYES (Alvarez), DANIEL BEER (Babbit)

"Fear causes hesitation, and hesitation will cause your worst fears to come true."

It's clear from the outset that *Point Break* is about a collision between two different ways of life; as the opening credits roll, the names of the movie's two stars are intermingled. Special Agent Johnny Utah (Keanu Reeves) comes to L.A. fresh from the Academy to help out in the investigation of a series of bank robberies. The members of the gang in question disguise themselves with masks of US Presidents, and Johnny's new partner Angelo Pappas (Gary Busey) suspects that they come from the surfing scene. Johnny is sent to work there undercover. Tyler (Lori Petty) teaches him to surf and introduces him to Bodhi (Patrick Swayze), for whom surfing is a way of life.

Bodhi fascinates Johnny and draws him into the surfing scene, but the investigation is beginning to get out of control. Johnny and his partner make a rushed attempt to bust a suspicious group of surfers and ruin months of work by their colleagues in the Drugs Department. In a moment of high spirits during their next surfing trip together, Bodhi thrusts his naked behind at his fellow surfers. This defiant gesture is exactly what the masked presidents do for the police security cameras at the end of their raids, and Johnny realizes that his surfing friends are the gang he has been looking for all along. He and his partner decide to confront them during their next robbery, but the plan goes wrong. His cover is blown, and the next day the surfers stand at his door and challenge him. First they take him parachuting then they force him to take part in the next bank raid. They take Tyler, now Johnny's girlfriend, as hostage.

During the getaway from the bank, Johnny's partner and one of the surfers are shot dead. Johnny himself is forced to get into the plane. The surfers jump out over the Mexican desert and leave him. In despairing rage he jumps out after them without a parachute and catches up with Bodhi in free fall. Once again they test each other's daring – neither of them wants to pull the ripcord – but Johnny loses once again. He lands in the desert and Tyler runs into his arms.

He has one last chance: the storm of the century has broken out in Australia and all the surfers flee the beaches except Bodhi, who stands waiting to take up Johnny's challenge. They fight, and this time Johnny manages to defeat Bodhi and handcuffs him, but he can't resist when Bodhi asks to be allowed to ride one last gigantic wave before Johnny's FBI colleagues arrive to take him away. The foam closes over the surfer, Johnny leaves the beach and throws his agent's badge over the cliff.

"*Point Break* makes those of us who don't spend our lives searching for the ultimate physical rush feel like second-class citizens. The film turns reckless athletic valor into a new form of aristocracy."

Entertainment Weekly

Kathryn Bigelow's *Point Break* is a celebration of speed and movement. During the opening sequences when Johnny goes to his new office for the first time, he is filmed in a long steadycam take which follows him down the hall and is directed – as is Johnny – by the pointing fingers of the other employees. In the surf scenes, the camera glides through the crests of the waves parallel to the boards in images that capture the absolute freedom of movement on water. The film's real climax is a chase scene through gardens, sitting rooms, and children's paddling pools, where Johnny pursues

Bodhi in his Ronald Reagan mask. Johnny sprains his ankle, and his only hope is to shoot Bodhi down, but he can't bring himself to do it. The fascination and intoxication of speed brings the power of the state to its knees.

Bigelow's *Point Break* is one of the best action movies of the '90s. Its excitement doesn't just come from its fantastic camera work and visuals, but also from the acting achievement of its two stars and their electrifying duel.

MS

---

1 Bodhi (Patrick Swayze) dreams of a single overwhelming wave that will sweep him away far beyond the reach of the justice of this world.

2 By disguising themselves as ex-presidents, the surfers express their contempt for a meaningless establishment.

3 Macho initiation rites: who'll be the last to pull the ripcord of his parachute?

4 The different careers of Keanu Reeves and Patrick Swayze make them an ideal choice to portray a tense and exciting friendship between two men.

5 The contrast between land and sea in this film represents the contrast between law and crime, and discipline and excess.

6 Like many other film gangsters, the ex-presidents are ultimately defeated by their increasing arrogance and self-styled image.

7 Hyper-motivated FBI agent Johnny (Keanu Reeves) lurches from one disaster to another.

STEADYCAM In the early '70s, cameraman Garrett Brown developed a portable tripod and vest which attaches a camera to the cameraman's body in such a way that all his movements are countered by a system of suspended rotating balancing weights. This made it possible for the first time for movies to be full of movement without the characteristic jiggling of the handheld camera. The steadycam can also produce running pictures in restricted spaces (for example, stairwells) without additional aids such as runners or cranes. One result of such filming – used for the first time in 1976 in *Rocky* and later in Kubrick's *The Shining* – is the pictures' independent dynamic. The camera seems freed from its limitations and is able to circle the action from all angles in one take so that place and time can be experienced in unbroken continuity.

THE BEAUTIFUL TROUBLEMAKER
LA BELLE NOISEUSE

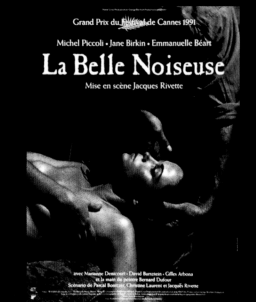

1991 – FRANCE – 240 MIN. (abridged version *DIVERTIMENTO*: 126 MIN.) – DRAMA, LITERATURE ADAPTATION

DIRECTOR JACQUES RIVETTE (*1928)

SCREENPLAY PASCAL BONITZER, CHRISTINE LAURENT, JACQUES RIVETTE, based on the short story *LE CHEF-D'ŒUVRE INCONNU* by HONORÉ DE BALZAC

DIRECTOR OF PHOTOGRAPHY WILLIAM LUBTCHANSKY **EDITING** NICOLE LUBTCHANSKY

MUSIC IGOR STRAVINSKY **PRODUCTION** PIERRE GRISE, MARTINE MARIGNAC for FR3 FILMS, PIERRE GRISE PRODUCTIONS, GEORGE REINHART PRODUCTIONS

STARRING MICHEL PICCOLI (Edouard Frenhofer), JANE BIRKIN (Liz), EMMANUELLE BÉART (Marianne), MARIANNE DENICOURT (Julienne), DAVID BURSZTEIN (Nicolas), GILLES ARBONA (Porbus), BERNARD DUFOUR (Hand of the painter), MARIE-CLAUDE ROGER (Françoise), MARIE BELLUC (Magali), LEILA REMILI (Maidservant)

IFF CANNES 1991 JURY PRIZE (Jacques Rivette)

"A cruel game."

"When I take art to its limits, there's blood on the canvas." – Art has always been about pushing back boundaries. It certainly is for artist Edouard Frenhofer (Michel Piccoli), once a famous painter, but now almost forgotten. Although he excels at the technical aspects of his art, he knows he has never succeeded in creating a masterpiece. When the film opens, we see that he has withdrawn to a solitary country house in Burgundy together with his partner Liz (Jane Birkin), and has more or less stopped painting altogether. Liz is no longer his muse: now she merely looks after him. She modeled for Frenhofer's last picture, "The Beautiful Troublemaker," which lies unfinished and hidden in his studio, and as a result she embodies his failure as much as the work itself. Both now live a life without art, locked into human and artistic stagnation.

The situation changes when their friend the art dealer Porbus (Gilles Arbona) comes to visit accompanied by the young painter Nicolas (David Bursztein) and his girlfriend Marianne (Emmanuelle Béart). Nicolas and Porbus insist on seeing "The Beautiful Troublemaker." Frenhofer refuses, but eventually they reach a compromise: Frenhofer will continue the work with Marianne as model and Porbus will buy the finished picture.

Outrage is followed by hestitation, until finally Marianne agrees to the deal which soon becomes a grueling test of endurance for both parties. Painter and model struggle with art and with themselves until they teeter on the verge of self-destruction.

For three of the total of four hours, director Jacques Rivette represents the finishing of "The Beautiful Troublemaker" as an existential challenge for

3

1   Edouard Frenhofer (Michel Piccoli) is in search of the ultimate masterpiece. After a lengthy period of artist's block, he accepts the challenge one last time.

2   Painter and model. Marianne (Emmanuelle Béart) has to suffer numerous humiliations at the hands of the eccentric artist. But she ends up the stronger.

3   The creative process begins by overcoming a fear of the empty canvas.

4   The beautiful muse. Marianne reluctantly agrees to the experiment.

"Whereas in his films about theatre Rivette looked for the truth in the set, the acting and the costumes, in *La Belle Noiseuse* he directs his search towards nakedness, gestures, line, as well as material

"We made every effort to produce a film that comes close to painting, rather than talking about it."

Jacques Rivette in *Der Spiegel*

painter and model. Frenhofer wrestles to assert himself as an artist, and his naked model is forced into painful poses by the sulky and despotic painter as she fights to defend her personality and her self-esteem.

"Let me be how I am," Marianne demands. In the end, she has to encourage the despondent painter to continue. But, by the time the painting is finished, Marianne has become the beautiful troublemaker herself, and can no longer bear the sight of the picture and the truth it reveals.

Liz's face on the canvas is replaced by the younger woman's naked buttocks; the creative process is, she concludes "a cruel game." For her, the real obscenity is the question of whether a whole life can be fixed in a couple of brushstrokes. She has sacrificed her life for Frenhofer's art and now she knows the price of such presumption.

Rivette's film is based on Honoré de Balzac's tale *The Unknown Masterpiece*, but whereas for Balzac, blood on the canvas was a reference to

the idea that under the painted skin, the observer should be able to imagine blood flowing, coming from Frenhofer it sounds like a threat of mental or physical violence. Balzac's Frenhofer, who is a kind of Pygmalion, comes to believe that the picture he is working on is a real woman. Everything else is a confusion of lines and colors under which the "unknown masterpiece" is hidden; only a perfectly painted foot can be seen in the corner of the canvas.

In the movie, the finished painting is walled up in Frenhofer's studio and no one ever sees it apart from those immediately concerned, and the public are passed off with a hastily produced replacement. Rivette's movie can also be taken as an eloquent commentary on literary models: if there is such a thing as creative truth beyond self-centered arrogance and artistic hubris, then it is only accessible to those who appreciate how painful the link between reality and the artistic imagination can be.

SH

FILM ADAPTATIONS OF LITERATURE Some of the best films of the '90s were adapted from literary models, like *The Silence of the Lambs* (Jonathan Demme, 1990) taken from the novel by Thomas Harris or *L.A. Confidential* (Curtis Hanson, 1997) based on the book by James Ellroy. Many movies from the '90s also show that filming best sellers is a lucrative business, as the film versions of John Grisham's books (including *The Firm* by Sydney Pollack, 1993 and *The Jury* by Joel Schumacher, 1996) undoubtedly demonstrate. When directors choose an older literary model, they must first decide whether to make a historical movie or a modernization. Whereas films such as *Hamlet* (Kenneth Branagh, 1996) concentrate entirely on historical authenticity, modernizations such as Al Pacino's *Looking for Richard* (1996) explore the contemporary aspects of historical material.

THELMA & LOUISE

1991 – USA – 129 MIN. – ROAD MOVIE, DRAMA
DIRECTOR RIDLEY SCOTT (*1937)
SCREENPLAY CALLIE KHOURI DIRECTOR OF PHOTOGRAPHY ADRIAN BIDDLE EDITING THOM NOBLE
MUSIC HANS ZIMMER PRODUCTION PERCY MAIN, MIMI POLK, RIDLEY SCOTT for PERCY MAIN
PRODUCTIONS
STARRING SUSAN SARANDON (Louise Sawyer), GEENA DAVIS (Thelma Dickinson),
HARVEY KEITEL (Hal Slocumb), MICHAEL MADSEN (Jimmy), CHRISTOPHER MCDONALD
(Darryl), BRAD PITT (J. D.), STEPHEN TOBOLOWSKY (Max), TIMOTHY CARHART (Harlan),
LUCINDA JENNY (Lena the waitress), MARCO ST. JOHN (Truck driver)
ACADEMY AWARDS 1992 OSCAR for BEST ORIGINAL SCREENPLAY (Callie Khouri)

"You've always been crazy, this is just the first chance you've had to express yourself."

The movie's first image is of a broad landscape that slowly brightens and then immediately sinks back into darkness. Two friends, Thelma (Geena Davis) and Louise (Susan Sarandon) are treating themselves to a weekend away. Thelma has to get ready in secret, as her helpless husband would never let her out of the house if he knew, as he needs her to make his coffee and fasten his gold bracelet every morning. The unfamiliar freedom is a revelation to her, and at the first stop she orders a drink and takes up a cowboy's invitation to dance. Things turn nasty and he tries to rape her, only giving up when Louise holds a pistol to his head. The crisis seems to have passed when the cowboy starts shouting unbearable obscenities after the two women. Louise turns round and shoots him dead with the

words, "You watch your mouth, buddy." Horrified at their own actions, the friends flee, convinced that no one would believe their version of events. Thelma's self-confidence has been sapped by long years of marriage and she reacts at first with childish despair, whereas Louise coolly organizes their escape to Mexico.

The film then develops a double perspective. The first follows the two women, who become more daring, more independent, and less tolerant with every obstacle that crosses their path. Thelma begins to get the hang of being free and getting her own way. She locks a policeman into his own trunk at gunpoint when he tries to arrest them, and then blows up an oil tanker when the driver directs a stream of sexist comments at them as he drives

4

ROAD MOVIE From the earliest days of the movies, train travel has been a popular motif, due to cinema's fascination with movement. When cars and motorbikes became more widespread, motion could be intimately connected with a character's individual development. From the '40s onward, outsiders and dropouts were continually portrayed as motorized nomads. The enormous success of Dennis Hopper's *Easy Rider* (1969) helped turn the road movie into a distinctive and familiar genre. Along with *Thelma & Louise* (1991), the road trips in other movies such as David Lynch's *Wild at Heart* (1990) and Oliver Stone's *Natural Born Killers* (1994) provide a way of dealing with what are often violent social conflicts. The protagonists in *The Straight Story* (1999) – also directed by David Lynch, *About Schmidt* (2002), and *Broken Flowers* (2005) adopt a more personal approach – searching for oneself, the uncertain future – in taking to the road.

by. The second perspective shows us the police investigations. Detective Hal Slocumb (Harvey Keitel) is a sensitive cop who suspects the truth about the murder and tries to mediate, but he is powerless to stop the machinery of the FBI once it begins to roll. Thelma spends a night with con man and playboy J. D. (Brad Pitt), who puts the detectives on the trail of the two women. Eventually, an entire flotilla of screeching police cars catches up with Thelma and Louise at the brink of a canyon. A standoff develops and the policemen cock their guns. In a moment of high emotion, Thelma urges Louise to drive on. Louise puts the car in gear and floors the pedal, and they roar off over the edge of the abyss to certain death. The picture freezes as the car hovers high over the canyon and gets brighter and brighter until all we see is pure white light.

Thelma & Louise is the story of a liberation. As the journey progresses, the frightened and helpless Thelma develops into a smart, strong woman. The more critical the friends' situation gets, the more assertive she becomes. Looking back on her married life, she realizes how her husband tyrannized her, and the tragedy of her seemingly normal life becomes clear.

Thelma & Louise is also a story about a journey into the light. In the course of the movie, the exterior scenes get brighter and brighter until they are almost overexposed. In jarring contrast, the interiors where the police carry out their interrogations are filmed in cold blue and green. Scott's movie doesn't map out an exclusively female pattern of behavior for the two friends, but rather lets them take on roles that are usually reserved for men. Reviewers in the US criticized the movie for its man-hating attitudes and glorification of violence, but in fact Thelma & Louise makes no generalizations about the sexes. It is one of the few movies where lines and actions were applauded or booed aloud during cinema screenings. Seldom does cinema tread so provocatively on society's fault lines.   MS

"These great 'heroines' bring Callie Khouri's furious screenplay to life with totally infectious energy." *Cinema*

1 Farewell domesticity: Thelma (Geena Davis) forces a policeman into the trunk of his car.

2 Pursued by hundreds of policemen, Thelma and Louise (Susan Sarandon) stare resolutely towards the future.

3 Portraying these two radically different women had a formative influence on the careers of Susan Sarandon and Geena Davis.

4 A sensational moment from the film: a tanker, the symbol of masculine power, is blown sky-high.

5 Brad Pitt came fresh from the world of advertising to star as a sex symbol in this film.

6 Composed and resolute, Louise reaches for her gun, having no other option.

7 The film repeatedly offers the two women a fleeting respite in the still of the night.

DELICATESSEN

1991 – FRANCE – 99 MIN. – BLACK COMEDY
DIRECTORS JEAN-PIERRE JEUNET (*1955), MARC CARO (*1956)
SCREENPLAY JEAN-PIERRE JEUNET, MARC CARO, GILLES ADRIEN
DIRECTOR OF PHOTOGRAPHY DARIUS KHONDJI **EDITING** HERVÉ SCHNEID **MUSIC** CARLOS D'ALESSIO
PRODUCTION CLAUDIE OSSARD for CONSTELLATION, UGC, HACHETTE PREMIÈRE
STARRING DOMINIQUE PINON (Louison), MARIE-LAURE DOUGNAC (Julie Clapet),
JEAN-CLAUDE DREYFUS (The Butcher), KARIN VIARD (Miss Plusse), TICKY HOLGADO
(Mr. Tapioca), ANNE-MARIE PISANI (Mrs. Tapioca), EDITH KER (Grandmother Tapioca),
MICKAEL TODDE, BOBAN JANEVSKI (Young rascals), JACQUES MATHOU (Roger)

"How much do you weigh?"

Something terrible has happened to the world. Everything is in ruins and permanent darkness reigns. Somewhere, a solitary apartment block remains standing. It must have been quite a distinguished residence at some point in the past. Now, the people here are better off than elsewhere – the downstairs of the house is a butcher's shop, run by an ingenious master butcher (Jean-Claude Dreyfus) who keeps the occupants supplied with fresh meat. The wares on offer at his "delicatessen" are the former neighbors, but this no longer seems to bother his customers: in times like these they can't afford to be choosy. When provisions run short at her funeral, Grandmother herself provides the refreshments – giving a whole new meaning to the expression "funeral baked meats."

Louison (Dominique Pinon), an unemployed clown, strays into this apocalyptic horror-idyll. The butcher, sharpening his knives, takes him on as a caretaker, and the rest of the gruesome crew look forward to a glut of fresh meat.

Despite the difficult times, Louison has retained his sunny character and he entertains the occupants of the house with his tricks – but that isn't enough to get him taken off the menu. Luckily for him the butcher's daughter Julie (Marie-Laure Dougnac) falls in love with him, and she does her utmost to save him from her father's meat grinder. In her hour of need she turns to the arch-enemies of the house's bizarre inhabitants: the vegetarians, who indulge their repulsive preference for corn and wheat in the Paris sewers …

Delicatessen was the first full-length movie by Jean-Pierre Jeunet and Marc Caro, French directors who had made their names with distinctive shorts. The film is a showcase for comic figures like Mrs. Interligator (Silvia Laguna), who constantly hears voices encouraging her to attempt suicide with a series of daredevil contraptions that are as inventive as they are unsuccessful. Then there's the elderly gentleman (Howard Vernon) who has turned his apartment into a pond to keep himself in frogs and snails: the plot is really just an excuse for the succession of peculiarities and monstrosities that Jeunet and Caro parade before our eyes.

The film's impact also depends on the details of its fairy-tale comic scenery, which is loving created. We learn to expect the unexpected from the walls, pipes, and shafts of the house, which, rather than providing shelter

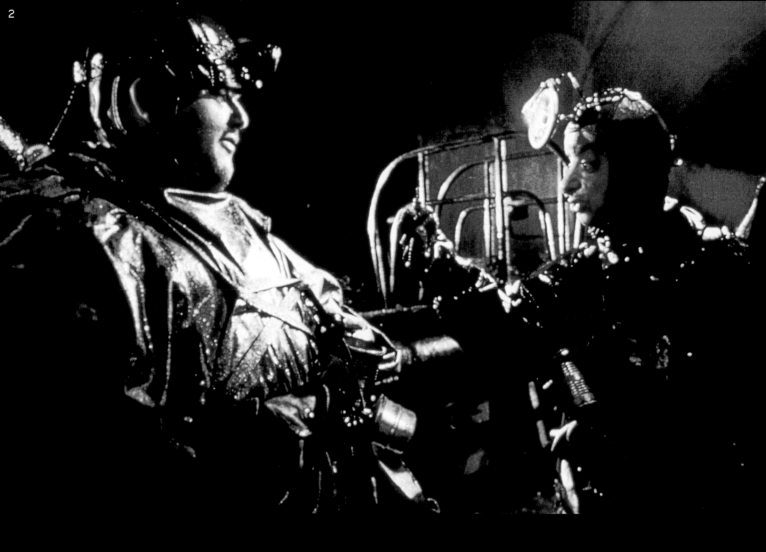

for its inhabitants, shifts and stirs like a prehistoric creature and seems to have swallowed them whole. Its crooked staircases and hallways mark it as a surreal motif with many forerunners in the history of the cinema, like the Bates Motel in Hitchcock's *Psycho* (1960) or the Overlook Hotel in Stanley Kubrick's The *Shining* (1980). But more than anything *Delicatessen* is a slapstick version of Roman Polanski's apartment house horror film *Le Locataire* (*The Tenant*, 1976) based on the novel by French writer Roland Topor.

Both the "living" house and the hero of the film call to mind Terry Gilliam's alarming apocalyptic vision *Brazil*. Like the willful civil servant Sam

Lowry, Louison is a naïve revolutionary who has remained human in an inhuman world and is therefore bound to antagonize the people who surround him. Louison forgives his tormentors by constantly reminding himself that it is the circumstances which have turned them to the bad. He respects his fellow men despite their cannibalism, and the fact that they kill his pet ape, who winds up in their stew pot.

Delicatessen does far more than push back the boundaries of bad taste. It's also an eloquent plea for humanity, solidarity, and – vegetarianism.

SH

SURREALISM – CINEMA AS DREAM The poet Guillaume Apollinaire used the term "surréel" for the first time in 1917. Following the ideas of Sigmund Freud, Surrealism tries to make man's internal reality visible. Motifs from dream experiences and intoxicated states distort the surrealists' view of the world and transform objective reality into a reflection of the soul. As surrealism coincided with the early days of film, it is not surprising that its images and ideas have influenced cinema history since its very beginnings. An early example is *Der müde Tod* (*Destiny*, 1921) by Fritz Lang. Surrealist set pieces can be found in all movie genres, although not always as explicitly as in Alfred Hitchcock's *Spellbound* (1945), whose dream sequences were designed by Salvador Dalí. Variations on surrealist themes and motifs have found their way into in a range of different genres, from horror to science fiction.

1 Will that be all, sir? Butcher Clapet (Jean-Claude Dreyfus) always seems to have the welfare of his fellow inhabitants at heart.

2 Living on rabbit food: militant vegetarians barricade themselves in the basement to fight for a meat-free diet.

3 Nobody is safe from the butcher's razor-sharp knife.

4 A Little Night Music … Louison (Dominique Pinon) and Julie (Marie-Laure Dougnac) meet and fall in love.

5 Circus artist Louison tries to survive in an inhuman milieu by using imagination and humanity.

"There's nothing remotely like the world of *Delicatessen.* It's a fragment of childhood miraculously intact. A mirage. A scrap of eternity. It's heart-breakingly lovely." *Le nouvel observateur*

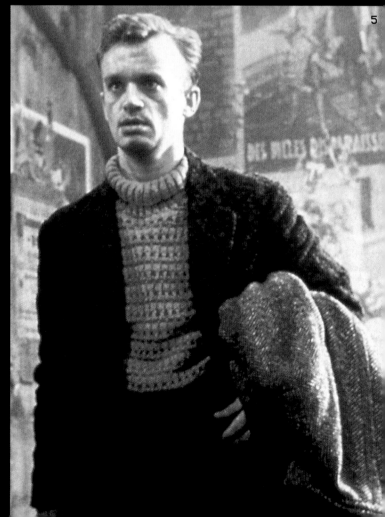

4

TERMINATOR 2: JUDGMENT DAY ♟♟♟♟

1991 – USA – 137 MIN. – ACTION FILM

DIRECTOR JAMES CAMERON (*1954)
SCREENPLAY JAMES CAMERON, WILLIAM WISHER DIRECTOR OF PHOTOGRAPHY ADAM GREENBERG
EDITING CONRAD BUFF, DODY DORN, MARK GOLDBLATT, RICHARD A. HARRIS
MUSIC BRAD FIEDEL PRODUCTION JAMES CAMERON, GALE ANNE HURD for
CAROLCO PICTURES, LIGHTSTORM ENTERTAINMENTS, PACIFIC WESTERN
STARRING ARNOLD SCHWARZENEGGER (Terminator T-800), LINDA HAMILTON
(Sarah Connor), EDWARD FURLONG (John Connor), ROBERT PATRICK (T-1000),
EARL BOEN (Dr. Peter Silberman), JOE MORTON (Miles Bennett Dyson), S. EPATHA
MERKERSON (Tarissa Dyson), CASTULO GUERRA (Enrique Salceda), DANNY COOKSEY
(Tim), JENETTE GOLDSTEIN (Janelle Voight)
ACADEMY AWARDS 1992 OSCARS for BEST VISUAL EFFECTS (Dennis Muren, Stan Winston,
Gene Warren Jr., Robert Skotak), BEST SOUND EFFECTS EDITING (Gary Rydstrom,
Gloria S. Borders), BEST MAKEUP (Stan Winston, Jeff Dawn), and BEST SOUND
(Tom Johnson, Gary Rydstrom, Gary Summers, Lee Orloff)

"You gotta listen to the way people talk. You don't say 'affirmative' or some shit like that. You say 'no problemo.'"

In the year 2029, war rages between intelligent machines and the last human survivors of an atomic attack launched against mankind by the computer network Skynet in 1997. But strangely, the outcome of that war is to be decided in the present day of the film, the early '90s, as both sides have sent a Terminator back in time to manipulate the course of history. The scene is the city by night, where two naked bodies materialize in quick succession. Unimpressed by attempts to stop him, the hefty T-800 (Arnold Schwarzenegger) robs a Hell's Angel of his leathers, motor bike, and shades. T-1000 (Robert Patrick) appears less muscle-bound, and he takes a policeman's car and uni-

form. Both set off in search of the ten-year-old John Connor (Edward Furlong), who will lead the human resistance forces in the year 2029, but is at present still living with his long-suffering foster parents. His mother Sarah (Linda Hamilton) has been institutionalized in a mental hospital. Her fearful tales of brutal fighting robots in human form – who the movie's audience recognize from the first *Terminator* film – are considered the ravings of a madwoman.

The two Terminators find John Connor practically at the same time in the dark corridors of an amusement arcade. T-800 rips out a pump-action shotgun from the gift-wrapped box under his arm, grabs John, deflects

2

3

"Visceral to the point of overkill (and beyond), a berserk blizzard of kinetic images, it doesn't even give you time to be scared." *The Washington Post*

MORPHING Of all the special effects used in *Terminator 2*, computer-generated morphing is both the simplest and the most original. Transformations from one form into another (the Greek word *morphe* means form) are shown as a seamless process. Two different images – for example, a man and an animal – are computer-manipulated to produce further images, enabling a seamless transition from one figure to the other. Previously, directors had to rely on the audience's imagination; the original figure was shown, then the successive shape, and the transformation took place in the audience's head. Since *Terminator 2*, the process can be shown in its entirety. Morphing has a surprisingly uncanny effect on screen. It interferes with our preconceptions of material stability and suggests that everybody and everything is interchangeable.

1 Clad head to toe in leather and armed to the teeth, the Terminator (Arnold Schwarzenegger) is the

2 In contrast to the angular figure of Schwarzenegger, Robert Patrick embodies a slippery, cynical liquid

4 … the T-800's stolen motorbike enhances Schwarzenegger's "image."

T-1000's shots with his bare torso and fires back. T-1000 is thrown back by the force of the gunfire, but instead of gunshot wounds, his upper body shows nothing but scratches which glimmer metallically and close over instantly.

T-800 escapes with John on his motorbike, but he only explains what is happening after they have blown up the tanker truck which the T-1000 is using to follow them. He explains to John that he is an old-fashioned robot (a mechanical skeleton covered with organic tissue) reprogrammed by the people of the future, but that the machines of the future have sent a more highly developed cyborg made of fluid metal who can fit itself to any shapes it touches. The glimmering metal figure of T-1000 emerges from the flames of the burning truck unharmed, and takes on the shape of a cop before our very eyes.

Once John has discovered that T-800 is programmed to obey his every instruction, his first act is to forbid him from killing people, and then orders him to free his mother Sarah from the mental hospital. The robot and Sarah have their hands full saving John from the attacks of T-1000, but Sarah goes one step further: she wants to stop the coming atomic war single-handed, and goes to find Dyson, the scientist who is developing the technology which will make the machines' domination possible. John and T-800 only just make it in time to stop her killing Dyson, but by cutting open the flesh of his arm to show the mechanics underneath, T-800 manages to convince the scientist of the dangers to come. He lets them into the compound of the Cyberdine Corporation, where they steal the remains of the

Terminators from the first movie, without which the deadly future developments will not be possible.

T-1000 remains hot on their heels, effortlessly gliding through iron bars and transforming his arm into steel spikes in a fraction of a second. They finally destroy him in a steel works, in a fight to the death the likes of which have seldom been seen on the screen. They blow up another tanker truck, but this time it is full of fluid gas, which freezes the amorphous Terminator. A shot from T-800 shatters the metal into millions of splinters. But as they begin to warm up, the drops of metal flow together to re-form the familiar figure of T-1000. In the fight that follows on the stairways and metal grids of the steel works, he is almost split in two and then grows back together, he takes on the shape of Sarah Connor and tries to deceive John, and the real Sarah fires at him until her bullets run out. At the last moment, T-800 appears on a conveyor belt and hurls the badly damaged metal hulk into a furnace full of glowing steel, where T-1000 runs through all its possible transformations with ear-splitting cries and screeches until it is mixed with the liquid metal forever.

One last test awaits Sarah and John. The chip in T-800's head could also be used for military research and as a departure point for future wars – it too must be destroyed. As the Terminator is incapable of self-destruction, Sarah has to push the button that sends him into the steel bath which swallowed up his enemy. Shortly before he disappears completely, he gives the thumbs-up sign, a "cool" greeting that John taught him during their escape.

A record budget

Terminator 2 is a movie that set standards for years to come. Although it was the most expensive movie of all time when it was made in 1991, it still made an enormous profit. Its effect relies on a continual assault on the senses. The opening credits are underscored by the pulsating music that structures the whole film. The action spectacle contains very few quiet moments, but even in the scenes reserved for developing the comic-sentimental relationship between John and T-800, the mood is dark and overshadowed by the final battle to come. The audience is spared none of the details of Sarah's vision of atomic fallout with a fireball, burning bodies, and disintegrating skeletons. But the apocalyptic mood comes above all from the special effects. The computer technology used was brand new in 1991, and rumor has it that the production crew were still not sure that some of the movie's scenes were actually possible when the filming started. But, despite their spectacular nature, the effects are so well integrated in the movie's plot that they never become a mere end in themselves. *Terminator 2* not only sketches a vision of the future, its special effects themselves are part of this future. The struggle between T-800 and T-1000 is the conflict between two different stages of technological development. While the mechanical skeleton and computing chip of T-800 are still materially fallible, T-1000 represents post-material technology thanks to the use of unprecedented special effects: its mimetic polyalloy allows it to "morph" between metallic machine and human form giving it an unnatural shapelessness. The two Terminators mirror the ambivalent relationship between the human beings and the technology they have created. On the one hand, we fear that research that has run out of control and that technology is becoming self-sufficient – the computerized defense network Skynet in *Terminator 2* is a reference to the SDI project. On the other hand, T-800 represents the fantasy of technology that compensates for the deficits in human society. As Sarah Connor says: "Of all the would-be fathers who came and went over the years, this thing, this machine, was the only one who measured up. In an insane world, it was the sanest choice."

MS

5 Being on the run with John Connor (Edward Furlong) teaches the Terminator how humans behave. On the orders of his protégé, fatalities become a thing of the past.

6 Linda Hamilton was one of the first female actors allowed to bare visibly trained muscles in a Hollywood movie.

7 No other film has ever shown off Arnold Schwarzenegger's face and body to such impressive effect.

7

8   As is often the case in Hollywood films, the
strong woman is never far from hysteria.

8

"After *Terminator 2*, Hollywood will have to think twice about making still another car chase movie."

New York

THE LOVERS ON THE BRIDGE
LES AMANTS DU PONT-NEUF

1991 – FRANCE – 126 MIN. – DRAMA
DIRECTOR LÉOS CARAX (*1960)
SCREENPLAY LÉOS CARAX   DIRECTOR OF PHOTOGRAPHY JEAN-YVES ESCOFFIER   EDITING NELLY QUETTIER
MUSIC Various, including LES RITA MITSOUKO, DAVID BOWIE, IGGY POP, ARVO PÄRT,
GILLES TINAYRE   PRODUCTION CHRISTIAN FECHNER, ALBERT PRÉVOST, HERVÉ TRUFFAUT,
ALAIN DAHAN for FILMS CHRISTIAN FECHNER, FILM A2
STARRING JULIETTE BINOCHE (Michèle), DENIS LAVANT (Alex), KLAUS-MICHAEL GRÜBER
(Hans), DANIEL BUAIN (Alex's friend), MARION STALENS (Marion), CHRICHAN LARSSON
(Julien)

*"I want to be drunk with you,
so I can see you laugh."*

The first scenes of Léos Carax's movie *The Lovers on the Bridge* are like a documentary shot in cinéma vérité style: a young man staggers along on the central reservation of a road, oblivious to the cars which roar past him. One of the cars knocks him over. A young woman, with a lost air, observes how he is finally picked up by a bus that takes homeless people to a night shelter. Later that night the two meet again on the Pont-Neuf, the oldest bridge in Paris, which is closed for renovation. And there begins Carax's love story, a tale of two outsiders whom life has not treated well.

The young woman is called Michèle (Juliette Binoche) and is a painter who is almost blind in one eye. She is haunted by her bourgeois origins and by an unhappy relationship that forces her to keep a pistol in her paint box. Alex, the young man (Denis Lavant), is hyperactive, antisocial, and permanently under the influence of drugs. He occasionally works as a fire-eater. One other memorable character is the old vagabond Hans (Klaus-Michael Grüber), the man who has lived on the bridge the longest. Alex falls in love with Michèle but has no words to express his love. In order to discover something about the woman he loves, he breaks into her apartment and reads her letters.

Léos Carax went to great lengths for the production of his movie and the re-creation of the homeless milieu in which it is set. He had the bridge copied and built in an almost life-size replica near Montpellier, complete with sham housefronts on the banks of an artificial Seine. The filming of the movie was dogged by misfortune. First the producer died and then the relationship between Léos Carax and his long-time partner and leading actress Juliette Binoche broke down. The movie took three years to finish and by the time it reached the movie theaters it was three times over budget. Its 160 million franc production costs made it the most expensive French movie ever made. Although strictly speaking it was not a box office success, the critics loved it, perhaps because its strengths lie in its opulent images rather than in its sparing dialogues. Visually, the movie is immensely stylized, but at the same time it also gives a strong impression of realism, so that the audience is never sure

whether what it is watching is the product of a fertile imagination or simply an intelligent and realistic film. There are two murders in the movie, which may be real or may just have taken place in Michèle's mind. The empty eye socket, which Alex sees when he lifts Michèle's eyelid, is probably only a figment of his imagination. The Lovers on the Bridge is an uncomfortable movie, compellingly filmed and open to many different interpretations.

Léos Carax has never been one for conventional cinematic idioms. The movie is a kind of cinematic litmus test which shows a great number of different visual layers and shades of emotion and mood. Some of its more exciting scenes have an almost hypnotic quality, as when Michèle and Alex dance wildly during the firework display commemorating the 200th anniversary of the French Revolution or when Michèle waterskis behind a stolen police boat.

The source of Carax's inspiration becomes clear in one of the last shots in the movie. The two lovers are shown in a pose which reminds us of the figurehead of a ship, a homage to Jean Vigo's film *L'Atalante* (1934), a masterpiece which combines a dreamlike atmosphere with the realities of Parisian life.   APO

4 The people who live on the bridge have the
   fireworks celebrating the bicentennial of the French
   Revolution in their front room.

5 A love without words: Alex (Denis Levant)
   and Michèle on their bridge.

"This wounded tarantella of a film is unique. The emotion wells from its form not its core, and is as pure and direct as the great never-to-be-forgotten prewar melodramas. Few words, music of every denomination, and so many breathtaking images that one drowns in them." *Le Monde*

JULIETTE BINOCHE Juliette Binoche won her first Academy Award in 1997 for her supporting role as the nurse in *The English Patient*. The daughter of an actress and a sculptor, her career as an actress began in the mid-'80s in her native land with movies such as Jean-Luc Godard's *Hail Mary* (*Je vous salue, Marie*, 1983) and Léos Carax's *Bad Blood* (*Mauvais Sang*, 1986). She and Carax were partners for many years until their relationship broke up during the filming of *The Lovers on the Bridge*. Her roles in Philip Kaufman's film of Kundera's novel *The Unbearable Lightness of Being* (1987), Louis Malle's *Damage* (1992), and Krysztof Kieślowski's *Three Colors: Blue* (*Trois Couleurs: Bleu*, 1993) won her an international reputation as the archetypal French actress. She confirmed her position as one of the top European stars with her roles in two films directed by Michael Heneke, *Code Unknown* (1999) and *Hidden* (2005), and in Abbas Kiarostami's *Certified Copy* (2010).

THE COMMITMENTS

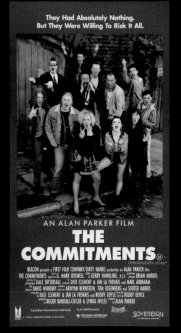

1991 – IRELAND / GREAT BRITAIN – 117 MIN. – MUSIC FILM, COMEDY
DIRECTOR ALAN PARKER (*1944)
SCREENPLAY DICK CLEMENT, IAN LA FRENAIS, RODDY DOYLE, based on the novel *DUBLIN BEAT* by RODDY DOYLE **DIRECTOR OF PHOTOGRAPHY** GALE TATTERSALL **EDITING** GERRY HAMBLING
MUSIC PAUL BUSHNELL, various soul songs **PRODUCTION** ROGER RANDALL-CUTLER, LYNDA MYLES for BEACON COMMUNICATIONS
STARRING ROBERT ARKINS (Jimmy Rabbitte), ANDREW STRONG (Deco), MICHAEL AHERNE (Steve Clifford), ANGELINE BALL (Imelda Quirke), MARIA DOYLE (Natalie Murphy), DAVE FINNEGAN (Mickah Wallace), BRONAGH GALLAGHER (Bernie McGloughlin), FÉLIM GORMLEY (Dean Fay), GLEN HANSARD (Outspan Foster), DICK MASSEY (Billy Mooney), JOHNNY MURPHY (Joey "The Lips" Fagan)

"The Irish are the blacks of Europe."

Anyone who grows up in the Catholic north of Dublin has three possible ways of escaping the rubble-strewn wastelands and washing lines. He can be a good boxer, a good footballer or, best of all, play music like U2. This is what Derek and Ray hope to do, although they start out by giving their best renditions of popular favorites at family get-togethers. They are still calling themselves "And, And, And" when Jimmy Rabbitte (Robert Arkins) offers to be their manager. Jimmy has narrow sideburns and knows all about music. He always has the latest records, but most of all, he is a man on a mission: to found the best soul band that Ireland has ever seen. Musicians are recruited through a small ad which reads "Have you got soul? If so, the hardest working band in the world is waiting for you!"

The next day, half of Dublin is lined up outside Jimmy's parents' kitchen and an endless parade of hopefuls show off their talents with the bagpipes, tin whistle, and banjo. The Commitments start to take shape, from the 16-year-old bus conductor Deco (Andrew Strong) with his Joe Cocker voice to Joey "The Lips" (Johnny Murphy), the trumpeter, who assures then that God has sent him to come to their aid. When that doesn't work he swears that he once played with Wilson Pickett. After a few weeks of rehearsals, The Commitments bring miserable community halls to their feet and the commercial breakthrough is not long in coming, and Jimmy founds his own record agency.

Alan Parker's *The Commitments* continues the rags-to-riches theme of his earlier movie *Fame* (1979). Both films are based on the "a star is born" ideology. Despite their slum backgrounds, his characters show remarkable wit and intelligence, and considering that they are a group of amateurs at the beginning of the movie, they develop a professional sound with admirable speed. Their musical success is guaranteed by cover versions of Soul classics like "When a Man Loves a Woman" and "Respect." Two years later Parker's fellow countryman Stephen Frears produced another Irish version of the same recipe for success. His portrayal of Dublin's working classes in *The Snapper* was also based on another novel by Irish writer Roddy Doyle, whose book *Dublin Beat* was the model for *The Commitments*.

Parker doesn't stint on sitcom elements and entertaining details. Jimmy, the manager's father, has a picture of the Pope hanging in his kitchen to show his loyalty to the Catholic Church, but as he is also an Elvis fan, there has to be a picture of Elvis as well. And as Elvis is God, not just his representative, Elvis hangs over the Pope. In one key scene in the film, The Commitments wait for Wilson Pickett who has promised to come to one of their concerts. Jimmy has spread the word and so the local press are out in full force. They wait in vain and Jimmy is accused of being a con man. After the premiere of *The Commitments* in Los Angeles, Wilson Pickett himself really did appear on stage. Cinema lives from such stories. RV

1 A white Prince of Soul surrounded by swinging sides of pork – an Irish dream of freedom through music.

2 The Commitments' backing singers at their first gig in a Roman Catholic community center: "Heroin(e) kills" can just be read in the background.

3 The sax and trumpet are called Gina (Lollobrigida) and Kim (Basinger); when they are played, the result is the coolest working rhythm in the world.

4 Deco (Andrew Strong), the heavyweight lead singer, hogs the limelight, but when he's pounding out Wilson Pickett's "Mustang Sally," soul reaches the Irish working class.

"Alan Parker's *The Commitments* is a loud, rollicking, comic extravaganza." *Chicago Sun-Times*

MUSIC MOVIES Someone is preoccupied with a dream – obsessed, even. He fights against all obstacles and adversity, against evil representatives of the industry and jealous competitors, struggles with inner demons and drugs and finally comes out on top – all of which happens under the spotlight and with plenty of music. This is the quintessential music film. Exponents of the genre tell the story of a real or, as in *The Commitments* (1991), fictional musician or group. From *The Glenn Miller Story* (1954) through *Great Balls of Fire* (1989, Jerry Lee Lewis) to *The Doors* (1991), music films have always been popular in Hollywood. The success potential of the screen product rises in proportion to the fame of the star portrayed: hence the biopics of Ray Charles (*Ray*, 2004), Johnny Cash (*Walk the Line*, 2005), and the legendary soul trio The Supremes (*Dreamgirls*, 2006) all won Oscars. Music films are made outside Hollywood as well, for example *La Vie en rose* (*La Môme*, 2007) about Edith Piaf.

BARTON FINK

1991 – USA / GREAT BRITAIN – 116 MIN. – DRAMA, MYSTERY
DIRECTOR JOEL COEN (*1954)
SCREENPLAY ETHAN COEN, JOEL COEN DIRECTOR OF PHOTOGRAPHY ROGER DEAKINS
EDITING ETHAN COEN, JOEL COEN (as RODERICK JAYNES) MUSIC CARTER BURWELL
PRODUCTION ETHAN COEN, JOEL COEN, GRAHAM PLACE for CIRCLE FILMS,
WORKING TITLE FILMS
STARRING JOHN TURTURRO (Barton Fink), JOHN GOODMAN (Charlie Meadows),
JOHN MAHONEY (W.P. Mayhew), JUDY DAVIS (Audrey Taylor), MICHAEL LERNER
(Jack Lipnick), JON POLITO (Lou Breeze), TONY SHALHOUB (Ben Geisler),
STEVE BUSCEMI (Chet), RICHARD PORTNOW (Detective Mastrionotti),
CHRISTOPHER MURNEY (Detective Deutsch)
IFF CANNES 1991 GOLDEN PALM, BEST DIRECTOR (Joel Coen) and BEST ACTOR (John Turturro)

"I'm a writer, you monsters! I create, I create for a living! I'm a creator!"

Barton Fink (John Turturro) is one of those characters who only the Coen brothers could have come up with. A lanky, insecure guy. With his round glasses, one is inevitably reminded of the silent film comedian Harold Lloyd, whose hair, from fear, always stood on end – except for the fact that Barton's hair, unfortunately, looks like this naturally. This is no coincidence, for what happens to the ambitious playwright in Hollywood is simply hair-raising.

In the early 1940s, Barton arrives on the West Coast. A young, ambitious author, celebrated on Broadway, he now wants to bring his social and engaging stage plays to the big screen and, in doing so, gain access to a broader audience.

His humble lodgings, the Hotel Earle, with its dark rooms and abandoned hallways, exudes a charm similar to that of the Overlook Hotel in Stanley Kubrick's The Shining (1980). And just like the writer Jack Torrance in the classic horror film, Barton Fink also suffers from an insurmountable case of writer's block – he can't get past the first few lines. Distraught, he stares at the blank pages and at the ceiling of his rundown hotel room. The camera perpetually allows us to take part in his hopeless view of the wallpaper gradually peeling from the walls. Actually, he is only supposed to write the

screenplay for a trivial wrestling movie with Wallace Beery in the lead role – an inconsequential flick to entertain the masses. The pressure grows; studio boss Jack Lipnick (Michael Lerner) and film producer Ben Geisler (Tony Shalhoub) are anxious to see the screenplay. Barton, however, is overly ambitious – he wants to create nothing less than his magnum opus. He seeks the help of his idol, the writer W. P. Mayhew (John Mahoney), but working in Hollywood has turned him into a sad alcoholic.

Barton loses his grasp on reality more and more. Even the viewers lose sight of whether what they see is reality or just a product of Barton's imagination. First, he has a short affair with Mayhew's secretary Audrey (Judy Davis), but the next morning, her bloody, dead body lies in bed next to him. Barton can't remember anything. His neighbor in the hotel Charlie Meadows (John Goodman), helps him dispose of the body. Two detectives show up and suspect Barton of being Meadow's accomplice who revealed himself to be a bloodthirsty serial killer and creates a truly diabolical finale. At the end, Barton becomes part of the Hollywood machine. He sits on the beach and meets the same mysterious woman from the picture in his hotel room. He is now "in pictures" himself – a part of his own films.

The Coen brothers relish in describing the misery of a writer in the entertainment industry. Hollywood is full of writers. Throw a rock and you'll hit one, as Ben Geisler says to Barton, not without smugly adding that he should please try to throw the stone as hard as he can. The studio bosses want to hear nothing of artistic freedom – a writer belongs to the film studio, and if he doesn't work, he'll be replaced by the next best one. The "Barton Fink feeling" could be created just as well by any other writer, Lipnick reveals at the end of the film. Barton's ego is crushed for good when he finds out that Mayhew's books were ghostwritten by his secretary. In his despair, Barton even imagines that the first three sentences of his script are printed word for word in the Bible.

Ultimately, Barton is a Kafkaesque antihero who struggles with the loss of his own identity. In him, the modern man's fear of losing himself in the anonymity of the masses is reflected. What should Barton write if everything has already been written and if anybody else could word it just as well? It seems as if the Coens unceremoniously moved the postmodern debate over the death of the writer up a few decades.

Towards the end of the film, Barton's spell finally seems to be broken. Feverishly, he begins to write and finishes his screenplay. However, as we

1   With a combination of arrogance and fear of failure, John Turturro shines in the lead role of Barton Fink. In Cannes, he was honored for his portrayal with the award for best actor.

2   Barton has to find out from Audrey (Judy Davis) that his W.P. Mayhew is now only a shadow of his former self.

3   Studio boss Jack Lipnick (Michael Lerner) brings Barton to Hollywood – whatever he does, he just shouldn't approach the situation too intellectually.

4   Charlie Meadows (John Goodman) is all too familiar with the plight of the common folk, and he also knows how he can free them from it.

"Though *Barton Fink* defies genre, it seems to work best as a tart self-portrait, a screwball film noir that expresses the Coens' own alienation from Hollywood." *Washington Post*

"Like all of the Coen productions, *Barton Fink* has a deliberate visual style. The Hollywood of the late 1930s and early 1940s is seen here as a world of Art Deco and deep shadows, long hotel corridors and bottomless swimming pools. And there is a horror lurking underneath the affluent surface." *Chicago Sun-Times*

7

5 Bloody nose? Detective Deutsch (Christopher Murney) and Detective Mastrionotti (Richard Portnow) wonder about the large blood stain on Barton's sheets.

6 In the infernal hotel hallway, Charlie reveals his true identity – he's the notorious serial killer "Madman Mundt."

7 Bound to his bed, Barton must helplessly watch as Mundt gets rid of the two detectives.

8 Charlie shows Barton the tricks he learned from his time as a wrestler. But even these do little to help him with his screenplay.

hear the last few sentences of the script, we realize that they are almost identical to the end of his Broadway hit. Barton has become an unimaginative copy of himself.

Even though the names of the characters and films are fictitious, there are, nevertheless, countless references to actual people. The model for the main character was the Jewish stage actor Clifford Odets, who came from the New York Group Theater to Hollywood. W.P. Mayhew clearly alludes to the famous southern actor William Faulkner, who began writing for the movies as

early as the 1930s and wrote, among others, the screenplay for *Flesh* (1932) in which Wallace Beery plays a wrestler.

With *Barton Fink*, the Coen brothers achieved something truly unique: never before had a film won all three of the most important prizes at Cannes – best film, best director, and best actor. Apart from that, the film also received rave reviews all around. Even so, the attendance figures remained rather low, and the film only grossed two-thirds of its production costs.

CZ

JOHN TURTURRO For the Coen brothers, it was clear from the beginning that John Turturro should play the lead role in Barton Fink. John Michael Turturro was born the son of Italian immigrants in Brooklyn in 1957. He studied acting in New York and at the Yale School of Drama. His big screen debut was as an extra in Martin Scorsese's classic boxing film *Raging Bull* (1980). In *Five Corners* (1987), Turturro played Heinz, an ex-con trying to make a fresh start in the Bronx. Director Spike Lee liked him so much that he cast him in *Do the Right Thing* (1989). The two worked together a total of nine times on, among other films, *Jungle Fever* (1991), *Clockers* (1995), and *He Got Game* (1998). For the Coens, Turturro has stood before the camera four times – the first time as Bernie Bernbaum, the hunted small-time criminal in *Miller's Crossing* (1990). Turturro has often played Jewish characters such as in the lead role of the dumped gameshow contestant, Herbie Stempel, in Robert Redford's *Quiz Show* (1994) or in the role of Primo Levi in Francesco Rosi's *La tregua* (1997). He achieved cult status in another Coen film with his portrayal of the Mexican bowling god Jesus Quintana in *The Big Lebowski* (1998), especially with his famous line: "Nobody fucks with the Jesus!" Turturro has also directed several films such as *Illuminata* (1998) and the strange musical *Romance & Cigarettes* (2005). The likeable actor has also proven he can play a villain as Johnny Depp's adversary in *Secret Window* (2004). Turturro can also be seen from time to time in blockbusters: he played the role of agent Simmons in all three of Michael Bay's *Transformer* movies (2007, 2009, 2011).

BASIC INSTINCT

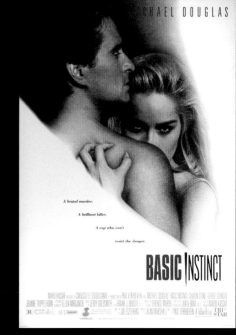

1992 – USA – 127 MIN. – EROTIC THRILLER
DIRECTOR PAUL VERHOEVEN (*1938)
SCREENPLAY JOE ESZTERHAS DIRECTOR OF PHOTOGRAPHY JAN DE BONT EDITING FRANK J. URIOSTE
MUSIC JERRY GOLDSMITH PRODUCTION MARIO KASSAR for CAROLCO, LE STUDIO CANAL+
STARRING MICHAEL DOUGLAS (Detective Nick Curran), SHARON STONE (Catherine Tramell),
JEANNE TRIPPLEHORN (Dr. Beth Gardner), GEORGE DZUNDZA (Gus), DENIS ARNDT
(Lt. Walker), LEILANI SARELLE (Roxy), BRUCE A. YOUNG (Andrews), CHELCIE ROSS
(Captain Talcott), DOROTHY MALONE (Hazel Dobkins), WAYNE KNIGHT (John Correli)

"She's the fuck of the century."

Sweaty bodies, rough sex, an ice axe, and lots of blood – from the opening shot of the movie, Paul Verhoeven makes it clear what the audience should expect for the next two hours. The director's third film appeals to our animal nature, although it's unclear whether the "basic instinct" of the title is a reference to hunting or the reproductive instinct. The story unfolds in a totally macho world where there is no place for weakness. Unfortunately, the hero, disillusioned cop Nick Curran (Michael Douglas), is powerless to resist temptation of any kind. Hot-tempered and partial to provocative women, he's also burdened with a past he would rather forget: ever since killing two innocent bystanders as part of a raid, he has struggled with an alcohol problem and had to endure the jibes of his colleagues. Douglas plays the role with his jaw clenched, but behind the foul temper and tough exterior lies a deeply insecure character whose private and professional life are constantly on the verge of breakdown, He comes across as thoroughly unlikeable, but Curran's weaknesses make him into a character with whom the audience can sympathize.

Despite his personal problems, he's given the job of investigating the murder shown so memorably at the beginning of the movie. The trail of clues leads him to Catherine Tramell (Sharon Stone), a crime writer who is as sexy as she is mysterious, who seems to have already anticipated the brutal act in one of her books. Could she have turned her evil imagination into reality? That solution is a little too obvious even for the police department. No one could be so stupid as to advertise a murder they were planning in a book in advance. Unless of course that is exactly what the murderer wanted the detectives to think.

1 Is she or isn't she? The public was more interested in whether or not Sharon Stone was wearing panties in this scene than they were in working out the whodunnit.

2 Detective Nick Curran (Michael Douglas) does battle with alcohol, nicotine, and sharp-tongued women writers.

3 Why would a woman who has everything commit such a senseless murder?

4 Intelligent, beautiful, and – lethal? Catherine Tramell (Sharon Stone) is always a few steps ahead of the investigators.

"The film is like a crossword puzzle. It keeps your interest until you solve it. Then it's just a worthless scrap with the spaces filled in." *Chicago Sun-Times*

Catherine Tramell certainly seems to be capable of such a calculating trick. Breathtakingly seductive, uncompromising in her search for sexual satisfaction, and rolling in money, she is a monstrous combination of male wish fulfillment and castration anxiety: a sex-hungry feminist and man-murdering vamp, intellectually far superior to the men who surround her.

The fearless detectives are helpless in the face of their provocative prime suspect. When they take her in for questioning at the police station, in what is undoubtedly the film's most famous moment and one of the main reasons for its success, she totally confuses them by crossing her legs and letting her skirt ride right up. The pressing question as to whether Catherine murdered her partner during sex is effectively overshadowed by the even more pressing one as to whether Stone was wearing panties during this

scene. Debate raged in the press, and there were even claims that during the love scenes, viewers were witnessing unsimulated sex. Such bizarre slippage of the boundaries between cinema and reality, between actual events and their interpretations is typical of Verhoeven's movies and ultimately part of their attraction.

Appropriately, given this double game with reality, there is also a female psychologist in *Basic Instinct*, in what seems to be the last straw for the beleaguered male characters. Dr. Beth Gardner (Jeanne Tripplehorn) plays a large part in the undoing of Curran. Her job is to test his psychological fitness for active police service, but he becomes hopelessly entwined in a labyrinth of sex, lies, and psycho trickery when he tries to use sexual humiliation to get his revenge for this professional degradation. Eventually

he inevitable happens and Curran succumbs to the charms of the prime uspect. Needless to say this does him no good whatsoever either as far as is resolve to give up smoking and drinking is concerned, or in his profession- l judgment. It is also highly dangerous, and to the very end the audience is ept guessing which trap the hero will finally fall into.

Sharon Stone's striking presence as a woman and as an actress makes oe Eszterhas's plot seem more complex to the viewer than it actually is. Verhoeven's strength – as his first two Hollywood films *Robocop* (1987) nd *Total Recall* (1990) show – lies in the calculated exaggeration of stereo- ypes: men crash through his films as city cops steaming with an excess of estosterone. They swill whiskey, slap each other on the back, and always have a pithy remark on their lips. His women are the complete opposite: unfathomable, and, when there is no "real" man to be had, lesbians. They

invariably spell disaster for the men. Verhoeven's characters are artificial fig ures that fall apart when confronted with the complexity of reality, precise because they are nothing but clichés. They are either figures to identify wit helpless prey of their own appetites like Curran, or they are victims lik Curran's dumb colleague Gus (George Dzundza). Gus spends the whole filr shooting his mouth off before he is forced to a direct, physical realizatio that reality is much more complicated than he imagined. Verhoeven play the double game even further, and behind the cool superficiality of his cine matic world there are always threatening depths. In a world of sex and vic lence, voyeurism becomes the most genuine form of perception, but at th same time – as in the scene at the police headquarters – the pleasure seeing is revealed to be a complex trap. Verhoeven's movies are reflectior on filmmaking. They do not just portray pleasurable illusions, but are then

"In Hollywood it's all down to nerve, not originality."
end Film

selves illusion as films. Verhoeven ensures that this self-reflexive level doesn't get lost in all the sex and violence by peppering his movies with allusions and quotations from the entire history of cinema. In *Basic Instinct*, for instance, Michael Douglas's role can be taken as an ironic commentary on the prototype of the good cop he played in younger years in *The Streets of San Francisco*.

Above all, Verhoeven quotes from Alfred Hitchcock's movies, so much so that *Basic Instinct* is almost a homage to the great director, with long drives along coastal roads, dialogues inside cars interspersed with meaningful glances in the rear-view mirror – these are all nice touches taken from the master. Hitch is also present in the Freudian motives and explanations that give the film an unexpected comic aspect – above all in the home-baked, slap-dash psychology of Dr. Beth Gardener, a cardboard cutout psychologist

if ever there was one. Verhoeven is not however the kind of director to create such an effect unintentionally.

Besides all that, he shows his mastery of the art of suspense. The audience may feel that they are a couple of steps ahead of the hero all the time, but the real danger is always unpredictable.

Some critics saw *Basic Instinct* as a mere glorification of sex and violence, but that fails to do it justice. Verhoeven and Eszterhas clearly intended to do much more than that: Catherine Tramell is presented as a highly intelligent woman who would be unlikely to describe in her books crimes she intended to commit. If the makers of *Basic Instinct* had really only been interested in serving their animal natures, they would have used their craftsmanship and knowledge of film history to conceal it far more skillfully. Unless of course, that was what they wanted film critics to think. SH

PAUL VERHOEVEN Born in Amsterdam in 1938, Verhoeven first indulged his liking for explicit scenes of sex and violence in Dutch movies like *Keetje Tippel* (*Katie Tippel*, 1974/75) and *De vierde man* (*The Fourth Man*, 1983). His first international production, *Flesh + Blood* (1985), which was set in the Middle Ages, continued the trend. Verhoeven then made his name in Hollywood with the sci-fi spectaculars *RoboCop* (1987) and *Total Recall* (1990). In both movies, he uses action cinema stereotypes to reflect on the voyeurism of the film industry and its inherent imbalance of illusion and reality. After *Basic Instinct* (1992) he came up with a flop slated by the critics, *Show Girls* (1995), which has since become a cult film for the gay scene. In *Starship Troopers* (1996) Verhoeven portrays a grim parody of a future totalitarian regime. His most politically committed film is the historical drama *Black Book* (2006), which shows the suffering of a Jewish woman in the Netherlands during the German Occupation.

UNFORGIVEN ♟♟♟♟

1992 – USA – 130 MIN. – WESTERN
DIRECTOR CLINT EASTWOOD (*1930)
SCREENPLAY DAVID WEBB PEOPLES DIRECTOR OF PHOTOGRAPHY JACK N. GREEN EDITING JOEL COX
MUSIC LENNIE NIEHAUS PRODUCTION CLINT EASTWOOD for MALPASO
STARRING CLINT EASTWOOD (Bill Munny), GENE HACKMAN (Little Bill Daggett),
MORGAN FREEMAN (Ned Logan), RICHARD HARRIS (English Bob), JAIMZ WOOLVETT
(Schofield Kid), SAUL RUBINEK (W. W. Beauchamp), FRANCES FISHER (Strawberry Alice),
ANNA THOMPSON (Delilah Fitzgerald), DAVID MUCCI (Quick Mike), ROB CAMPBELL
(Davey Bunting)
ACADEMY AWARDS 1993 OSCARS for BEST PICTURE, BEST DIRECTOR (Clint Eastwood),
BEST FILM EDITING (Joel Cox), and BEST SUPPORTING ACTOR (Gene Hackman)

"Did Pa used to kill folks?"

The story begins with the ultimate affront in a male-dominated society: a young horse trader goes to town with a friend looking for a good time, but when he drops his trousers in front of prostitute Strawberry Alice (Frances Fisher) she bursts out laughing. tragic consequences follow. The humiliated man slashes Strawberry Alice's face with a knife, robbing her of her good looks, which are all she has. As far as Little Bill Daggett (Gene Hackman), the tyrannical sheriff of Big Whiskey is concerned, the only injured party is the owner of the brothel. The cowboys have to pay him horses in compensation and the disfigured whore comes away empty-handed. But the girls she works with are not prepared to leave it at that, and they scrape together their savings to put a prize on the head of the cowboys.

News of the whores' plot reaches former gunslinger-turned-farmer Bill Munny (Clint Eastwood) at exactly the right, or rather, exactly the wrong moment. His pigs are dying in scores from an epidemic, and the widowed

father of two children, now a convert to pacifism and godliness, can see no way out other than taking up the immoral offer.

Despite the fact that he can no longer hold his hand nor his horse steady, he sets off to Big Whiskey together with his old friends Ned Logan (Morgan Freeman) and the almost blind would-be gunman Schofield Kid (Jaimz Woolvett). Little Bill is waiting for them, determined to make an example of every bounty hunter who turns up.

The first man to suffer is English Bob (Richard Harris), who is also attracted by the money offered by the whores. Little Bill crushes him physically, before humiliating him and exposing him as a fraud.

Meanwhile, Munny and his accomplices begin their sorry work. Munny has never shot anyone sober but he soon realizes that death is a wretched business that has nothing to do with heroism. Schofield Kid is forced to the same conclusion after shooting his unarmed victim on the toilet. Horrified

1

2

3

"A moral film which comes over as an allegory of the increasingly violent world in today's large American cities."

film-dienst

by his own deed, he drowns himself and we begin to realize why Munny had to drown his past in alcohol.

In *Unforgiven*, the time of the great Western heroes is long gone. The sagas of fearless settlers and liberty-loving outlaws glorifying American history appear instead as a collective illusion, covering up a seemingly endless spiral of murder and slaughter. There is no forgiveness in this world: when the two cowboys offer Strawberry Alice a pony as compensation out of court, they are pelted with horse dung by the outraged whores.

If institutionalized violence in the shape of the sheriff is a mere tool in the machinations of the powerful, killing in the name of justice is also nothing but a farce. Munny and his friends magnify Strawberry Alice's mutilation in their imagination until they have convinced themselves that her injuries are appalling enough to justify their return to their ways of old.

"Is it true, Pa used to shoot people?" asks Munny's youngest daughter. The truth is he can hardly remember himself. All he knows of his past identi-

ty comes from the tales that others tell, and so he has become a legend even to himself. His return to action – and this is the movie's real adventure – is a journey into his own past.

A Freak Show of Lost Souls

Eastwood bought the screenplay for *Unforgiven* in the early 1980s but let it lie so he could "grow into the role." The movie was originally to have been directed by Francis Ford Coppola. It is the quintessence of Eastwood's previous Westerns and at the same time a swan song for the part of the solitary avenger he played so often; he dedicated the movie to the directors who "spotted" him, Sergio Leone and Don Siegel. Although he has been accused – by critics like Pauline Kael for example – of reactionary views and of excusing rough justice, in *Unforgiven* he tells a sad tale of the senselessness of violence

1   A man at the end of the road: Bill Munny (Clint Eastwood) sets off on a journey into his past and has to drown the memories of his own misdeeds in booze.

2   A powerful misanthrope: Sheriff Little Bill Daggett (Gene Hackman) has built himself his own little realm of terror.

3   The Big Whiskey whores are up in arms, demanding vengeance for the mutilation of one of the girls.

4   Old partners. Bill Munny and Ned Logan (Morgan Freeman) on their way to Big Whiskey. Once they sowed fear and terror in their path, now they are shadows of their former selves.

and of the existential and moral desperation of individuals. The casts of what Georg Seesslen termed "phantom Westerns" like *High Plains Drifter* (1972) or *Pale Rider* (1985) – the solitary avenger, the cowardly small town citizens, the corrupt town mayor – all come together here in a freak show of lost souls whose last resort for survival is cynicism. At times like these there is nothing left worth fighting for. All the protagonists seem to have reached their final destination and even the whores' revenge will not change their fate. Men like Little Bill are incapable of laying the solid foundations necessary for a home, and not meant for a settled existence. The movie's tragic irony is that the characters who have found their place in life set off once again to repeat the mistakes of their past. They got away with their lives the first time round, but the relapse is unforgivable, and this unholy crusade ends fatally for Munny's accomplices.

The boundless desolation of the movie is reflected in its scenery. The endless expanse of the American West is no longer a grandiose setting for adventure, but is transformed instead into a barren wasteland, a never-ending desert of stones and dust whose limitlessness implies the pain of homelessness and desertion rather than a sense of freedom. Even the prairie has become a melancholy reminder of a time that maybe never even existed. Those who embroider their own legend, like English Bob, end up even more ridiculous than the rest.

The famous feats of the "Duke of Death" are shown to be the embarrassing appearances of a ham actor. English Bob is shadowed by a writer called Beauchamp (Saul Rubinek), whose aim is to conserve the memory of a supposedly heroic epoch, but his efforts are as hopeless as the sheriff's attempts to patch his leaky roof. "Maybe you should hang the carpenter," a hapless visitor suggests as the master of the house tries in vain to catch the drips in pails and bowls. A remark like that might have cost him his life in the "good old days," as a grim look from Little Bill tells us: now it almost passes unnoticed.

"I thought it was about time there was a film showing that violence not only causes pain, but is also not without consequences for the perpetrators as well as the victims."

Clint Eastwood in *film-dienst*

THE ANTIHERO Whenever and wherever the hero suffers an identity crisis, the hour of the antihero has struck. This was how spaghetti Westerns reacted to the Wild West clichés propagated by Hollywood in the '70s, for example, when the antihero appeared on the scene as an assault on stagnant genre conventions. As antiheroes don't need moral justification, they can help break up stereotyped storytelling mechanisms, as in Quentin Tarantino's *Pulp Fiction* (1994). This also explains why antihero figures are often used when formal innovation is a director's first priority, as in Oliver Stone's *Natural Born Killers* (1994).

5 Unforgiven: Ned Logan has walked into the brutal sheriff's trap.

6 An ill-matched trio: the almost blind Schofield Kid (Jaimz Woolvett) joins forces with his heroes and has to learn the meaning of killing someone.

7 Bill Munny says goodbye to his children.

8 A startling finale: contrary to the conventions of the genre, the showdown is no storm that clears the air, and the hero is denied salvation.

5

The dime novel writer Beauchamp is Eastwood's merciless portrait of everyone who propagates the myth of the Wild West. Beauchamp panders to criminals' vanity by shrouding their deeds in mystery and praise, but literally wets himself at the first sign of real violence. In settling the score with the myth itself, *Unforgiven* also settles with all those who helped to create it. This extends of course to naturally the actor/director Eastwood himself, who has the self-same legends and clichés to thank for his fame and has often embodied and glorified them on the silver screen. Eastwood does not allow himself a nostalgic look back, however, and his most famous role of solitary avenger has lost all its moral justification in *Unforgiven*.

In the end, the movie's deconstruction of old-style heroes amounts to a thorough deglorification of violence and its perpetrators. In classic Westerns the final showdown is like a storm which clears the air and allows justice to emerge triumphant. The finale of *Unforgiven,* by contrast, brings no salvation, and Munny is forced to realize that his past has caught up with him. He returns home victorious and yet defeated: a hero who has lost his mask, and one who is even denied a hero's death at the end.

SH

TWIN PEAKS: FIRE WALK WITH ME

1992 – USA – 134 MIN. – MYSTERY DRAMA

DIRECTOR DAVID LYNCH (*1946)

SCREENPLAY DAVID LYNCH, ROBERT ENGELS **DIRECTOR OF PHOTOGRAPHY** RON GARCIA

EDITING MARY SWEENEY **MUSIC** ANGELO BADALAMENTI **PRODUCTION** GREGG FIENBERG for LYNCH-FROST PRODUCTIONS, CIBY PICTURES

STARRING SHERYL LEE (Laura Palmer), RAY WISE (Leland Palmer), KYLE MACLACHLAN (Dale Cooper), MOIRA KELLY (Donna Hayward), CHRIS ISAAK (Chester Desmond), DANA ASHBROOK (Bobby Briggs), KIEFER SUTHERLAND (Sam Stanley), DAVID BOWIE (Phillip Jeffries), HARRY DEAN STANTON (Carl Rodd), PEGGY LIPTON (Norma Jennings)

IN A TOWN LIKE TWIN PEAKS NO ONE IS INNOCENT.

"A freaky accident."

Teresa Banks is murdered in Deer Meadow, Washington, and when FBI Agent Chester Desmond (Chris Isaak) and his young colleague Sam Stanley (Kiefer Sutherland) are sent to investigate local police make things difficult. The case (a young girl wrapped in a plastic tarpaulin found murdered on a riverbank) bears a clear resemblance to the murder which happens one year later in the small town of Twin Peaks. In the course of the investigation Agent Desmond disappears without a trace and Agent Dale Cooper (Kyle MacLachlan) is sent to replace him. Several inauspicious signs, including a letter of the alphabet found under a fingernail of the victim, convince Dale Cooper that the murderer will strike again. But who knows where and when…

The film of the television series begins appropriately with an imploding television set, followed by the famous place name sign from the series opening credits and Angelo Badalamenti's atmospheric film music – we're back in Twin Peaks alright. Laura Palmer is still alive, and what we see are her last days, in the hope of finding out what the series left unclear.

Lynch claimed that his main reason for developing the TV series *Twin Peaks* (1989–1991) into a lengthy feature film was the feeling that he had not yet finished with the material. The series creators, David Lynch and Mark Frost, had originally hoped that the crime story of *Twin Peaks* would gradually fade into the background and eventually become completely unimportant. The unexpected success of the series meant that they were eventually forced to present their audiences and producers with a murderer. As Lynch had warned, viewer numbers then fell and he ended up suffering for a mistake that was not his own.

However the bizarre, imaginary world of Twin Peaks and the inconsistencies of its main characters continued to haunt Lynch, and before long he began work on the movie *Twin Peaks: Fire Walk with Me.* Accusations that he was trying to cash in on the success of the TV series are unfair. The movie brings together some of the plot strands which had been lost in the increasingly complex weave of the story. The incest theme, which only emerged slowly in the series, is one of the main elements in this process, and Lynch was also able to give more space to the sexual aspects of the story in general, as he no longer had to worry about TV regulations in the many countries where *Twin Peaks* was broadcast. Numerous hints and questions

left open in the series are explained, and in the movie Lynch does his characters more justice by working on their psychic conflicts and making them more convincing. As obscure hints and contradictions were the lifeblood of the series, clarifying matters in the movie was a risk. In the final edit, a number of scenes were omitted, some offbeat marginal figures were cut to fit the material to film length and a more clearly defined plot framework was provided. Many ironic allusions fell by the wayside, and so for instance regular viewers of the TV series were disappointed to see that the frequent references to doughnuts and cherry pie had disappeared. Much of what was cut

were the elements that served to lighten the mood of the series, and so the movie turned out much darker than its TV model. The bizarre atmosphere of Twin Peaks and the threatening presence of the forest condense into a claustrophobic nightmare. Audiences unfamiliar with Lynch's earlier work are unsure how to react, but, the movie remains a monument to Lynch's single-mindedness and versatility. He did more than continue the series: he fitted his material to the demands of a different medium. The message makes uncomfortable viewing, but his treatment of it is clear.

SH

FILM AND TV The sequel or "resurrection" of a TV series on the big screen – still the exception in 1992 – has long since become the rule: examples include *Charlie's Angels* (2000), *Starsky & Hutch* (2004), and *Miami Vice* (2006). The fear of contamination between film and TV has disappeared. Even famous filmmakers work in television as well: *Sideways* director Alexander Payne produced the series *Hung* (2009–2011) and also directed the pilot episode; and Martin Scorsese (*The Departed*, 2006) produced the series *Boardwalk Empire* (2010). Both come from the stable of American cable TV company HBO, which kicked off the new wave of quality television with series like *The Sopranos* (1999–2007) and *Six Feet Under* (2001–2005). The new series use the extra time available to them in comparison with film to give more nuanced character development. They also tackle unusual story lines and narrative styles, which makes them exciting for the discerning film fan.

---

1 During his investigation, Agent Dale Cooper (Kyle MacLachlan) visits a bizarre dream world, where he is given puzzling tip-offs by a dwarf.

2 Beautiful but flawed: before her murder Laura Palmer (Sheryl Lee) did not lead the completely blameless life she would have had people believe.

3 *Twin Peaks: Fire Walk with Me* is a prequel to the TV series. The viewer is given insights into Laura Palmer's double life and in the end finds out who the real killer was.

4 There can't always be cherry pie: many ironic allusions fell victim to editorial cuts, including Dale Cooper's fondness for local specialities.

5 The cryptic dream symbolism has a clearer role to play in the much darker film version.

3

"People want to forget the world around them, but at the same time they're scared of it. Watching a film at home is much safer. There are worlds I'd rather not experience — but if I go to the cinema, I want to be right in the middle of the action." David Lynch

4

5

THE LAWNMOWER MAN

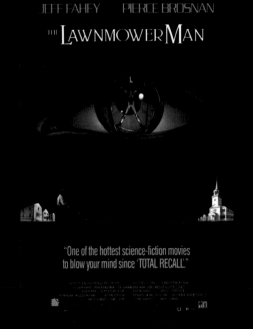

1992 – USA – 108 MIN. – SCIENCE FICTION, THRILLER
DIRECTOR BRETT LEONARD (*1959)
SCREENPLAY GIMEL EVERETT, BRETT LEONARD, based on the story of the same name by
STEPHEN KING **DIRECTOR OF PHOTOGRAPHY** RUSSELL CARPENTER **EDITING** ALAN BAUMGARTEN
MUSIC DAN WYMAN **PRODUCTION** GIMEL EVERETT for ALLIED VISION, LANG PRINGLE
STARRING PIERCE BROSNAN (Dr. Lawrence Angelo), JEFF FAHEY (Jobe Smith),
JENNY WRIGHT (Marnie Burke), JEREMY SLATE (Pater McKeen), AUSTIN O'BRIEN
(Peter Parkette), MARK BRINGELSON (Sebastian Timms), ROSALEE MAYEUX
(Carla Parkette), GEOFFREY LEWIS (Terry McKeen), JOHN LAUGHLIN (Jake Simpson),
COLLEEN COFFEY (Caroline Angelo)

"I am a God here!"

From loser to ruler of the world: mentally retarded assistant gardener Jobe Smith (Jeff Fahey) discovers the blessings of modern technology – until his flight into virtual reality becomes a trip to hell.

Based on a short story by Steven King, *The Lawnmower Man* is a re-telling of the old tale of the sorcerer's apprentice who calls up spirits he cannot control. "Virtual Reality Specialist" Dr. Lawrence Angelo (Pierce Brosnan) is conducting research into ways of increasing the intelligence of apes with the help of computer simulations until the government blunders in on his work. They aren't interested in intelligent primates, but they do want expendable fighting machines, so they start to manipulate his experiments until one day Angelo's ape runs amok and has to be killed. The research project seems doomed to failure.

By chance the scientist then happens upon Jobe, who leads a miserable existence exploited and abused by his foster father and the local minister, and is a butt for the jokes and spite of his fellow men. Jobe is known as the Lawnmower Man not because he mows the doctor's lawns, but because he also has a talent for repairing machines of all kinds. He knows that a broken lawnmower doesn't just need mending, but that it also needs a few words of encouragement every now and again. This innocent, naive relationship to machines foreshadows of Jobe's fate as a man-machine. Professor Angelo sees in Jobe a chance of saving his work. Attracted by colorful cyber trips and the professor's promise to make him more intelligent, Jobe becomes his apprentice.

In this movie computer games increase the intellect, and Jobe's trips into the world of bits and bytes turn him to an intelligent beast in a literal sense: but unbeknownst to the professor, the military still has an evil hand in the game. Jobe soon overtakes his master and throws to the wind his warnings that the human spirit should not be overtaxed – a principle which in the eyes of some critics the movie itself also failed to heed.

"A modern version of *Frankenstein*, which attempts to put across new visual experiences using computer graphics." *film-dienst*

In no time at all, like everybody too clever for their own good, Jobe wants to rule the world. Disappointed with cybersex and the limitations of the human race from which he has become completely alienated, he wants to be exalted as the immortal god of cyber space in the form of a worldwide network: the internet as global techno-divinity.

The makers of this movie were not primarily interested in either realism or a critique of technological progress. Their main concern was spectacular video animation, so for example there is no explanation of how all the multi-colored 3D effects make Jobe into a super brain. Critics loathed *The Lawnmower Man,* and had a field day tearing it to pieces. But at a time when only a small minority used the Internet, words like cyberspace and cybersex had a far more mysterious ring to them than they do today, and the idea of being able to have sex without touching someone was particularly attractive in the age of AIDS. As an early example of the fascination with new digital production possibilities, *The Lawnmower Man* is thoroughly worth the journey to the land of computer dreams. SH

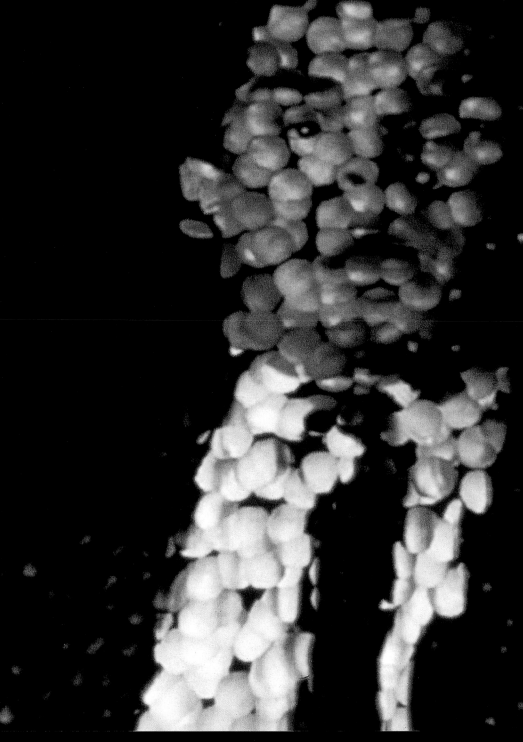

1   A brave new multi-colored cyber world? In the early 1990s *The Lawnmower Man* made a strong impression with vivid computer animation, warning of the dangerous temptations presented by technology.

2   The computer as weapon. Those who stood in the way of the Lawnmower Man were shot off into the void of cyberspace without further ado.

3   What began as a seemingly harmless computer game soon became deadly serious.

4   Between worlds. Soon nobody can tell what is real and what is simulated.

5   From gardener to superhero: as ruler of cyber-space, the Lawnmower Man Jobe Smith (Jeff Fahey) then turns his attentions to domination of the real world.

CYBER THRILLER   In the 1990s, computers were no longer simply tools used in the process of making movies, but featured more and more often as their subject matter too. The idea of fusing man and machine emerges as particularly fascinating, as in movies such as *The Lawnmower Man* (1992), *Johnny Mnemonic* (1995), or *Strange Days* (1996). Portrayals of how computers or the Internet actually change particular aspects of everyday life don't come until later and remain exceptions (for example, *The Net,* 1995). *The Matrix* (1999) can be seen as a provisional climax of the computer theme: the decade ends with the idea that the whole world surrounding modern man is nothing but a vast computer animation.

THE PLAYER

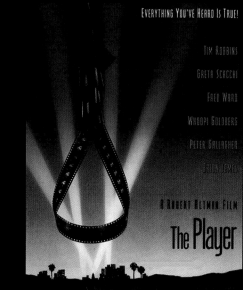

1992 – USA – 117 MIN. – SATIRE, THRILLER, LITERATURE ADAPTATION
DIRECTOR ROBERT ALTMAN (1925–2006)
SCREENPLAY MICHAEL TOLKIN, based on his novel of the same name
DIRECTOR OF PHOTOGRAPHY JEAN LEPINE EDITING MAYSIE HOY, GERALDINE PERONI
MUSIC THOMAS NEWMAN PRODUCTION DAVID BROWN, MICHAEL TOLKIN, NICK WECHSLER for
AVENUE PICTURES, SPELLING ENTERTAINMENT, DAVID BROWN-ADDIS WECHSLER
PRODUCTIONS
STARRING TIM ROBBINS (Griffin Mill), GRETA SCACCHI (June Gudmundsdottir), FRED WARD
(Walter Stuckel), WHOOPI GOLDBERG (Detective Susan Avery), DEAN STOCKWELL
(Andy Civella), PETER GALLAGHER (Larry Levy), VINCENT D'ONOFRIO (David Kahane),
DINA MERRILL (Celia Beck), SYDNEY POLLACK (Dick Mellen), RICHARD E. GRANT
(Tom Oakley)
IFF CANNES 1992 BEST DIRECTOR (Robert Altman), BEST ACTOR (Tim Robbins)

"No stars!"

"I hate your guts, asshole!" Griffin Mill (Tim Robbins), executive at a big Hollywood studio, is not exactly popular. He's known this for a long time, and he doesn't need the anonymous death threat he gets at the end of the eight-minute opening sequence of *The Player* to spell it out for him. In a single take, a reference to Orson Welles's *Touch of Evil*, director Robert Altman introduces 20 characters and outlines what his movie is all about: the everyday madness of Hollywood studio life. In the faceless machinery of Hollywood, there is no place for personal preferences or artistic ambition – although that thesis is flatly contradicted by Altman's extraordinarily mannerist opening.

However, as long as people like Griffin Mill have a say in whether an idea becomes a movie or not, the only things that matters are internal power games and perhaps, in a pinch, box-office success. Mill is an obstacle which screenplay writers have to surmount on their way to fame. It's his job to get rid of the authors of "witty yet touching political thriller romances" or "High-School Graduation, Part 2," and no one does it as cold-bloodedly as, smooth career man Mill. His own life is like a farcical movie: "I guess they must breed guys like him some place," says Burt Reynolds (in the role of Burt Reynolds) at one point in the second half of the film. People like Mill have no friends. They only have contacts and victims.

The anonymous letter seems to point – unsurprisingly – to a disgruntled writer who hates Mill. Mill goes to find him to offer him a "deal," but this time it is the offended and somewhat drunken writer who gives the studio parasite the brush-off ("What would you do if you were out of a job? I can write at least, but what can you do?") In the heat of the moment, Mill kills him, only to discover the next day that he has murdered the wrong man. "Surprise" says the fax. Mill then realizes that there were witnesses to his crime.

Although not unduly troubled by the fact that he has killed a man, the murder is the beginning of a downward turn in Mill's life, and things get worse by the minute. Intrigues brew behind his back and suddenly even his own plotting and planning threatens to blow up in his face. The slide continues until finally his whole career is at stake, by which point it is clear to the movie's audience that the end of his career would be the end of him. To make matters worse, cynical police inspector Susan Avery (Whoopi Goldberg) is on his case.

The Player does more than question the divide between screenplay and reality where its main character is concerned. Altman plays a sophisticated game; he does not even present himself from the outside as an uninvolved bystander, but as a worker in the dream factory from which there is no ultimate escape.

3

4

"This film uses Hollywood as a metaphor for our society. It shows greed and corruption, and these are not exclusive to the film industry."

Robert Altman in *Der Spiegel*

5

"No stars!" is the demand of a young screenplay writer naive enough to want to make a realistic film. But when Bruce Willis rescues Julia Roberts from the electric chair at the end, he's the one who applauds the loudest.

Increasingly, Griffin Mill's life seems to follow the sort of trajectory to be found in one of the screenplays he rejects by the dozens every day. In the bizarre parallel universe of Hollywood, no one cares whether life imitates art or art life. Seeing movie stars on the street is an everyday occurrence. Around 50 well-known Hollywood greats, including actors, many directors,

writers, and studio people appear in *The Player* in small cameo roles, but in a setting like that, the only people who stand out are the ones who aren't famous.

It's only logical that the studio bosses in *The Player* eventually have the bright idea of saving money by getting rid of screenwriters altogether. After all, movies only quote from each other, and real life provides the best stories, as the wonderfully ironic, double bind at the happy end of *The Player* shows.

SH

1   The usual suspects? Producer Griffin Mill (Tim Robbins, no. 5) gets into trouble not only with crazy screenplay writers and the authors of anonymous threatening letters, but also ultimately with the police.

2   Inside Hollywood's high society, Griffin Mill has forgotten that there's another world out there.

3   "No stars!" Rarely has there been such an array of famous names in a movie. Even Bruce Willis and Julia Roberts got a chance to mimic themselves in *The Player*.

4   A relationship seems to be in the offing between the murdered writer's partner, mysterious Icelander June Gudmundsdottir (Greta Scacchi), and Griffin Mill.

5   Walter Stuckel (Fred Ward) philosophizes at great length about classic and contemporary cinema.

A FEW GOOD MEN

1992 – USA – 138 MIN. – THRILLER, COURTROOM DRAMA
DIRECTOR ROB REINER (*1945)
SCREENPLAY AARON SORKIN, based on his play of the same name
DIRECTOR OF PHOTOGRAPHY ROBERT RICHARDSON EDITING ROBERT LEIGHTON, STEVEN NEVIUS
MUSIC MARC SHAIMAN PRODUCTION DAVID BROWN, ROB REINER, ANDREW SCHEINMAN for
COLUMBIA PICTURES, CASTLE ROCK ENTERTAINMENT
STARRING TOM CRUISE (Lt. J. G. Daniel Kaffee), JACK NICHOLSON (Col. Nathan R. Jessup),
DEMI MOORE (Lt. Comm. JoAnne Galloway), KEVIN BACON (Capt. Jack Ross),
KIEFER SUTHERLAND (Lt. Jonathan Kendrick), KEVIN POLLAK (Lt. Sam Weinberg),
JAMES MARSHALL (Priv. Louden Downey), J. T. WALSH (Lt. Col. Matthew Andrew
Markinson), CHRISTOPHER GUEST (Comm. Doctor Stone), J. A. PRESTON (Judge Col.
Julius Alexander Randolph)

"We're supposed to fight for people who couldn't."

Lieutenant J. G. Daniel Kaffee (Tom Cruise) is a defense attorney with the American army. His speciality is settling cases with the public prosecutor out of court to avoid them ever having to come to trial. For him, law is not a matter of justice, but of pragmatism; he only has a cynical smile to spare for moral issues. This is also all Lieutenant Comm. Galloway (Demi Moore) gets from him when she is assigned to work on a case with Kaffee: at Guantanamo Bay, an American base in Cuba, two members of an elite troop of marines have bound, gagged, and beaten a comrade. He dies as a result of the attack and those responsible stand accused of murder. It soon becomes clear that the victim suffered from poor health and had asked for transfer to another base. Galloway suspects that a Code Red was behind the attack, a disciplinary measure carried out by the marines themselves. At first, the accused stand together against Kaffee's efforts as defense attorney. He wants to get them the mildest possible sentence on the condition that they admit their guilt. The two marines admit to the deed, but claim that they acted on orders. Although they risk the heaviest penalty, it is a matter of honor for them to bring the truth to light. Initially, smart Kaffee cannot understand this attitude at all, but the two marines are supported by their other attorney Galloway, who also begins to influence her partner Kaffee.

Rob Reiner's movie addresses the fundamental dilemma of the justice system within the military: does an order free a soldier from personal responsibility? In the course of the investigations, the young attorney is gradually forced to ask himself such questions. The son of a famous lawyer, he has always stood in his father's shadow, and now he has to reconsider his strategy of trying to keep cases out of court: in court it is at least possible to lose. When he finally takes on the challenge of a trial, it is partly because he wants finally to be worthy of his dead father.

His opponent is Colonel Jessup, the commander of the marine base played by Jack Nicholson with the arrogance of someone who believes himself to be morally irreproachable. Kaffee is only able to live his carefree yuppie existence because he, Jessup, looks after things down in Cuba with his boys. He feels quite safe from this inexperienced upstart, who in his eyes has no right to be in the army anyway. When all's said and done, his orders and his daily struggle with the enemy uphold national security – who cares if they are legal are not. Kaffee discovers Jessup's weak point – his self-satisfaction.

The investigations are difficult and full of unexpected turns, they prepare the young lawyer for the final test, the trial. The two accused marines come to understand that even within the chain of military command, mora

> "A dramatically and technically gripping courtroom thriller, which passes harsh judgment on the army and rigorously resists action for its own sake."
>
> film.de

1 Col. Nathan R. Jessup (Jack Nicholson), arrogant, powerful, and narrow-minded.

2 Lt. J. G. Daniel Kaffee (Tom Cruise): a photo fit for a job application.

3 Jessup is the victim of his own arrogance. Titles and military decorations count for nothing in the courtroom, where reason free of prejudice triumphs.

4 Lt. Commander Galloway (Demi Moore) finds it hard to persuade the jury. Rob Reiner gives us a series of penetrating portrait shots.

responsibility still has to lie with he who acts. Only the seemingly all-powerful Colonel Jessup remains unaltered and eventually gets his just desserts. At their best, courtroom movies are showcases for the leading actors. Both Tom Cruise and Jack Nicholson throw themselves into the verbal battle with all guns blazing and the result is real movie-star cinema. The film as a whole also gains by resisting the temptation to involve Tom Cruise and Demi Moore in a love story following their initial disagreements about legal theories and defense strategies. Even if the moralistic undertone is unmistakable at the end of the film, *A Few Good Men* remains a straightforward and exciting courtroom thriller.

SL

"Reiner falls back on a tried and tested formula and creates first-rate cinema."
epd Film

5   Nice people must play baseball, at least they have to if they are American.

6   The army is a man's world. JoAnne Galloway's outfit during a conversation after work is evidence of this.

7   She's in uniform and is carrying out her duty; he's wearing casual clothes and has given up the case up for lost. Hardly a basis for good communication.

TOM CRUISE Born in 1962 in Syracuse, New York, Thomas Cruise Mapother IV has always been considered a successful actor. Yet it was only after the respect he won with his work on Stanley Kubrick's marital drama *Eyes Wide Shut* (1999) that his earlier roles were reappraised. In *Rain Man* (1988), for instance, he did a reasonable job alongside Dustin Hoffman, whose outstanding performance as the autistic brother won him the Oscar. Often seen as a sex object, Cruise is now rightly regarded as an action star, thanks to roles in *Top Gun* (1986) and the *Mission: Impossible* series (1996–2011). Yet he has also played increasingly demanding roles in dramas like *The Color of Money* (1986), *Jerry Maguire* (1996), and *Magnolia* (1999). A committed member of the Scientology movement, Cruise came under fire for his role as the would-be Hitler assassin in *Valkyrie* (2008).

ARIZONA DREAM

992/1993 – FRANCE – 142 MIN. – COMEDY, TRAGICOMEDY
DIRECTOR EMIR KUSTURICA (*1955)
SCREENPLAY EMIR KUSTURICA, DAVID ATKINS **DIRECTOR OF PHOTOGRAPHY** VILKO FILAC
EDITING ANDRIJA ZAFRANOVIC **MUSIC** GORAN BREGOVIC **PRODUCTION** CLAUDIE OSSARD for
CONSTELLATION, UGC, HACHETTE PREMIÈRE, CANAL+
STARRING JOHNNY DEPP (Axel Blackmar), JERRY LEWIS (Leo Sweetie), FAYE DUNAWAY
(Elaine Stalker), LILI TAYLOR (Grace Stalker), VINCENT GALLO (Paul Leger),
PAULINA PORIZKOVA (Millie), CANDYCE MASON (Blanche), ALEXIA RANE (Angie),
POLLY NOONAN (Betty), ANN SCHULMAN (Carla)
IFF BERLIN 1993 SILVER BEAR (SPECIAL JURY PRIZE)

"Wake up, Columbus!"

Strange people have strange habits. Some take doors for a walk in the desert; others put dozens of wrecked cars on stilts and sweep sand under them. We are in the land of liberty and adventure, Arizona, USA. Axel (Johnny Depp), a 20-year-old Parsifal, runs away from this place of solitary obsessions to New York, where he counts fish for an obscure research project. His cousin Paul (Vincent Gallo) gets him drunk and takes him back home.

Axel is an orphan and was brought up by his Uncle Leo (Jerry Lewis), who is about to marry for the umpteenth time and would like Axel as his best man. The bride, who is as young as Axel, bursts into tears when she lays eyes on her future husband's nephew. Leo tries to get Axel to stay. He has made a fortune as a car salesman and wants Axel to work for him although his nephew is violently opposed to the idea.

Solitary obsessions again: Leo's father, who started up the car sales business, dreams of a ladder to heaven completely made up of cars. Leo dreams of big business and young women. Paul dreams of being a famous actor as he sits in the movie theater and repeats all the lines of the films by heart while dogs pee on the screen.

One day, the stylish widow Elaine (Faye Dunaway) appears on the scene with her stepdaughter Grace (Lili Taylor). Axel instantly falls in love with Elaine. They have dinner and he discovers Elaine's great passion: flying.

The couple are constantly disturbed by the moody daughter, who is lost in her own obsessions – accordion music, her love of tortoises, and her hatred of her stepmother. Nevertheless, Axel decides to stay and allows himself to be carried away by a passionate affair and numerous breakneck attempts at flying. He has strange visions, but he is the only one who has no dreams and his naïveté and innocent curiosity make him irresistible to the others. But day-to-day life with an egocentric woman gradually takes its toll, and Axel loses his naturalness and eventually falls in love with the neurotic daughter.

At a talent-spotting evening they go to together, Paul makes a fool of himself. To prove his acting talent, he chooses the scene from Alfred Hitchcock's *North by Northwest* (1959) where Cary Grant is strafed by a crop sprayer. As he doesn't have a plane at his disposal, he tries to reproduce the scene alone amid the mocking laughter of the audience. Leo also breaks down: he takes an overdose of sleeping pills shortly before his wedding and Axel promises him in the ambulance that he will go back to New York.

They all celebrate Elaine's birthday together, giving her a flying machine that really works. In the meantime, the stepdaughter Grace has let her tortoises go and bent a lampshade into an antenna to kill herself with a lightning bolt during a violent storm; in Arizona, even death is a strangely comic

"The true greatness of American cinema is revealed in the panoramic shot, says Kusturica." *Der Spiegel*

affair. Axel often quotes his mother who used to wake him up every morning with the words: "Wake up, Columbus!" He thinks she meant to tell him that America has already been discovered.

All European directors who work in America seem to feel the need to dissect America's most sacred values and lay them bare to the bone. The Bosnian Emir Kusturica takes as his theme the promise anchored in the Declaration of Independence that all Americans are free to seek their happiness in the way they see fit. Visually, *Arizona Dream* is one of the most powerful movies of recent years. But it portrays a grotesque world filled with unhappy people and we are not sure whether we should laugh or cry about the abyss that separates American reality and the American dream.

JOHNNY DEPP Born in 1963, Johnny Depp actually wanted to become a rock star, and managed to get as far as Iggy Pop's support band before landing an acting part in the TV series *21 Jump Street.* When he took on the title role in *Edward Scissorhands* in 1990, it established the first constant factor in Depp's later career: since then he has collaborated regularly with director Tim Burton, on films including *Alice in Wonderland* (2010) and horror movie *Dark Shadows* (2012). The second recurring element in Depp's career is the role of the pirate captain, Jack Sparrow, the actor clearly relishing his four appearances in this swashbuckling costume drama to 2011: the *Pirates of the Caribbean* series has become one of the most successful movie franchises of all time.

1 A strange flying machine: dreams come true if you stretch out your arms.

2 Even if you pose as a pro (Faye Dunaway, Johnny Depp), you're still a complete amateur.

3 People's spiritual wounds can be seen when they look you in the eye.

4 Even threats only arouse pity in those involved.

5 Breaking every rule of cinema, all the actors (Lili Taylor) look directly at the camera. They seem as confused as the viewers.

6 Rather than stunning landscapes, the panorama with cars on stilts features weird and impossible things.

6

BAD LIEUTENANT

1992 – USA – 96 MIN. – DRAMA, CRIME FILM
DIRECTOR ABEL FERRARA (*1952)
SCREENPLAY ABEL FERRARA, ZOË LUND DIRECTOR OF PHOTOGRAPHY KEN KELSCH
EDITING ANTHONY REDMAN MUSIC JOE DELIA PRODUCTION EDWARD R. PRESSMAN for
BAD LT. PRODUCTIONS
STARRING HARVEY KEITEL (The Lieutenant), VICTOR ARGO (Bet Cop), ZOË LUND (Junkie),
PAUL CALDERON (Cop One), LEONARD L. THOMAS (Cop Two), ROBIN BURROWS (Ariane),
FRANKIE THORN (Nun), PEGGY GORMLEY (Wife), ANTHONY RUGGIERO (Lite),
VICTORIA BASTEL (Bowtay), PAUL HIPP (Jesus)

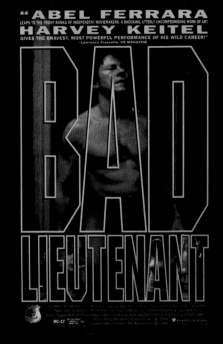

"Forgive me, please! Forgive me, Father!"

The lieutenant in question (Harvey Keitel) lives with his wife and children in a suburb of New York. He's a man who can't find peace – and has long been part of the urban hell of violence, drug dealing, and prostitution in which he works every day. As a corrupt, competitive junkie cop, he thinks nothing of abusing his power. He's a cheat and a bully, and has given up fighting against temptation of any kind. He is inextricably enmeshed in a life of gambling, drug taking, and sexual excess. When a nun (Frankie Thorn) is raped and the Catholic Church offers a high reward to anyone who tracks down the perpetrators, the lieutenant sees a final chance to pay off his debts to the mafia. Although the nun remains silent, she knows who did it. She has forgiven her rapists – an act of mercy which the cynical cop cannot even begin to understand.

Bad Lieutenant is a journey into the darkness of existential despair. Like Martin Scorsese's *Taxi Driver* (1975), Abel Ferrara's movie presents New York as an inferno where ideas like justice or the difference between right and wrong have no place. A world abandoned by God, where the anonymous protagonist – a "fuckin' Catholic" as he describes himself – has lost all faith and where there is no hope of redemption. The lieutenant suffers terribly. He is a driven man who tries to deaden his despair through sex, drugs, and gambling. The lower he sinks, the more he seems to disappear into the gloomy chaos of the city, in the hysterical tumult of a techno disco, or in dark back

rooms and stairwells. Increasingly he feels like an alien in the comfortable bourgeois world of his family, and he staggers through the clean sterility of his home in a daze. The coldness of his family life makes it clear that they can never help him, and that they are in fact one of the reasons for his fall. The few moments of real warmth and intimacy he experiences are elsewhere, with prostitutes and a junkie friend (Zoë Lund). Ferrara directs the story in uncompromising, almost documentary-style shots which he only interrupts when the nun appears or when the cop experiences religious visions under the influence of drugs and his moral crisis. The rape of the nun uses the artificiality of a video clip as though it were just one more of the cop's nightmare hallucinations. The appearance of Jesus shortly before the end of the movie is made in the same way. Here, the religious dimension hinted at in various points of *Bad Lieutenant* is made visible: the nun heralds the divine principle against which the lieutenant has sinned and without which he has no hope of forgiveness. Only when he realizes this can he find redemption.

The movie's provocative intensity comes above all from Harvey Keitel's outstanding acting, without which the powerful directness of Ferrara's production would not be possible. Keitel's grotesque howl when faced with his own guilt is so overwhelmingly heartfelt that it seems laden with all the tragedy of our human existence.

JH

1 Confession of a sinner: face-to-face with the capacity to forgive, the lieutenant acknowledges his guilt (Frankie Thorn and Harvey Keitel).

2 The film has a clearly religious dimension: a Christ figure (Paul Hipp) appears to the shattered cop.

3 Acting that reaches the limits of self-revelation: Harvey Keitel's performance makes the lieutenant's existential despair almost physically tangible.

4 A nightmare-like sequence: director Abel Ferrara stages the rape of the nun in video-clip style.

5 A showpiece role for Harvey Keitel: the corrupt cop as a mirror image of a violent society.

HARVEY KEITEL After training at the famous Actors Studio in New York and appearing in various theater productions Off Broadway, Harvey Keitel, who was born in New York in 1939, made his film debut in Martin Scorsese's *Who's That Knocking at My Door* (1968). He went on to make four more films with Scorsese, including *Taxi Driver* (1975). Keitel had long been considered an excellent character actor, thanks to numerous appearances in American and European films, when the '90s heralded the beginning of a new era in his career. Roles in a series of spectacular artistic successes finally made him a star, including Abel Ferrara's *Bad Lieutenant* (1992), Ridley Scott's *Thelma & Louise* (1991), Quentin Tarantino's *Reservoir Dogs* (1991) and *Pulp Fiction* (1994), Jane Campion's *The Piano* (1993), James Mangold's *Cop Land* (1997), and István Szabó's *Taking Sides* (2001).

"Make no mistake, Ferrara and his *Bad Lieutenant* are on a trip that's nothing to do with transport; out of phase, rude but by no means routine, their philosophy of cinema is one of borderline aesthetic and human experience. They're playing with fire, by turns unsettling and inspiring, and it's a pleasure to see." *Cahiers du cinéma*

BATMAN RETURNS

MICHAEL KEATON DANNY DeVITO MICHELLE PFEIFFER

1992 – USA – 126 MIN. – COMIC, SCIENCE FICTION

DIRECTOR TIM BURTON (*1958)

SCREENPLAY DANIEL WATERS, based on a story by DANIEL WATERS, SAM HAMM and characters by BOB KANE **DIRECTOR OF PHOTOGRAPHY** STEFAN CZAPSKY **EDITING** BOB BADAMI, CHRIS LEBENZON **MUSIC** DANNY ELFMAN **PRODUCTION** DENISE DINOVI, TIM BURTON for WARNER BROS.

STARRING MICHAEL KEATON (Batman / Bruce Wayne), DANNY DEVITO (The Penguin), MICHELLE PFEIFFER (Catwoman / Selina), CHRISTOPHER WALKEN (Max Shreck), MICHAEL GOUGH (Alfred Pennyworth), MICHAEL MURPHY (Mayor), CHRISTI CONAWAY (Ice Princess), ANDREW BRYNIARSKI (Chip), PAT HINGLE (Commissioner Gordon), VINCENT SCHIAVELLI (The Organ Grinder)

"I guess I'm tired of wearing masks."

There are some dreadful parents around. A wealthy aristocratic couple in Gotham City, seeing that their babe is born with flippers instead of hands and is generally far removed from human ideals of beauty, summarily dump the deformed offspring along with its black carriage in a nearby riverbed. The baby disappears down the sewers and nothing more is heard of it. Years later, tycoon Max Shreck (Christopher Walken) is about to turn on the lights on the biggest Christmas tree that Gotham City has ever seen when an enormous Christmas present to the city turns out to be a horrific joke, concealing skeletons armed with machine guns who jump out and gun down bystanders and municipal dignitaries. Naturally, there's only one man to call: Batman (Mi-

chael Keaton), who confronts not just that abandoned mutant son who has become The Penguin (Danny DeVito), but also the seductive yet easily ruffled Catwoman (Michelle Pfeiffer). As inscrutable as her animal model, Catwoman first makes the hero's life difficult and then completely turns his head. Tycoon Shreck quickly turns out to be the baddy and soon nobody seems to know whose side they're really on.

Tim Burton's second *Batman* film is a desolate comic opera that owes more to Sigmund Freud than it does to the characters invented by Bob Kane. Flashy effects and scenic spectacle aside, it is the psychology of the main figures that most interests Burton. As in *Batman* (1989), the cityscape of

3

4

"*Batman* isn't a film, but an American state of trance. A monologue of the collective subconscious."

Der Spiegel

1 Batman (Michael Keaton) and The Penguin (Danny DeVito): a meeting between creatures of the night. The dividing line between good and evil is not at all clearly defined in *Batman Returns*.

2 Supervillain with a giant rubber duck: Burton skillfully mixes fantastic childhood images and imaginary terrors to form a comic nightmare.

Gotham City is one of the real stars of the movie. The production designer Bo Welch creates a comic nightmare version of Manhattan where cinematic predecessors such as Fritz Lang's *Metropolis* merge with expressionism and borrowings from fascist architecture to form a threatening artificial world. Gotham City was completely remade for *Batman Returns*, and the scenery left over from the first *Batman* movie remained untouched, a clear sign that Burton wanted to use the sequel to correct what he saw as the mistakes of his first *Batman* film – mistakes caused above all by too many concessions to the production company.

Batman Returns is something like an artistic liberation: Burton is not interested in constructing a consistently logical plot and the actual story is

5

3 The Penguin, a son disowned by his aristocratic family, subjects Gotham to a reign of terror, when all he really wants is to be loved.

4 From goody-goody secretary to horror vamp with bloody claws: Michelle Pfeiffer makes a fascinating, erotically feline Catwoman.

5 Stop that: Batman goes into action.

6 The queen of the cats with her subjects. Whose side is the enigmatic Catwoman on?

7 Sometimes the real villains are hard to be found: Christopher Walken as tycoon Max Shreck, who has everything except the welfare of his employees in mind.

COMICS AND MOVIES The links between comics and movies are often underestimated. Both are dynamic media that depend on a series of exciting pictures where the right attitudes or perspectives are just as important as dramatic events. From their earliest days, comics have always taken up cinematic motifs and themes, and they have also always served as inspiration for new movies. The same is true of their characters. Cinema is particularly interested in the world of the super hero: Superman, Spider-Man, and above all Batman have fired the imaginations of filmmakers for generations now.

marginal to the movie. The real plot is the story that lies behind the bizarre main characters. Catwoman and The Penguin are lost souls who have been turned into horrific figures by unkind fate and the actions of their fellow men. The Penguin is really only looking for his parents and some recognition, Catwoman is actually a frightened secretary who has seen too much of her boss's affairs. It is hardly surprising that these fantastic figures are what interest Burton most in the Batman story; his favorite cast members have always been the misunderstood, like the subversive freak Pee-Wee Herman in *Pee-Wee's Big Adventure* (1985), or outsiders like the "normal human"

The Penguin and Catwoman are the result of their own internal contra-dictions: the salvation they long for would ultimately rob them of their iden-tity. That is also true of the figure of Batman himself. Ironically, given the title of the movie, Batman himself retreats into the background and his adversar-ies take center stage. Michael Keaton plays his sparing appearances with an air that varies from laconic to melancholic, giving the impression of a super-hero tired of his job who would like nothing better than the chance to hang up his mask forever. Batman witnessed the murder of his parents as a young

HUSBANDS AND WIVES

1992 – USA – 108 MIN. – DRAMA, COMEDY
DIRECTOR WOODY ALLEN (*1935)
SCREENPLAY WOODY ALLEN DIRECTOR OF PHOTOGRAPHY CARLO DI PALMA EDITING SUSAN E. MORSE
MUSIC GUSTAV MAHLER ("9TH SYMPHONY"), various jazz numbers
PRODUCTION ROBERT GREENHUT, JACK ROLLINS, CHARLES H. JOFFE for TRISTAR
STARRING WOODY ALLEN (Gabe Roth), MIA FARROW (Judy Roth), JUDY DAVIS (Sally),
SYDNEY POLLACK (Jack), JULIETTE LEWIS (Rain), LIAM NEESON (Michael),
LYSETTE ANTHONY (Sam), BENNO SCHMIDT (Judy's ex-husband), BLYTHE DANNER
(Rain's mother)

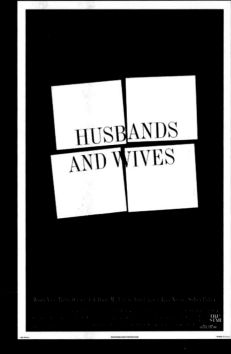

"Do you ever hide things from me?"

Judy and Gabe (Mia Farrow and Woody Allen) are absolutely convinced that Sally and Jack (Judy Davis and Sydney Pollack) are a happily married couple. They are completely taken aback when their two friends take the opportunity of a dinner party to announce their planned separation. They do not seem to have argued and are calm, almost cheerful about it. They explain to their friends how they have grown apart over the years. Separation seems the best solution, as their children are now almost grown up. Judy and Gabe needn't worry, as it's nowhere near as bad as it sounds. Needless to say, once they taste freedom again the harmonious atmosphere between Sally and Jack doesn't last long, and when Sally discovers that Jack is living with a young aerobics instructor (Lysette Anthony) she is completely distraught. This confirms Judy and Gabe's negative view of the whole affair, but gradually it becomes apparent that their friends' separation has also shaken up their own marriage. Judy tries to match Sally with her attractive colleague Michael (Liam Neeson) but eventually has to admit that she is the one who is really in love with him. Gabe, a literature teacher, may have been outraged by Jack's new relationship, but the friendship which he develops with a talented student called Rain (Juliette Lewis) is neither platonic nor mere professional interest.

The cinema release of *Husbands and Wives* was overshadowed by the scandalous circumstances of Woody Allen's separation from his long-term partner Mia Farrow. The media saw the film as a depiction of the director's failed relationship, and the desires and problems of the couples in the movie were equated with those of the real-life couple. This interpretation is undoubtedly justified to some extent as Allen's figures are always closely related to his own personality and he is regarded as synonymous with the New York neurotics who populate his films. Meditations on the relationship between fact and fiction are a constant feature of his movies, as in the fictional film biographies *Zelig* (1983) and *Sweet and Lowdown* (1999). In *Husbands and Wives* he treats this aspect in playful documentary fashion: the protagonists and those who have accompanied them in important phases of their life as a couple are interviewed by a television team, as if they were being psychoanalyzed. The television team never appears on camera, but this interview triggers a series of flashbacks in which hectic handcamera work captures the action in a seemingly lifelike way. We get the impression that the main figures are being shown to us directly from various perspectives, as if the film really could give us an objective view of events. This is an ironic construction, as the movie's plot reveals subjective truth as essential to interpersonal relationships. Each individual has a completely different view of what is happening, and fact and fiction are inextricably combined in that view. Personal bitterness on Allen's part aside, *Husbands and Wives* is much more than a complex, sensitive, and amusing look at the relationship between the sexes. It is also an illuminating commentary on the media's fatal tendency to drag private matters into the public sphere, forcing them into wholly unsuitable categories of guilt and innocence.

JH

3

"The best scenes in *Husbands and Wives* are between the characters played by Allen and Farrow. If we can judge by the subsequent events in their lives, some of this dialogue must have cut very close to the bone." *Chicago Sun-Times*

WOODY ALLEN The director, actor, author, and musician Woody Allen was born in 1935 in Brooklyn, New York, as Allen Stewart Konigsberg. He began his career in the '50s as a joke writer, before appearing in person as a stand-up comedian. His first film role was in Clive Donner's *What's New Pussycat?* in 1965. He made his debut as a director in 1969 with *Take the Money and Run*. Since then, with impressive regularity, he has directed a movie virtually every year, most of which have been comedies. The main theme of his films is the eternal struggle between the sexes, which he presents from many different perspectives. Allen acts in most of his own movies, often as the vulnerable, urban neurotic with which his personality is also identified in real life. His most famous films include *Annie Hall* (1977), *Manhattan* (1978), and *Mighty Aphrodite* (1995). While all of his films up to this time had been set in New York, in 2005 Allen "re-invented" himself with *Match Point*: from then on he made films mainly in Europe. The whimsical time-travel comedy *Midnight in Paris* became the biggest commercial success of Allen's career in 2011.

1 A typical city-dwelling neurotic: writing is a poor form of therapy for Gabe (Woody Allen).

2 A relationship that is over: as so often in Allen's films, the woman is the first to realize that her partner is drifting away from her (Mia Farrow).

3 A richly cast film with outstanding actors: Judy Davis (left) received an Oscar nomination for her portrayal of the highly-strung Sally.

4 Two master directors in dialogue: the conversation between Jack and Gabe (Sydney Pollack) is typical of the film's pseudo-documentary style.

5 In comparison to earlier Allen films, Mia Farrow as Judy comes across as much more egotistical and ambitious (Mia Farrow and Liam Neeson).

6 Juliette Lewis was still at the debut of her career in Allen's film. Shortly beforehand, she had had a breakthrough in Martin Scorsese's *Cape Fear*.

JURASSIC PARK ♟♟♟

1993 – USA – 126 MIN. – ACTION FILM
DIRECTOR STEVEN SPIELBERG (*1946)
SCREENPLAY MICHAEL CRICHTON, DAVID KOEPP, based on the novel *DINOPARK* by
MICHAEL CRICHTON **DIRECTOR OF PHOTOGRAPHY** DEAN CUNDEY **EDITING** MICHAEL KAHN
MUSIC JOHN WILLIAMS **PRODUCTION** KATHLEEN KENNEDY, GERALD R. MOLEN
for AMBLIN ENTERTAINMENT
STARRING SAM NEILL (Dr. Alan Grant), LAURA DERN (Ellie Sattler), JEFF GOLDBLUM
(Dr. Ian Malcolm), RICHARD ATTENBOROUGH (John Hammond), SAMUEL L. JACKSON
(Arnold), BOB PECK (Robert Muldoon), MARTIN FERRERO (Donald Gennaro),
B. D. WONG (Dr. Wu), JOSEPH MAZZELLO (Tim), ARIANA RICHARDS (Lex),
DENNIS NEDRY (Wayne Knight)
ACADEMY AWARDS 1994 OSCARS for BEST VISUAL EFFECTS (Dennis Muren, Stan Winston,
Phil Tippett, Michael Lantieri), BEST SOUND (Ronald Judkins, Shawn Murphy,
Gary Rydstrom, Gary Summers), BEST SOUND EFFECTS EDITING (Richard Hymns,
Gary Rydstrom)

"You should have more respect."

John Hammond (Richard Attenborough) has a vision: he wants to build the biggest and most unusual theme park in the world. As is so often the case in mainstream cinema, his vision compensates for a personal shortcoming – he has a pronounced limp. On a secluded island off the coast of Costa Rica, his idea is to present the public with the most extraordinary thing imaginable: living dinosaurs. Thanks to advances in genetics, such a thing is now possible, and by reactivating the DNA of dinosaur blood from mosquitos trapped in fossilized tree resin, Jurassic Park's scientists clone dinosaurs back into existence after millions of years of extinction.

Unfortunately, the plan begins to go wrong when a park employee is fatally injured by particularly dangerous species of dinosaur as it is being unload-

ed. His family sues for compensation and the park's insurers and investors commission a safety report. To carry out the investigation, Hammond invites a group of experts to the park including palaeontologist Alan Grant (Sam Neill), his girlfriend Ellie Sattler (Laura Dern) – a biologist who specializes in extinct plants of the dinosaur age, an insurance expert, and chaos theoretician Ian Malcolm (Jeff Goldblum). Hammond hopes that the giant lizards will impress the scientists so much that they will abandon their critical attitudes and leave filled with enthusiasm for his project. When the helicopter with the scientists approaches the island and the movie's memorable theme tune is heard for the first time, the audience is also convinced that they are about to see something really amazing. Grant and Sattler are only used to dealing with the dinosaurs'

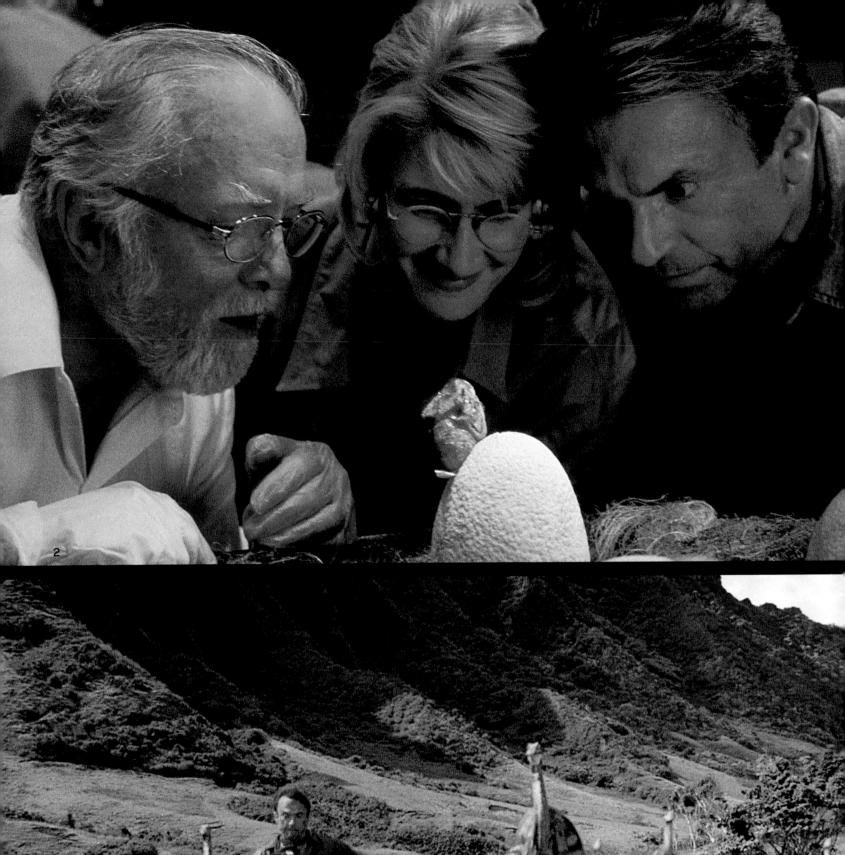

4

"Spielberg plays like a virtuoso on the keys of the visual arts industry. He takes our longing for the miraculous, and then makes the miraculous accessible to people like you and me."

epd Film

excavated skeletons and they fall in love with the prehistoric creatures at first sight. The insurance expert is positively bursting with enthusiasm and greed. Only Ian Malcolm takes a pessimistic view of the park and predicts that messing around with nature can only bring catastrophe.

It's hard not to be impressed with the computer animated dinosaurs of *Jurassic Park*, which stride majestically across the screen. Spielberg knows how to make the most of them and builds an exciting plot around them.

Before *Jurassic Park*, dinosaurs had only ever been seen on the screen when scientists took a trip back in time or discovered lost continents in the earth's interior where primitive nature survived. But when Steven Spielberg came to make his movie, advances in genetics had added a new motif to the dinosaur story. If it's possible to decipher the human DNA code, why not the genes of an animal which lived on the earth many millions of years ago? The explosive potential of such experiments when combined with human greed soon become all too clear to the protagonists of the movie.

Disaster strikes on the island when Dennis Nedry (Wayne Knight, a greedy Park employee), decides to sell embryos to the competition and deactivates the security system for a few minutes to carry out the theft. Muldoon

chooses a weekend when the security staff is on the mainland. As in a traditional horror film, all the prerequisites are prepared, and preparation for a night of spectacular terror, the weather forecast predicts violent storms. The nightmare begins: fences are ripped up, high-voltage cables tear and flail, bridges are flooded, mudslides sweep away the sides of the mountains, there's thunder and lightning, the heavens send forth fire and brimstone and there's also a *Tyrannosaurus rex*, one or two *Velociraptor*, a poisonous *Dilophosaurus* and a herd of *Brachiosaurus*. The electricity fails and the visitors' computerized jeeps come to a standstill. Alan Grant, Ian Malcolm, Hammond's two grandchildren, and the insurance expert are in extreme danger. The latter falls victim to a *Tyrannosaurus* attack. The chaos theoretician survives, but is wounded and has to be left behind. Grant escapes with the two children.

One of the movie's most memorable scenes is the second attack by the *Tyrannosaurus*. We see vibrations in a puddle of water which become stronger and stronger until it is filled with small waves and the earth trembles under the creature's claws. The hunted visitors try to escape in the jeep, but it can't get up enough speed on the swampy ground.

1 "What used to fascinate me even as a child was King Kong." Steven Spielberg.

2 Man playing God. Their eyes (Richard Attenborough, Laura Dern, Sam Neill) may be shining, but they are blinded by their enthusiasm.

3 Nature unleashed. Rarely a recipe for success.

4 What looks like a hermetically sealed world turns out to have a few loopholes.

Most impressive of all is the precarious balance that Spielberg maintains on the knife-edge between horror film and family entertainment. He carefully avoids showing the dinosaur's brutal and horrific behavior in any great detail, while still managing to keep up the tension to please the horror and animation fans. *Jurassic Park* once again proves the cinematic truism that it is more effective to show the consequences of horrific happenings than to show the events themselves. Rather than seeing the blood spurt when a cow is devoured by a *Velociraptor*, we see the waving grass and then hear ear-piercing bellows of fear followed by slurping noises and the sound of bones.

In the morning after the night of terror it seems as if nothing has happened: Alan Grant has found a safe haven in the treetops with the children. A *Brachiosaurus* peacefully grazes under their feet and even allows itself to be stroked. It shows its appreciation by grunting like a walrus and the children feel they could befriend this extinct giant.

But the peace does not last. A small group fights its way into the command bunker of the park. In the meantime the others have managed to re-boot the park's computer and have telephoned for a helicopter to come and take them off the island. They await their rescue in the Jurassic Park museum, where fossilized dinosaurs are exhibited to whet the visitors' appetite for the real thing. Finally, past and present clash for one last time. Two murderous *Velociraptor* attack the group, but a *Tyrannosaurus* appears which fights back and saves the survivors. The dream ends, and once again humans and dinosaurs are separated by a distance of millions of years.

SL

SOUND DESIGN The simulated dinosaurs seem so overwhelmingly convincing because they are the result of a combination of many different high-tech techniques. The model animators worked closely with computer animators, blue screen experts, and animal trainers. Spielberg often uses sound to reinforce the impression of terror and danger, so boffins and sound engineers were kept particularly busy on this movie, where they found themselves on completely new acoustic territory. The dinosaurs had to sound lifelike, but no one could say what an enraged dinosaur attacking two children in a kitchen might have sounded like: the solution they finally arrived at was to mix dolphin noises with walrus grunts until the whole thing sounded sufficiently aggressive. Another challenge was to produce an acoustic effect to mirror the optical effect of dinosaur's footsteps making rings in a water glass. Sound engineers solved that problem by placing the glass on a guitar and plucking the strings. Effects like that provided plenty of acoustic thrills for the new sound systems of the multiplex cinemas.

5 Sceptics (Jeff Goldblum) may not be heroes, but in the end they are usually right.

6 The hunt for the kill in a shiny chrome kitchen. The boy (Joseph Mazzello), rigid with fear, is trying to hide from the dinosaurs.

7 An American nightmare: the monster doesn't even respect the cars.

5

FOUR WEDDINGS AND A FUNERAL

1993/1994 – GREAT BRITAIN – 117 MIN. – COMEDY
DIRECTOR MIKE NEWELL (*1942)
SCREENPLAY RICHARD CURTIS DIRECTOR OF PHOTOGRAPHY PHILIP SINDALL EDITING JON GREGORY
MUSIC RICHARD RODNEY BENNETT PRODUCTION DUNCAN KENWORTHY for WORKING TITLE
(for POLYGRAM, CHANNEL FOUR)
STARRING HUGH GRANT (Charles), ANDIE MACDOWELL (Carrie), KRISTIN SCOTT THOMAS
(Fiona), SIMON CALLOW (Gareth), JAMES FLEET (Tom), ANNA CHANCELLOR (Henrietta),
CHARLOTTE COLEMAN (Scarlett), CHARLES BOWER (David), SARA CROWE (Laura),
TIMOTHY WALKER (Angus)

"Marriage is just a way of getting out of an embarrassing pause in conversation."

It's just another normal Saturday morning. At a shrill ring from the alarm clock, Charles (Hugh Grant) falls out of bed, staggers into his tailcoat, and rushes off to church. Hardly a weekend goes by when he and his friends are not invited to some wedding or other. Charles is always late. He may be invited to lots of weddings, but he has no intention of marrying himself. As his friends get hitched one by one, the shy and chaotic bachelor remains a "serial monogamist" as he says himself, apparently unable to sustain any serious relationship. But at this particular wedding reception he meets Carrie (Andie MacDowell) – the woman of his dreams, and it's a classic case of love at first sight. Carrie seduces him and they spend the night together. The next morning, Charles hesitates a moment too long and suddenly the American beauty has disappeared from his life – if not from his thoughts.

Of course they meet again – at the next wedding. Before Charles can pluck up the courage to speak, Carrie introduces him to her future husband, who she marries at the movie's third wedding. The fourth, which is only stopped at the last minute by the courageous intervention of Charles's deaf brother, is Charles's own – but the bride's name isn't Carrie.

The succession of wedding celebrations is interrupted by a burial: one of Charles's friends, the bon vivant and cynic Gareth (Simon Callow), dies of a heart attack at Carrie's wedding. When his friend Matthew holds the funeral speech, Charles suddenly realizes that despite the absence of a wedding certificate and the accompanying celebrations, Matthew and Gareth had also made a real commitment for life.

These four weddings and one funeral are the main events of Mike Newell's light-hearted satire on the fossilized code of conduct and behaviour of the British upper classes. The only couples held together by true love are those who will never marry. If Gareth is to be believed, marriage is simply a way of dealing with the embarrassing pauses in conversation which become more frequent as a relationship progresses. Charles's other friend Tom (James Fleet) is equally pragmatic: he hopes to find a nice girl who won't feel nauseous when she looks at him and with whom he can simply be happy.

The script of Four Weddings and a Funeral was written by Richard Curtis, one of Britain's most productive film writers and the creator of many

"Mike Newell's film finds its premise in one of modern life's minor truths: if you are a sociable specimen of the yuppie breed, you spend much of your spare income suiting yourself up for friends' weddings." *Time Magazine*

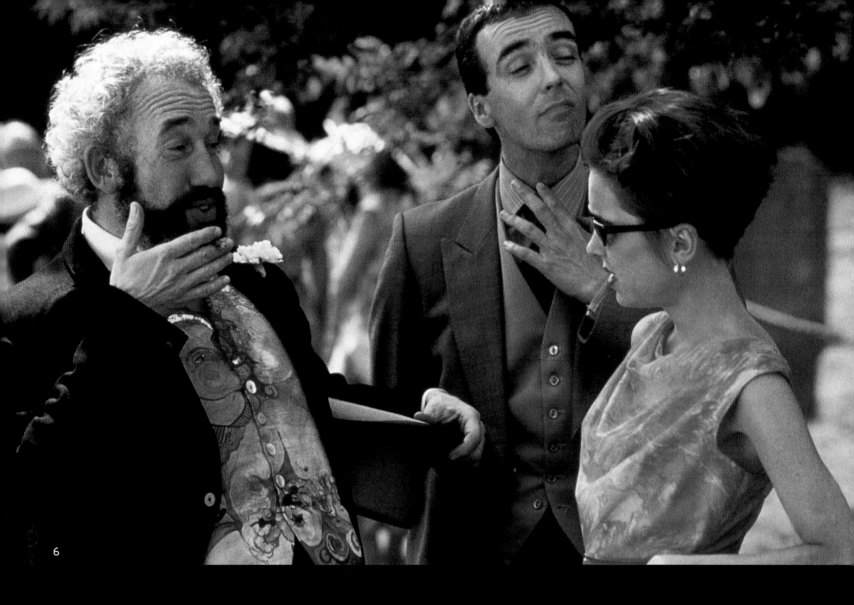

6

successful television series and feature films. He wrote the series *Blackadder* and *Mr. Bean* together with Rowan Atkinson, who plays a small but hilarious role in this movie as a stuttering priest. *Four Weddings and a Funeral* was a small budget production, but it became Britain's most successful movie to date and was only knocked off the number one spot when Roger Michell's romantic comedy *Notting Hill* came along in 1999, also starring Hugh Grant and written by Richard Curtis. Mike Newell's movie shows as little of the everyday life of its characters as it shows of the real social conditions in Britain. His

protagonists all come from "good" families and we only see them in their Sunday best, either at weddings or on their way there. The audience's gaze sweeps through the party like that of a curious guest. Interesting people catch the eye, and the witty dialogue catches the ear. From the very first ring of the alarm clock to the last kiss, the timing of this brilliant farce is perfect, and it combines all the best elements of comedy and melodrama.

APO

BAFTA AWARD The British Academy of Film was founded in 1947 by a committee of 14 people under the director David Lean. Its aim was to promote excellence in the British movie industry. In 1958 it fused with the professional body of television producers and directors and in 1978 it was renamed the British Academy of Film and Television Arts (BAFTA). The BAFTA award is the most important film and television prize in Britain and is awarded yearly in various categories. The golden mask that commemorates each award was designed by the artist Mitzi Cunliffe.

1 The role of the shy young bachelor who attends wedding after wedding turned British actor Hugh Grant into a superstar.

2 David (Charles Bower, center), the speech- and hearing-impaired brother of Charles, saves him at the last minute from making the biggest mistake of his life.

3 Hats off: the role of the independent and self-assured American lady Carrie could have been tailor-made for Andie MacDowell.

4 Suffering in silence: Fiona (Kristin Scott Thomas), who's been in love with Charles for years, is just a "good friend" as far as he's concerned.

5 Last minute rush: Charles and his flatmate Scarlett (Charlotte Coleman) dash from one wedding to the next.

6 An arch commentator: the long drawn out parties wouldn't be half so much fun without Gareth's (Simon Callow, left) witty observations.

RAINING STONES

1993 – GREAT BRITAIN – 91 MIN. – DRAMA

DIRECTOR KEN LOACH (*1936)
SCREENPLAY JIM ALLEN **DIRECTOR OF PHOTOGRAPHY** BARRY ACKROYD **EDITING** JONATHAN MORRIS
MUSIC STEWART COPELAND **PRODUCTION** SALLY HIBBIN for PARALLAX, FILM FOUR
STARRING BRUCE JONES (Bob Williams), JULIE BROWN (Anne Williams),
GEMMA PHOENIX (Coleen Williams), RICKY TOMLINSON (Tommy), TOM HICKEY
(Father Barry), JONATHAN JAMES (Tansey), MIKE FALLON (Jimmy), RONNIE RAVEY
(Butcher), LEE BRENNAN (Irishman)
IFF CANNES 1993 JURY PRIZE (Ken Loach)

"When you're down it's raining stones seven days a week."

Bad things don't just come in threes. Bob (Bruce Jones) has seen enough of life to know the truth of these sayings: he's 40, unemployed, supports his family with state allowances and occasional labor and lives in a comfortless council flat somewhere in the north of England. You could live and die here, and no one would notice, as his wife Anne (Julie Brown) says.

Despite these miserable living conditions, Bob always bounces back. His family is sacred to him and his Catholic faith a rock in stormy seas. They give him the strength to keep his humor and his self-respect despite the continual bad luck. When he and his best mate Tommy (Ricky Tomlinson) steal a sheep, things go badly awry – they can neither slaughter it themselves nor sell it to a butcher. Bob's old delivery van is stolen from the yard while they are trying to get rid of the sheep in the pub, and finally, having tried in vain to get paid work cleaning drains with borrowed tools, he finds himself up to his neck in filth at the church – and that for free!

Bob's daughter Coleen (Gemma Phoenix) is about to celebrate her First Communion, and he wants to buy her a new dress, even though the full outfit with the shoes, stockings, and veil costs over 100 pounds. The priest (Tom

Hickey) tries and fails to talk Bob into buying a second-hand dress – after all, it's a very important family occasion.

Bob borrows the money from a loan shark, who sells the IOU on to Tansey (Jonathan James), a professional debt collector. When Bob can't pay the money back and Anne and Coleen are threatened at home by Tansey's brutal hitmen, Bob can't take it any more. During the resulting showdown between Bob and Tansey in an underground garage, Tansey is killed. Although Bob is not directly responsible, he feels guilty and wants to turn himself in to the police. He can find no peace until the parish priest, an exceptional man, grants him absolution, saying "You only want justice." He realizes that Bob won't find it in secular society and offers him the forgiveness of the church instead.

Despite its grimness, *Raining Stones* has many comic moments. When Bob, Tommy, and a couple of mates see a perfect lawn outside a Conservative Club one day, they neatly take it up and sell it as turf. But most of the humor is extremely black. The daily humiliations these men have to face often make it difficult for the audience to laugh. When someone is as desperate as

Tommy, we don't laugh when his daughter gives him pocket money, as that would be too much like a kicking a man when he's down.

Raining Stones is the opposite of a Hollywood movie. Ken Loach filmed it in a 16 mm format and worked with a hand camera and original sounds instead of expensive technology and synchronization, and like most of his movies, *Raining Stones* is cast with amateur actors drawing on their own experiences. What counts for Loach in front of the camera and the microphone is not appearance, but the reality behind it.

For that reason, he's often been labeled "the social conscience of Great Britain." The name suits him: all of his movies criticize the political system, even if they don't all have the effectiveness of the BBC television film *Cathy Come Home* (1966), which had a part to play in influencing changes made to British vagrancy laws ten years later. He has often had problems with censorship. In the '80s, almost all of his works were banned on the order of the IBA (Britain's Independent Broadcasting Authority) and even as late as 1997, Channel 4 refused to broadcast his film *Ladybird, Ladybird* (1994).   APO

"The credit sharks' heavy boys lurk in front of the social security office, to collect overdue debts. Social imagination seems to be infinitely inventive only when it is a case of exploiting those in serious difficulties even more cruelly." *epd Film*

COPRODUCTION Coproduction refers to joint projects carried out by producers and production companies. This form of cooperation arose due to financial and material difficulties in Europe in the years following the Second World War. Production companies and producers in other countries joined together to finance expensive European films and to gain access to newer, larger markets. Coproduction is still general practice today for the same reasons.

1   Her big day: Bob's innocent young daughter Coleen (Gemma Phoenix) has no idea that her First Communion dress costs someone their life.

2   Guilt and expiation: Father Barry is a human being first and the Church's representative second. He acquits Bob (Bruce Jones) of the death of the debt collector.

3 Dogged by bad luck: while Tommy (Ricky Tomlinson, right) is trying to unload the worthless mutton on the man in the pub, his car gets stolen.

4 Sympathetic: the pulpit is the only place where Father Barry (Tom Hickey) speaks to his people with raised forefinger.

5 Up hill and down dale: survival artists Bob and Tommy struggling to bring someone else's flock into the dry.

PHILADELPHIA ♟♟

1993 – USA – 125 MIN. – DRAMA, COURTROOM DRAMA
DIRECTOR JONATHAN DEMME (*1944)
SCREENPLAY RON NYSWANER DIRECTOR OF PHOTOGRAPHY TAK FUJIMOTO EDITING CRAIG MCKAY
MUSIC HOWARD SHORE PRODUCTION EDWARD SAXON, JONATHAN DEMME for
COLUMBIA TRISTAR, CLINICA ESTETICO
STARRING TOM HANKS (Andrew Beckett), DENZEL WASHINGTON (Joe Miller),
JASON ROBARDS (Charles Wheeler), MARY STEENBURGEN (Belinda Conine),
JOANNE WOODWARD (Sarah Beckett), ANTONIO BANDERAS (Miguel Alvarez),
RON VAWTER (Bob Seidman), JEFFREY WILLIAMSON (Tyrone), CHARLES NAPIER
(Judge Garnett), LISA SUMMEROUR (Lisa Miller)
ACADEMY AWARDS 1994 OSCARS for BEST ACTOR (Tom Hanks) and BEST SONG
(Bruce Springsteen, "The Streets of Philadelphia")
IFF BERLIN 1994 SILVER BEAR for BEST ACTOR (Tom Hanks)

"Forget everything you've seen on television and in the movies."

Andrew Beckett (Tom Hanks) and Joe Miller (Denzel Washington) are two ambitious young lawyers. They have just presented opposing sides of a civil law case; afterwards in the elevator they simultaneously pull their dicta-phones out of their pockets to record the case results; somewhere a cell phone rings and without interrupting their dictation, both search for their phones. Youth, ambition, and lots of energy – that's what they have in com-mon, but nothing more: Joe Miller is black, a legal eagle who advertises his work in local TV commercials; Andrew Beckett is a WASP, graduate of an eli-te university and employed by one of Philadelphia's most prestigious law firms. He is also gay. A few days later things start to happen: Beckett is made a senior partner of the firm by his mentor Charles Wheeler (Jason Robards) and is entrusted with a very important case. A blood test shows that he has HIV. No one in the firm is supposed to know about his illness. But when a vital document disappears under mysterious circumstances and he is fired

for incompetence, he suspects his disease is the real reason for the dismissal and decides to sue his former employers for discrimination. Unfortunately, there is not a single lawyer in the city who is prepared to take on his case – apart from Joe Miller, who as a black man knows what it's like to be discrim-inated against. After a long period of hesitation he decides to help Beckett, above all because the case will bring both money and publicity.

The years 1993/94 seemed to herald a new trend in Hollywood. Two films were released which confronted audiences with historical and social reality. Hard on the heels of Steven Spielberg's Holocaust movie *Schindler's List* came Jonathan Demme's *Philadelphia*, and more than ten years after "gay cancer" first became public knowledge, the first big budget movie about AIDS had appeared.

The interesting thing about *Philadelphia* is that it is not what it claims to be. It is a complete failure as a film about gays and AIDS. It succeeds

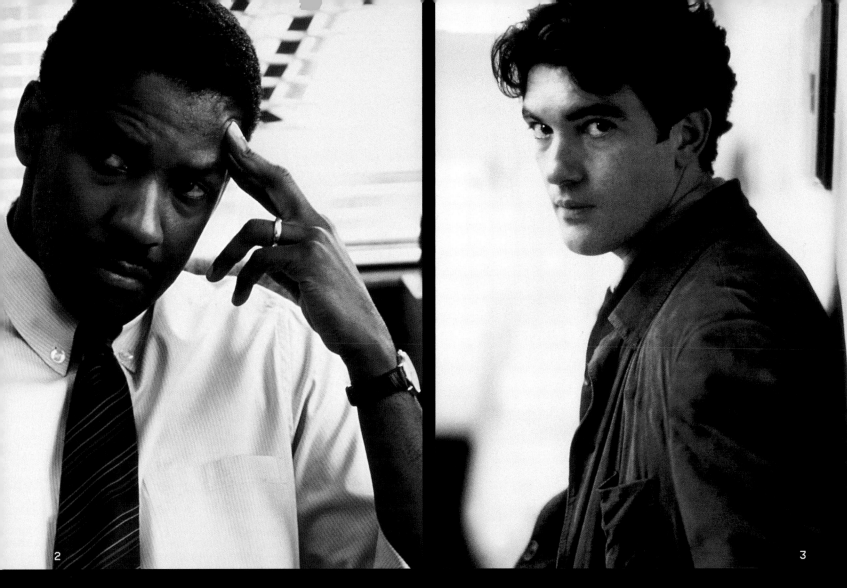

"It is, at the very least, a giant step forward for Hollywood, which tends to portray homosexuals as either psychopathic cross-dressers or the giddy fruitcakes who live next door." *The Washington Post*

6

however as a tension-filled and exciting courtroom drama about deep-seated social prejudices against those who think, look, and love differently. In this respect it resembles Stanley Kramer's movie *Guess Who's Coming to Dinner?* (1967) where parents Spencer Tracy and Katharine Hepburn have to get used to the idea of a black son-in-law. Beckett's lawyer Joe Miller, convincingly portrayed by Denzel Washington, is the prototypical normal person. His hatred of gays is deeply rooted and his ignorance of the disease astonishing. When Beckett goes to visit him for the first time in his office, they shake hands. A few moments later, Miller discovers that Beckett has AIDS. The camera reveals his fear, it follows his eyes to the objects Andrew has touched like the cigars Miller keeps for his clients and a photo of his new-

born daughter. When Andrew has left, he immediately makes a doctor's appointment. But the irony is that Beckett could not wish for a better lawyer: Miller forces the jury to examine its own prejudices, just as the cinema audience is forced to do.

Philadelphia was classified as suitable for children. No bodily fluids are exchanged between gay men, and there is nothing more explicit than a peck on the cheek. The same fears demonstrated by Joe Miller's dealings with gays are mirrored in the movie's treatment of what is supposed to be its main theme. Despite, or perhaps because of this, Demme's attempt to make contact was rewarded with a clutch of international film prizes, including two Oscars.   APO

HOMOSEXUALITY IN THE MOVIES For many years following the inception of cinema, homosexuality hardly featured. Social acceptance was extremely limited and pressure from the industry was enormous. One of the first movies that still survives, *The Gay Brothers* (William Dickson, 1895), shows two men dancing a waltz. From the mid-1930s onward the portrayal of homosexuality in film became virtually impossible in the USA, thanks to the industry's self-imposed production code. Homosexuality in movies has only ceased to be an issue since the 1980s. Since 1987, the Teddy Award for best gay or lesbian film has been presented at the Berlin Film Festival.

1   The courage to play an outsider: the role of the attorney (Andrew Becket) suffering from AIDS presented a real challenge for Hollywood star Tom Hanks.

2   Worried he might catch something: homophobic attorney Joe Miller (Denzel Washington) knows all about discrimination.

3   Faithful unto death: Andrew's partner Miguel Alvarez (Antonio Banderas) knows he caught the disease by playing around.

4   A plausible façade: as long as Andrew can keep up appearances, the partners in his chambers still think he's the best.

5   Overstepping the mark: Denzel Washington is outraged when someone in a supermarket thinks he's gay.

6   Andrew's mentor Charles Wheeler (Jason Robards, left) holds the ambitious young attorney in high esteem – perhaps because he recognizes in him something of himself. He is inconsolable when he learns the truth about his protégé.

GROUNDHOG DAY

1993 – USA – 101 MIN. – COMEDY

DIRECTOR HAROLD RAMIS (*1944) SCREENPLAY DANNY RUBIN, HAROLD RAMIS

DIRECTOR OF PHOTOGRAPHY JOHN BAILEY EDITING PEMBROKE J. HERRING MUSIC GEORGE FENTON

PRODUCTION TREVOR ALBERT, HAROLD RAMIS for COLUMBIA PICTURES

STARRING BILL MURRAY (Phil Connors), ANDIE MACDOWELL (Rita Hanson), CHRIS ELLIOTT (Larry), STEPHEN TOBOLOWSKY (Ned Ryerson), BRIAN DOYLE-MURRAY (Buster), MARITA GERAGHTY (Nancy), ANGELA PATON (Mrs. Lancaster), RICK DUCOMMUN (Gus), RICK OVERTON (Ralph), ROBIN DUKE (Doris the waitress)

"I got you babe ..."

"I Got You Babe" thunders from Phil Connors's (Bill Murray) radio alarm at six in the morning. Connors, the embodiment of the cynical, streetwise modern city dweller, is a TV presenter who has been sent to cover an annual event in weather prediction. In Punxsutawney, deep in provincial America, a groundhog is taken out of its cage at the end of every winter and asked what the weather will be like in the following weeks. This curious ritual is broadcast across the land. Regardless of the predictions of the groundhog, everyone has a good time and enjoys the celebrations. Connors on the other hand considers the whole thing to be the annually recurring height of stupidity. He reports the event without any vestige of enthusiasm and even cuts the last few sequences so he can go home early. However a blizzard stops the television team from leaving and they have to spend another night in Punxsutawney. Phil is awakened the next morning by the sound of his radio playing "I Got You Babe." The other guests and the landlady greet him with the same friendly, conventional phrases as the day before and everyone is looking forward to the groundhog. Connors realizes that he is stuck in a time loop with no way of escape: stuck in everyday life in the sticks.

While everyone around him experiences the day for the first time, from now on everything is repetition for Connors – every morning, the same presenters' voices boom out from the radio to begin the day with "I Got You Babe."

The movie develops the funniest situations out of this idea of endless repetition. One day Phil does his work professionally, the next he refuses completely. He meets his old school friend Ned (Stephen Tobolowsky) again and again and reacts to his offensive cheerfulness differently every time, he shouts at him, strikes up a friendly conversation, or takes the stupid jokes right out of his mouth. Every time, though, the scene ends the same way: Phil runs away from Ned and without thinking steps into an ankle-deep puddle of ice-cold water, so that Ned has the opportunity to call one last joke after him. The running gag is an important element in comedy and a movie whose

"Director Harold Ramis stage-manages these days with a wealth of ideas and precision timing, and after his initial shock the hero enjoys his lack of responsibility."

epd Film

structural principle is repetition can been seen as a virtuoso play on the running gag. Even when Phil commits suicide, it has no effect on the next morning: "I Got You Babe." Again and again he meets the same people, but he always treats them differently: at first he is curious, then bored, until finally he becomes, compassionate. For Connors it may be sheer repetition, but the audience witness a rebirth, as his hatred for the backwoods disappears as he grows to appreciate the people of Punxsutawney. Slowly his cynicism begins to dissolve and eventually the self-satisfied egocentric has to admit that he is in love with his producer Rita (Andie MacDowell). Every day he tries repeatedly to conquer her affections and for each new attempt he is better prepared. Naturally it is this love which saves him in the end.

The movie promotes virtues like genuine sentiment and rural simplicity so blatantly that it could be disregarded as kitsch. However, it's also possible to enjoy the gradual conversion of the arrogant, smug Connors, who at first believes he has everything under control. His sarcasm is shown as a mask that he can only lay aside if he is prepared to break out of the vicious circle of self-importance and throw himself into life with no regard for the consequences. *Groundhog Day* is one of the most intelligent comedies of the '90s. It is one of the few romantic comedies to give us a love story and leave something over for the viewers who will find this too sugary: some will find Phil Connors most entertaining when he is obnoxious and shrugs off every human feeling with a mocking grin.

SL

BILL MURRAY Born in 1950 in Wilmette, Illinois, Murray was popular as a radio and TV comic long before his film career began. He made his movie debut in 1979 in Ivan Reitman's *Meatballs*. In the years that followed, Murray became a popular star of the so-called animal comedies – movies characterized by anarchic humor. He landed his first big hit with Reitman's *Ghostbusters* (1984) and proved his talent in a more serious role in John Byrum's *The Razor's Edge* in the same year. *Quick Change* (1990) has been his first and only attempt at directing to date. Murray continued his '80s successes with the romantic comedy *Groundhog Day* in 1992. In Wes Anderson's *Rushmore* (1998) he played a depressed millionaire and showed for the first time that he knows better than most US comics how to give depth to his roles. More recently, he has developed his unique blend of misery and extreme quirkiness in what are surely his best roles to date: in Sofia Coppola's *Lost in Translation* (2003) and Jim Jarmusch's *Broken Flowers* (2005).

1 The sceptical face of presenter Phil Connors (Bill Murray), before the miracle starts to happen.

2 In films, shower scenes are always moments on the brink of madness.

3 American holidays have strange heroes: groundhogs, turkeys, and pumpkin heads.

4 Dancing never fails to bring people (Andie McDowell) closer together.

5 Happiness is only possible if you lay yourself completely open.

IN THE LINE OF FIRE

1993 – USA – 128 MIN. – POLITICAL THRILLER
DIRECTOR WOLFGANG PETERSEN (*1941)
SCREENPLAY JEFF MAGUIRE DIRECTOR OF PHOTOGRAPHY JOHN BAILEY EDITING ANNE V. COATES
MUSIC ENNIO MORRICONE PRODUCTION JEFF APPLE for CASTLE ROCK ENTERTAINMENT,
COLUMBIA PICTURES
STARRING CLINT EASTWOOD (Frank Horrigan), JOHN MALKOVICH (Mitch Leary /
John Booth / James Carney), RENE RUSSO (Lilly Raines), DYLAN MCDERMOTT
(Al D'Andrea), GARY COLE (Bill Watts), FRED DALTON THOMPSON (Harry Sargent),
JOHN MAHONEY (Sam Campagna), GREG ALAN-WILLIAMS (Matt Wilder), JIM CURLEY
(President), SALLY HUGHES (First Lady)

"Why not call me Booth?"

America is traumatized by its dead presidents, from Abraham Lincoln, murdered by John Wilkes Booth in 1865 while watching a play from a box at the theater, right up to JFK, whose death became one of the most disturbing and macabre events in the history of television. The amateur film of Kennedy's murder in 1963 is probably the most minutely analyzed pieces of celluloid of all time, and the pictures were broadcast repeatedly in a constant reexamnation of the murder, an early example of reality TV.

In the Line of Fire uses that idea as a plot mechanism, but Petersen's movie is really about the ancient duel between good and evil. At first glance the divide seems simple enough: undercover cop Frank Horrigan (Clint Eastwood) is tough and hands-on, his evil opponent Mitch Leary (John Malkovich) thoughtful and intellectual. They are both cynics. But at a second glance another perspective begins to appear. We see Frank play beautiful ballads on the piano and tenderly court his colleague Lilly (Rene Russo), whereas Leary murders two women in their apartment and kills two hunters in cold blood while practicing his aim.

Clint Eastwood plays aging bodyguard Frank Horrigan, a man who feels he failed President Kennedy. The role goes against his image as an unscrupulous supporter of lynch justice, which he owes above all to the Dirty Harry movies. The impatient individualist of In the Line of Fire also hates bureaucrats but he has a kindly side too. Eastwood's Frank Horrigan doesn't hide the signs of age or the unhealed wounds on his soul. Leary, his diabolic opponent, also suffers; the system that taught him the art of perfect killing suddenly no longer wants him. Once part of a special unit that planned and carried out assassinations on the government's orders, he has now been discharged. Malkovich's Leary is an intellectual killer who carries out his plan to revenge his dismissal by assassinating the president of the USA with supercool precision. His sudden outbreak of rage when Frank manages to talk with him on the telephone only makes him seem even more dangerous and unpredictable. Eastwood's stony face contrasts with Malkovich's changing disguises, from eccentric hippy to smart software manager.

Combined with Petersen's fine sense for the right dose of suspense, this constellation carries the movie throughout its length despite occasional narrative shallows. Leary sometimes calls himself Booth after Lincoln's murderer, and plays a gripping cat and mouse game with Frank who sees the case as a chance to make good his previous failure. Booth's real concern is no

2

1 Frank Horrigan (Clint Eastwood): patriotism is a question of honor.

2 The horrors of the past keep catching up with Officer Horrigan, who is as uncompromising as he is fearless.

3 Loss of honor to be avenged: John Malkovich as the demonic adversary Mitch Leary.

4 If Frank Horrigan ever smiles ...

5 ... it's only because of his good-looking colleague Lilly (Rene Russo).

the president's personal safety. The movie distances itself from politics and reveals a clear satirical undertone when it presents an election campaign as a carnivalesque parade, and when the president is removed from the line of fire of a presumed assassin during a public appearance there are strong overtones of slapstick.

The movie concentrates instead on the duel between Leary and Horrigan and plays with the closeness between criminal and victim. Whenever Frank and his colleagues try to locate him, Leary is constantly one step ahead. Leary is a brilliant strategist, and can even manipulate the telephone wires to cover his tracks.

Thanks to the extreme economy of John Bailey's camera work (*Silverado*, 1985) and Anne Coates's (*Lawrence of Arabia*, 1962) masterful editing, Petersen manages to balance and combine the two diverging halves of the movie, its hectic action scenes and the romance between Frank and Lilly. He constantly inserts ironic breaks, as when the CIA and the FBI attack each other in Leary's empty apartment as they have no idea that the other would be there. In the end, however, after a last-minute showdown where Frank throws himself in front of the president and saves his life, there can only be one winner.

BR

WOLFGANG PETERSEN *Das Boot (The Boat)* is the best-known German production by Wolfgang Petersen (*1941). He made it between 1979 and 1981 as a television series and as a feature film, which later was nominated for six Oscars. He began his career in 1960 as a director's assistant at the Ernst Deutsch Theater in Hamburg. After studying at the Berlin Film and Television Academy, he first made a name for himself with TV productions, particularly with *Reifezeugnis* (High School Graduation, 1977), a feature-length episode of a crime series with the young Nastassja Kinski. He made his most expensive movie to date in 1984 – *The NeverEnding Story*, about postwar Germany. Petersen has worked in Hollywood since 1985, achieving his important breakthrough with *In the Line of Fire* (1993), starring Clint Eastwood. Later work includes the largely computer animated, shipwreck blockbuster *The Perfect Storm* (2000), starring George Clooney, and two more big adventure movies – *Troy* (2004) and *Poseidon* (2006).

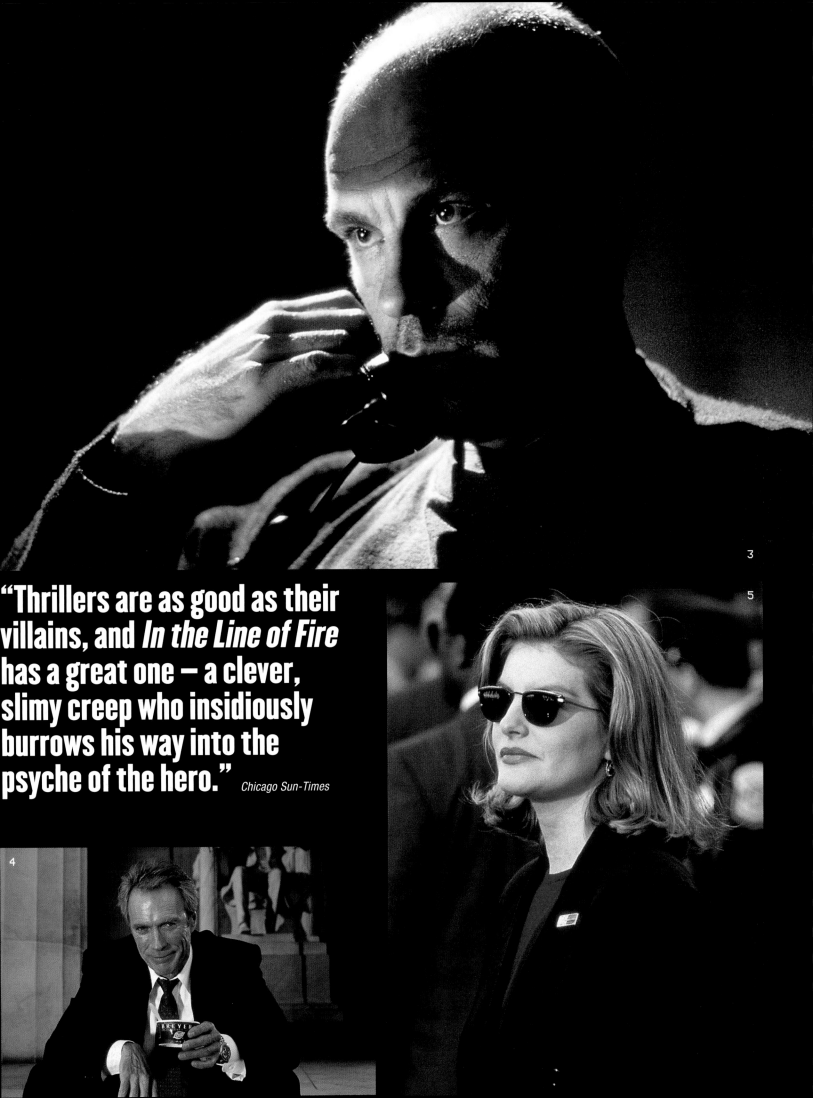

3

5

"Thrillers are as good as their villains, and *In the Line of Fire* has a great one – a clever, slimy creep who insidiously burrows his way into the psyche of the hero." *Chicago Sun-Times*

4

THREE COLORS: BLUE
TROIS COULEURS: BLEU

1993 – FRANCE – 97 MIN. – MELODRAMA

DIRECTOR KRZYSZTOF KIEŚLOWSKI (1941–1996)
SCREENPLAY KRZYSZTOF KIEŚLOWSKI, KRZYSZTOF PIESIEWICZ
DIRECTOR OF PHOTOGRAPHY SLAWOMIR IDZIAK EDITING JACQUES WITTA MUSIC ZBIGNIEW PREISNER
PRODUCTION MARIN KARMITZ for MK2 PRODUCTIONS, CED PRODUCTIONS, CAB PRODUCTIONS, TOR STUDIO
STARRING JULIETTE BINOCHE (Julie), BENOÎT RÉGENT (Olivier), FLORENCE PERNEL (Sandrine), CHARLOTTE VÉRY (Lucille), HÉLÈNE VINCENT (Journalist), PHILIPPE VOLTER (Broker), CLAUDE DUNETON (Doctor), HUGUES QUESTER (Patrice), YANN TRÉGOUËT (Antoine), EMMANUELLE RIVA (Mother)
OF VENICE 1993 GOLDEN LION for BEST FILM, SILVER LION for BEST ACTRESS (Juliette Binoche)

"If I have all knowledge …"

Like so many artists, Krzysztof Kieślowski likes to use motifs that allow him to work inside a wider framework. His earlier work for instance includes a series of films about each of the Ten Commandments. His movie trilogy on the French Revolution is also based on underlying motifs. Liberty, equality, and fraternity are the driving forces behind each film. Kieślowski uses the tricolor as his guide and defines blue as the color of liberty. His main concern is with how those revolutionary principles affect our private lives. How can we free ourselves from tragic, shocking, terrifying experiences? How can we become free to live again?

Julie (Juliette Binoche) is the only survivor of a car crash in which her husband Patrice (Hugues Quester) and daughter die. In the hospital she half-heartedly attempts suicide. When she is discharged she gives her house to a broker (Philippe Volter) to sell and tries to rid herself of all her memories. Patrice was a famous composer and had been working on a symphony for the unification of Europe. Julie was his coworker rather than his muse, and she destroys all the drafts of it. When Patrice's assistant, Olivier (Benoît Régent) visits her, she sleeps with him to prove to herself how unmoved she is by the tragedy. Nothing matters anymore.

But her protective shield is scratched again and again. A flautist on the street plays a melody from the Europe Symphony which he can't even know. An old woman strains to throw a glass bottle into the recycling bin. A mouse moves into the pantry of Julie's new apartment and gives birth. Julie borrows the neighbor's cat to eat up the naked mice which symbolize life and reproduction. Afterwards however she can't bring herself to return to the

apartment, and her only friend, a prostitute, offers to go in and clean up. In contrast to Julie, she suffers from too great a hunger for life, too much sex, and too many contacts. When she sees her father in the first row at the live sex show where she works, she can't go on and asks Julie for help. The two women sit opposite each other, neither knowing which way to turn. A documentary about Patrice and his work on television shows her dead husband embracing a young woman tenderly, and when Julie makes contact with this secret mistress, she sees that she is pregnant and begins to understand. However much she tries to shut out the past and stop her loss from tearing her soul in two, she will never be able to wipe it out. Patrice's music and his child will live on. She decides to give the house to the child and together with Olivier, whom she loves, she finishes the symphony for the unification of Europe. The final chorus of the work is also the final scene of the film, the words of the apostle Paul to the Corinthians: "If I have all knowledge and if can move mountains but am without love, I am nothing." Julie sleeps with Olivier again. She can cry for the first time. By making peace with the wounds inflicted by fate, she finds the strength to live on.

SL

KRZYSZTOF KIEŚLOWSKI Kieślowski, born in Warsaw in 1941, described himself as an "optimistic fatalist," perhaps as the result of many successful documentary films he made about Eastern Europe. It was only when he met the defense lawyer Krzysztof Piesiewicz (who much preferred to write screenplays) that he turned his attention to feature films. Together, they made ten films about the Ten Commandments for Polish television, including *A Short Film About Love* (*Krótki film o milosci*, 1988) and *A Short Film About Killing* (*Krótki film o zabijaniu*, 1988), which were also cinema successes in the West. In 1990, he went to France, and it was there that he made his later films. He dreamed of showing 17 different montage versions of the movie *The Double Life of Veronique* (*La Double Vie de Véronique*, 1991) simultaneously in 17 Paris cinemas. Kieślowski died during heart surgery in 1996. Even posthumously, several of his screenplays have been made into films, including *Heaven* (2000) by Tom Tykwer.

1 Turning your back on everything always makes you more vulnerable.

2 When those who have stumbled talk to those who have fallen, there's no place for glamour.

3 The camera has to love a person's face in order for people to understand the person: Juliette Binoche as Julie.

2

"It's the tenderness in the eyes of someone who is beginning to be sure of themselves and their freedom."

end Film

SCHINDLER'S LIST ♟♟♟♟♟♟♟

1993 – USA – 195 MIN. – HISTORICAL FILM, DRAMA
DIRECTOR STEVEN SPIELBERG (*1946)
SCREENPLAY STEVEN ZAILLIAN, based on the novel of the same name by THOMAS KENEALLY
DIRECTOR OF PHOTOGRAPHY JANUSZ KAMINSKI EDITING MICHAEL KAHN MUSIC JOHN WILLIAMS
PRODUCTION STEVEN SPIELBERG, GERALD R. MOLEN, BRANKO LUSTIG for
AMBLIN ENTERTAINMENT, UNIVERSAL PICTURES
STARRING LIAM NEESON (Oskar Schindler), BEN KINGSLEY (Itzhak Stern), RALPH FIENNES
(Amon Goeth), CAROLINE GOODALL (Emilie Schindler), JONATHAN SAGALL
(Poldek Pfefferberg), EMBETH DAVIDTZ (Helen Hirsch), MALGOSCHA GEBEL
(Victoria Klonowska), SHMULIK LEVY (Wilek Chilowicz), MARK IVANIR (Marcel Goldberg),
BÉATRICE MACOLA (Ingrid)
ACADEMY AWARDS 1994 OSCARS for BEST PICTURE, BEST DIRECTOR (Steven Spielberg),
BEST ADAPTED SCREENPLAY (Steven Zaillian), BEST CINEMATOGRAPHY
(Janusz Kaminski), BEST FILM EDITING (Michael Kahn), BEST ART DIRECTION –
SET DECORATION (Allan Starski, Ewa Braun) and BEST MUSIC (John Williams)

"It is said that he's a good man."

Can the horrors of the Holocaust be filmed without trivializing them? Can life under fascism be filmed without showing images which everybody has seen before? Steven Spielberg came up with one solution in his film about the German industrialist Oskar Schindler. The story he tells is unique, eccentric even, but the message is crystal clear: responsibility cannot be passed on to someone else, but is always a matter for the individual.

When the film starts, the German army has occupied Poland. The occupiers make a ghetto for the Jews in Krakow, and force them to register. We see their faces, one by one, individual people in great distress, many of whom are later tortured and murdered. This is no anonymous mass.

When we see Oskar Schindler (Liam Neeson) for the first time our eyes are drawn irresistibly to his Nazi party badge. He is an opportunist womaniz-er, and is building an enamel factory in Poland for the German army. Jewish workers are cheaper than Polish ones, so he takes Jews. His accountant Itzhak Stern (Ben Kingsley) turns out to be an organizational genius and becomes the real director of the factory. Schindler's job is to bribe the Nazi officials. He is more hard-bitten businessman than hero, and at first his humanity is a more a question economics than it is of morals: happy workers, he reasons, produce more than discontented ones.

In 1942, the ghetto is destroyed and all the Jews are deported to a work camp in Plaszow. Schindler observes the harrowing events. A little girl wanders silently through the chaos, seemingly oblivious to events around her. Her red coat is the only spot of color in this film, which is shot almost exclusively in documentary black and white. We later see her corpse in Auschwitz.

Through a bizarre friendship with sadistic camp commander Amon Goeth (Ralph Fiennes), Schindler manages to keep his workers although they are forced to live in the detention center. This protects them from being tortured by the guards and means that they can trade on the black market, without which it is impossible to survive. Eventually Plaszow is dissolved and all its inmates are transported to Auschwitz, so Schindler has to make a decision. He uses his entire capital to bribe the Nazis and buy the lives of his workers. He saves over 1100 people, who he transports with two trains, one for men, one for women, to his hometown of Brünnlitz to open a munitions factory. Since the factory produces goods for the war effort, his workers are considered indispensable and their lives are saved. Even when the women's train arrives in Auschwitz by mistake, through fearlessness and bribery

Schindler manages to get the women out again. His strengths are his stubbornness and deviousness. He pretends to be a money-grabbing businessman long after his motivation has changed and he has a real desire to help as many Jews as possible to survive. His weaknesses for drink, women, pleasure, and luxury lead the Nazis to think of him as one of their own, but his factory in Brünnlitz produces munitions of such poor quality that the army has no use for them. With the rest of his money, he bankrupts himself making sure that all of "his" Jews survive until the end of the war. As he is listed as a collaborator and Nazi Party member, he is forced to flee to Argentina before the Allies arrive. Today, the descendants of his Jewish workers outnumber the total population of Jews living in Poland.

SL

3

An inscrutable face (Liam Neeson as Oskar Schindler) – is this scepticism or self-assurance?

Camp commander Amon Goeth's (Ralph Fiennes) uniform matches his facial expression. His lips are pinched and his gaze is haughty.

Horrific pictures, like snapshots in some satanic photo album.

Hands cannot type as fast as they would like to in the attempt to prevent disaster.

"I just want to tell an interesting and true story." Steven Spielberg

STEVEN SPIELBERG When Spielberg announced that he wanted to make a movie about the Holocaust, everyone was appalled. The Jewish World Congress forbade him to film on the Auschwitz site. Spielberg's image was too strongly associated with *Raiders of the Lost Ark* (1981), *E. T. – The Extra-Terrestrial* (1982), and *Jurassic Park* (1992): he was considered too lightweight. Today, his Holocaust Foundation has the biggest archive of materials on Holocaust survivors in the world. Not only has he been extraordinarily successful in bridging the gap between entertaining and challenging cinema, he is now also considered to be the most successful director of all time. Spielberg continues to make both serious films, such as *Saving Private Ryan* (1998) and *War Horse* (2011), and entertainment epics like *War of the Worlds* (2005) and *The Adventures of Tintin* (2011), the latter was his first movie in 3D.

4

"'The film deals with survival, where it ought to be talking about death,' is an objection raised by Claude Lanzmann against Spielberg. 'But the Jewish people and Jewish culture survived Hitler,' is Spielberg's response." *epd Film*

5 The broken and traumatized prisoners are momentarily disoriented after their liberation.

6 Itzhak Stern (Ben Kingsley) is an organizational genius. Many Jews owe him and Schindler their lives.

A PERFECT WORLD

1993 – USA – 138 MIN. – DRAMA, CRIME FILM
DIRECTOR CLINT EASTWOOD (*1930)
SCREENPLAY JOHN LEE HANCOCK DIRECTOR OF PHOTOGRAPHY JACK GREEN EDITING JOEL COX,
RON SPANG
MUSIC LENNIE NIEHAUS PRODUCTION MARK JOHNSON, DAVID VALDES for MALPASO
(for WARNER BROS.)
STARRING KEVIN COSTNER (Butch Haynes), CLINT EASTWOOD (Red Garnett), LAURA DERN
(Sally Gerber), T. J. LOWTHER (Philip Perry), KEITH SZARABAJKA (Terry Pugh),
LEO BURMESTER (Tom Adler), BRADLEY WHITEFORD (Bobby Lee), JENNIFER GRIFFIN
(Gladys Perry), RAY MCKINNON (Bradley), LESLIE FLOWERS (Naomi Perry)

"I don't know nothing."

We are in Eastwood land. The themes of the movie are masculinity and the question of how to live a responsible life in a world that is far from perfect. Butch Haynes (Kevin Costner) breaks out of jail with the help of a cellmate he despises. Looking for a getaway car, the cellmate climbs into the kitchen of a single mother who is busy making breakfast for her family. He tries to rape her, but Haynes intervenes and knocks him down. A neighbor with a gun tries to overpower the convicts, but they take eight-year-old Philip as a hostage and flee.

Philip is an unwilling outsider. His mother, a Jehovah's witness, and his two sisters do everything they can to stop him having fun. Haynes himself feels that he too has been cheated out of a large portion of his life and he starts to feel increasingly responsible for the small boy with the big brown eyes. When his cellmate begins to harass Philip, Haynes kills him.

The other focus of the story is Sheriff Red Garnett (Clint Eastwood). He is under pressure: the governor is in the middle of an election campaign, and has assigned a young criminologist (Laura Dern) to track down Haynes together with some agents from the FBI. Years ago, it was Sheriff Garnett who ensured that Haynes was given several years' youth custody for a petty crime. His idea was to save him from his violent father, but now he's not sure if he didn't lay the foundations for his criminal career instead. Garnett has no faith in carefully planned police actions, and knows all too well that even the best-planned chase can end in bloody failure. "In the

end, all it's about is who has the stomach ulcer and the regrets," he snaps at his young colleague.

In the course of their flight, Haynes and Philip become friends. The man encourages the boy's growing self-confidence, and the boy dares to do more and more things which his mother would never allow. He also helps Haynes get out of tricky situations, and kidnapper and victim slowly become father and son on their journey through rural America. They meet a black farming family who take them in for the night. But when Haynes forces the loveless and brutal grandfather to apologize to his grandchild next morning, the situation escalates. Philip thinks he has been deceived in Haynes, and shoots at him and flees.

The two meet again in the middle of an open field. They are now surrounded by a ring of police who are closing in, and Haynes is gradually bleeding to death. Sheriff Garnett, unarmed, tries to calm the situation, and Haynes gives himself up. But an FBI agent misunderstands his gestures and shoots him dead. At the end of the movie, the only real victim is the criminal himself. There are no winners in Eastwood land.

This was the first film in Clint Eastwood's career where he gave up the main role to another star, and like *Unforgiven* (1992), his previous film, it was another melancholy swan song on the end of innocence. Kevin Costner took the opportunity to give a little more depth to the persona of the bad-tempered boy with a heart of gold that we first saw in *Bodyguard* (1992). Si

"This film by the mature Clint Eastwood, like numerous other road movies, is also about the father who was lost and then found." *Der Spiegel*

1 Despite appearances, these two are sadly not father and son (Kevin Costner and T. J. Lowther).

2 The viewer feels liking shouting, "What are you all staring at? Do something!"

3 Waiting for a better world. Butch Haynes and Philip Perry are standing at the side of a road to nowhere.

CHILD STARS Drew Barrymore, who starred in *E.T.* (1982) as a child, said she must have been the youngest heroin addict in Hollywood. Fortunately she recovered and went on to make a career for herself in adulthood. Many child actors felt the devastating consequences of early fame. River Phoenix (*Stand by Me*, 1986) and Brittany Murphy (*8 Mile*, 2002) paid with their lives. Others – like Macaulay Culkin (*Home Alone*, 1990) and Edward Furlong (*Terminator 2: Judgment Day*, 1991) – hit rock bottom as a result of drugs or social scandals. Some were little more than one-hit wonders, like David Bennent (*The Tin Drum*, 1979), although a small number have been able to succeed as adult actors, such as Jodie Foster (*Taxi Driver*, 1976) and Scarlett Johansson (*The Horse Whisperer*, 1998).

"This isn't the first time that Eastwood has turned the tables on our expectations, but he's never been this bold in the past, or this sure of himself." *The Washington Post*

4 The wide-open eyes of children seem to look into our souls.

5 There's real affection here, despite the chain-smoking, the guns, and the many misdemeanors.

THE FIRM

1993 – USA – 154 MIN. – THRILLER

DIRECTOR SYDNEY POLLACK (1934–2008)

SCREENPLAY DAVID RABE, ROBERT TOWNE, DAVID RAYFIEL, based on the novel of the same name by JOHN GRISHAM **DIRECTOR OF PHOTOGRAPHY** JOHN SEALE

EDITING FREDRIC STEINKAMP, WILLIAM STEINKAMP **MUSIC** DAVE GRUSIN

PRODUCTION SCOTT RUDIN, JOHN DAVIS, SYDNEY POLLACK for MIRAGE

STARRING TOM CRUISE (Mitch McDeere), JEANNE TRIPPLEHORN (Abby McDeere), GENE HACKMAN (Avery Tolar), ED HARRIS (Wayne Tarrance), HOLLY HUNTER (Tammy Hamphill), DAVID STRATHAIRN (Ray McDeere), HAL HOLBROOK (Oliver Lambert), TERRY KINNEY (Lamar Quin), WILFORD BRIMLEY (William Devasher), GARY BUSEY (Eddie Lomax)

"It's against the law."

Sydney Pollack's *The Firm* is as elegant as it is exciting. The movie has John Grisham's brilliant novel to thank for most of its excitement, while the elegance comes from the combination of Dave Grusin's music and the masterful editing, so much so that one of the key features of the film is the way in which the music determines the rhythm of the images. With breathtaking speed we are introduced to the life of Mitch McDeere (Tom Cruise), a Harvard student who is about to take his final law exams. Many law firms have contacted him and made enticing offers.

We see Mitch at job interviews, playing basketball with his lecturers, and working as a waiter. His father is dead, he has no contact to his mother, and his brother Ray (David Strathairn) is in jail. Unsurprisingly, the job that he accepts is with the company that offers the most money. Bendini, Lambert & Locke in Memphis, known as "the Firm" for short, don't just offer 20 percent more pay than the competition but also favorable loans for buying a house and leasing a Mercedes-Benz. Mitch and his young wife are amazed by so much wealth. After years of living in a modest student apartment and suddenly they have a spacious house, a big car, membership at the country club, and everything that makes for a comfortable, bourgeois existence. The Firm helps Mitch prepare for his exam but also expects him to begin work right away. He is assigned a mentor, Avery Tolar (Gene Hackman), who is as friendly as he is experienced – a replacement father for the fatherless lawyer.

While Abby (Jeanne Tripplehorn) finds some of the customs and principles of the Firm strange, particularly the exaggerated, studied friendliness of its employees, Mitch only wants to see the best in everything, the big career and the rosy future. In this way trust and mistrust are held in balance. It soon becomes clear, however, that the new job has its price. Their life together has a mere veneer of normality – in fact they are completely under the control of the Firm. The house is bugged, Mitch is being watched, and colleagues die in mysterious circumstances. What seemed like a serious law firm turns out to be a Mafia organization. Finally, Mitch is blackmailed by the FBI to appear as chief witness against his firm.

Director Pollack manages to tell two stories at once. On the one hand we see a young lawyer struggling to maneuver between professional idealism and corrupt practice, and on the other we see how these difficulties increasingly threaten his previously happy relationship with his partner Abby. Mitch is pressured into a one-night stand on a business trip and then blackmailed. The plot constantly twists and turns to maintain the tension until the very end. As the threats get bigger and his enemies start to mount up, Mitch becomes ever more inventive. He fakes a deal to get his brother out of prison and defends himself against the killers that the Firm sends out to get him. But Mitch's real struggle is with himself, until he understands the greatest danger is the temptation to betray his profession and join the side of the lawless.

SL

172

1 Trust is the name of the game, and knowing what to do when all is not what it seems – even in a marriage (Jeanne Tripplehorn and Tom Cruise).

2 The betrayers betrayed: a frantic search (Ed Harris, left) for Mitch McDeere's brother, who is on the run from the FBI.

3 Appearances can be deceptive: Tammy Hamphill (Holly Hunter) is anything but a naive secretary.

4 Even successful men (Gene Hackman as Avery Tolar) lose their way: he doesn't know friend from foe anymore.

5 Faking it: sophisticated furniture and elegant clothing notwithstanding, this is the Mafia's advocate (Hal Holbrook as Oliver Lambert).

JOHN GRISHAM Born in 1955, the US novelist John Grisham studied law and worked primarily as a criminal lawyer from 1981 through 1991. For a while, the commercial potential of his novels remained undiscovered, but he soon emerged as the best-selling novelist of the '90s. Now, all of his legal thrillers have been made into films: *The Firm* (1993), *The Pelican Brief* (1993), *The Client* (1994), *A Time to Kill* (1996), *The Chamber* (1996) and *The Rainmaker* (1997). His main theme is the relationship between justice and the authorities, and the issue of how a lawyer can maintain his integrity. Other novels he has written since 2000 include *Skipping Christmas*, which was made into the movie *Christmas with the Kranks* (2004).

"The good thing about the film is that Mitch doesn't have to be an idealist in order to carry out his plan."

epd Film

FAREWELL MY CONCUBINE
BAWANG BIE JI

1993 – HONG KONG / CHINA – 169 MIN. – COSTUME FILM, DRAMA
DIRECTOR CHEN KAIGE (*1952)
SCREENPLAY LILIAN LEE, LU WEI, based on the novel by LILIAN LEE
DIRECTOR OF PHOTOGRAPHY GU CHANGWEI **EDITING** PEI XIAONAN **MUSIC** ZHAO JIPING
PRODUCTION HSU FENG for TOMSON FILMS, CHINA FILM, BEIJING FILM STUDIOS
STARRING LESLIE CHEUNG (Cheng Dieyi), ZHANG FENGYI (Duan Xiaolou), GONG LI (Juxian),
LU QI (Guan Jifa), YING DA (Na Kun), GE YOU (Master Yuan), LI CHUN (Young Xiao Si),
LEI HAN (Old Xiao Si), TONG DI (The eunuch Zhang), LI DAN (Laizi)
IFF CANNES 1993 GOLDEN PALM

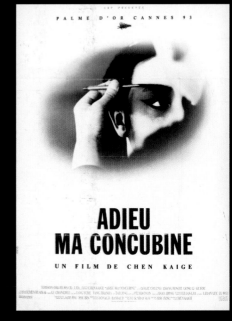

"How will we survive the days of real life with real people?"

A woman hurries through the streets of a Chinese town, dragging her small son behind her. In a square, pupils of the Peking opera school demonstrate their virtuoso talents. The mother is a prostitute whose son can no longer live with her in the brothel. She tries to get the director of the school to take the boy and when he refuses, displeased by a vulgar finger gesture the child makes, the furious mother is beside herself with despair and chops her son's little finger off. This is the first of many injuries that Cheng Dieyi (Leslie Cheung) has to suffer before he becomes a star of the Peking opera playing female roles.

The movie gets its title from the opera of the same name, a story of faithfulness and unconditional love: when Xiang Yu, the great king of Chu, finds himself surrounded on all sides by his enemies in battle, his concubine Yu dances the sword dance for him one last time before slitting her own throat with his sword.

In this world, anyone who wants to become an outstanding artist must suffer. The pupils at the opera school are abused and tortured, both physically and mentally. Most of them are orphans or foundlings, and they have no prospects other than the dream of an opera career. When Dieyi can bear it no longer and runs away with a friend, the two go to see a real performance of a Peking opera and are so moved that they return to the school. His friend hangs himself to escape future punishment, but for Dieyi, the self-punishment of the daily routine soon becomes normal. He makes a new friend in Duan Xiaolou (Zhang Fengyi), who also becomes his partner in the theater, playing King Yu to his concubine. When an opera house owner visits the school and his eye falls on Dieyi, an uproar ensues. As a performer of female roles, he makes the mistake of talking of himself as a man, and therefore immediately loses the visitor's favor. Duan, normally straightforward and relaxed, is overcome with rage and thrusts his king's scepter into

GONG LI Chinese actress Gong Li was born in 1965 and is one of the few Asian actresses to build a successful career without playing in martial arts films. Her longstanding partner, director Zhang Yimou, made her a star with his film *Red Sorghum* (*Hong gao liang*, 1987), and her subsequent films include *Ju Dou* (1990), *Raise the Red Lantern* (1991), and *Curse of the Golden Flower* (2006). Gong Li mostly plays serious, self-confident women, who are never victims and are in charge of their own lives. She combines a strong will with intelligence and sex appeal. In the 2000s she also appeared in American productions like *Memoirs of a Geisha* (2005) and *Miami Vice* (2006).

1 Things aren't what they seem, especially in Chinese opera.

2 Audiences see a man playing a woman in love with a man. In reality, it's a man playing a woman so that nobody finds out he's in love with a man.

3 Even on stage and behind a mask, reality catches up with you.

4 Everyone knows they are being watched. The question is, by whom?

Dieyi's mouth until he performs the concubine's part enchantingly and flawlessly.

Eventually they both become stars of the Peking opera, although their friendship fails due to their differences and the situation in 20th century China. Dieyi lives only for the opera. He turns to opium in moments of crisis, and the life of his best friend, his king on stage, puzzles and repulses him. Duan meets a high-class prostitute called Juxian (Gong Li) in a brothel and marries her. To Dieyi's horror the couple try to build a bourgeois life together, but the political situation in China will not allow this. The new revolutionary government disapproves of all artists who previously performed under other rulers. But the Japanese occupying forces, Chinese liberators, and Communist masses all agree about the quality of the opera and are keen to let it continue. The private and political story of obsession and treachery escalates in the Cultural Revolution. No one is safe; Dieyi denounces his friend (the lover he aspires to), Duan his wife, and his wife Dieyi. A decade later, years after they have both left the stage, they perform the final scene from *Farewell My Concubine* one last time. Dieyi takes the king's sword at the end of his aria and beheads himself. This is his answer to the recurring question: "How will we survive the days of real life with real people?" The road to becoming an artist was tortuous and inhuman, and the final answer for Dieyi can be "Not at all." Few viewers will be familiar with the music and stylized masks used in this movie, but it is impossible not be moved by the despairing pessimism of human beings whose only real home is the stage.

SL

"Chen Kaige's take on cinema makes no claim to solve the problems of humanity. Instead, it helps to make them bearable, not by dreamy escapism, but by bringing to the everyday a component of dreams, ideals and grace." *Cahiers du cinéma*

4

THE PIANO ♟♟♟

1993 – AUSTRALIA / FRANCE / NEW ZEALAND – 120 MIN. – DRAMA, HISTORICAL FILM
DIRECTOR JANE CAMPION (*1954)
SCREENPLAY JANE CAMPION DIRECTOR OF PHOTOGRAPHY STUART DRYBURGH EDITING VERONIKA JENET
MUSIC MICHAEL NYMAN PRODUCTION JAN CHAPMAN for MIRAMAX, CIBY 2000
STARRING HOLLY HUNTER (Ada McGrath), HARVEY KEITEL (George Baines), SAM NEILL
(Stewart), ANNA PAQUIN (Flora McGrath), KERRY WALKER (Aunt Morag),
GENEVIÈVE LEMON (Nessie), TUNGIA BAKER (Hira), IAN MUNE (Reverend),
PETER DENNETT (Sailor), PETE SMITH (Hone)
ACADEMY AWARDS 1994 OSCARS for BEST ACTRESS (Holly Hunter), BEST SUPPORTING ACTRESS
(Anna Paquin), BEST ORIGINAL SCREENPLAY (Jane Campion)
OF CANNES 1993 GOLDEN PALM, SILVER PALM for BEST ACTRESS (Holly Hunter)

"The voice you hear is not my speaking voice but my mind's voice."

A woman's fate around 1850, at the other end of the world and on the edge of civilization: in the days when fathers were still able to decide what was to become of their daughters, Ada McGrath (Holly Hunter) is married off in New Zealand. There is a chronic lack of womenfolk on the island, and her husband, settler Stewart (Sam Neill), has never clapped eyes on her before the wedding. But he doesn't seem to mind her nine-year-old daughter, nor does he care about the fact that Ada has not spoken at all for six years. "The good Lord loves mute creatures as well as those who speak," as he writes to her father in Scotland. But he is more puzzled by the piano that she brings with her, and it remains on the beach where she lands as he doesn't have enough men to carry all her luggage. The instrument is Ada's real voice, and Stewart fails to understand how much it means to her. Her playing has an intensity which expresses the whole force of her personality. Stewart is not a cruel man, but for him Ada represents a level of civilization which is a different realm to

the wild nature he hopes to tame and cultivate, worlds apart from the forest fires and land clearing which are the settlers' main concerns. Mother and daughter, clad entirely in black with bonnets and crinolines, appear to have arrived from another planet as they wade through the mud of the impenetrable New Zealand bush.

In her despair at the loss of her piano, Ada turns to George Baines (Harvey Keitel) who lives a little ways outside the settlement in a forest hut. We discover nothing about the illiterate Baines other than the fact that he has abandoned his British roots and gone native. He is covered with tattoos and speaks the Maori's language, and is therefore useful to the settlers as a negotiator and translator. Baines is what Fenimore Cooper would have called a frontiersman. He bridges the gap between two cultures; and despite his familiarity with the wilderness he also transmits his native culture. Ada comes to trust Baines because like her he is an outsider. Unlike Stewart, he

...stantly realizes what the piano means to her. Stewart accepts immediately when Baines offers him a stretch of forest in exchange for the instrument. He doesn't ask Ada.

Outraged, she rushes to Baines, who has had the piano carried to his house. "The piano belongs to me!" she scrawls in desperation on a page of the notebook which hangs around her neck. Holly Hunter won an Oscar for her portrayal of the role of Ada, and it is extraordinary how much aggression she manages to inject into the diminutive person of the unbending, contrary, small-lipped mute.

Ada demands that Baines return the instrument, but he suggests a deal: she can earn it back key by key with piano lessons. Ada beats him down to just the black keys, but George doesn't want to learn to play; he wants to listen to Ada, watch her, and "do certain things" to her as she plays. They agree on a rate of exchange. The closer he gets to her, the more keys he has to let her have. Finally she agrees to lie naked next to him for the last ten keys, and the piano is hers once more. But she still returns to Baines.

Ada is strengthened by her feelings for Baines and excited by the sensuality of their erotic meetings, which gradually free her from the fear of her own body that her Victorian upbringing has given her. She attempts to win her husband's affection and one night even tries to seduce him. Up until then, she had always remained distant when Stewart tried to claim his marital rights, but now it is he who pushes her away. Ada belongs to him, but now she wants him as a sexual object.

Stewart is annoyed. The movie's audience was also unsettled, accustomed above all to the primacy of male desire in American cinema and the male gaze on the female body. Jane Campion sees her story with the distance

"*The Piano* is a miracle of violence and repose, refinement and cruelty, passion and restraint." *Positif*

1 A surreal moment: washed up on a deserted beach in the wilderness with only music as a comfort.

2 People take familiar cultural objects with them to foreign lands – but why? (Holly Hunter and Anna Paquin).

3 For contact between different cultures to be successful, it must be gentle (Harvey Keitel as George Baines).

of 20th century eyes. Her literary inspirations, like the love triangle in Emily Brontë's *Wuthering Heights*, are not just set in an atmosphere of Victorian narrow-mindedness, they are also products of it. A story like *The Piano* in which the reality of society's sexual drives is revealed would have been absolutely unthinkable at the time in which it is set.

When Ada's daughter Flora (Anna Paquin) tells her stepfather about her mother's secret meetings with Baines, Stewart is beside himself with jealousy and rage. He follows his wife to Baines's house and tries to rape her. Stewart cannot help himself, he is a man of his times whose mental limitations "border on the tragic" as critics were keen to point out. He hacks off one of her fingers, so that she can no longer play the piano. He has finally understood her, or at least has realized how he can hurt her most. He sends Baines the finger – and gives up.

Ada leaves the island together with George on the boat in which she arrived. The piano is now nothing but ballast to her, and she wants it thrown overboard. As the rope holding it unwinds, she puts her foot in one of the loops and is nearly dragged down into the depths: She manages to break free, and at the end is shown sitting at the piano again with a metal finger which Baines has forged for her. The clacking of the artificial finger on the keys lends an ironic distance to the emotions of the music. And she begins to learn to speak again.

SL

4

"These characters don't have our 20th century sensitivity as far as sexuality is concerned. They aren't prepared for its intensity and power."

Neue Zürcher Zeitung

HOLLY HUNTER Her collaboration with Ethan and Joel Coen had an unusual start. In their debut movie, *Blood Simple* (1984), Holly Hunter (*1958) doesn't appear at all – we only hear her voice on an answering machine. Her breakthrough as a film actress came in one of the Coen brothers' wild, anarchic comedies. Alongside Nicolas Cage, she played the charming policewoman who longs for a child in *Raising Arizona* (1987). In the same year, Hunter received her first Oscar nomination for her role as a bubbly journalist in *Broadcast News*. Just 5 ft 2 in (1.57 m) tall, with thin lips and a sometimes pinched facial expression, Holly Hunter certainly doesn't fit Hollywood's conventional image of female beauty. She was so keen to have the role of Ada in Jane Campion's movie *The Piano* (1993) that she applied for it unsolicited, with a stream of faxes. Her performance won her the Best Actress Oscar at the 1994 Academy Awards. In the comedy *O Brother, Where Art Thou?* (2000) she plays the faithless wife, Penelope, whose husband (George Clooney) sets off on a crazy odyssey to find her. In 2005, she appeared in the black comedy *The Big White*, and from 2007 to 2010 starred in the crime series *Saving Grace*.

4 Love finds its voice first and foremost in music.

5 A picture beautiful enough to be a painting by an Old Master.

THE FUGITIVE ⚇

1993 – USA – 127 MIN. – THRILLER, POLICE FILM
DIRECTOR ANDREW DAVIS (*1946)
SCREENPLAY JEB STUART, DAVID N. TWOHY, based on characters by ROY HUGGINS
DIRECTOR OF PHOTOGRAPHY MICHAEL CHAPMAN EDITING DON BROCHU, DAVID FINFER,
DEAN GOODHILL, DOV HOENIG, RICHARD NORD, DENNIS VIRKLER
MUSIC JAMES NEWTON HOWARD PRODUCTION ARNOLD KOPELSON for WARNER BROS.
STARRING HARRISON FORD (Dr. Richard Kimble), TOMMY LEE JONES (Samuel Gerard),
SELA WARD (Helen Kimble), JULIANNE MOORE (Dr. Anne Eastman), JOE PANTOLIANO
(Cosmo Renfro), JEROEN KRABBÉ (Dr. Charles Nichols), ANDREAS KATSULAS (Sykes),
DANIEL ROEBUCK (Biggs), L. SCOTT CALDWELL (Poole), TOM WOOD (Newman)
ACADEMY AWARDS 1994 OSCAR for BEST SUPPORTING ACTOR (Tommy Lee Jones)

"This could be his lucky day."

Dr. Richard Kimble (Harrison Ford) is a successful and well-loved children's surgeon, married to a beautiful, wealthy woman and popular among his influential colleagues. He is warm-hearted and interested in the well being of his patients; all in all, he's a good person and a happy man. One day, when he is on his way home from a charity function, he is called to the hospital to perform an emergency operation, and when he finally gets home that night, he finds his wife murdered. Although he pleads his innocence and claims to have struggled with the murderer, a man with an artificial arm, all the evidence seems to be against him. The court's decision is that Dr. Richard Kimble be sentenced to death by lethal injection.

This plot was the starting point of one of the most successful TV series of the '60s, and it's also the 15-minute opening of one of the cleverest action movies of the decade. The TV series *The Fugitive* was an updated version of Victor Hugo's novel *Les Misérables*. In every episode Kimble tried once more to settle down, taking on a new job or starting a relationship with a new woman. According to the rules of the series, after 45 minutes his attempts invariably failed. It was hugely popular, and the last episode, in 1967, had a record Nielsen share of 72 percent.

The movie concentrates on two central questions – how Dr. Kimble always manages to evade his pursuers, and whether he will ever find the actual murderers. A balance is created between his escape and his search for the real culprits. The fugitive doctor is locked in a gripping ongoing struggle with investigating police marshal Samuel Gerard (Tommy Lee Jones). Driven by his will to succeed, the obsessive marshal will brook no criticism of his strategies in chasing the doctor. Gerard may work in a team, but this one gives him more scope to live out his unrelenting ambition. When the two meet for the first time, Kimble shouts: "I didn't kill my wife!" Gerard roars back, "I don't care!" Kimble, at least, then knows what he's up against. He always has to be a step ahead, always a shade cleverer than his pursuer. In the end, the marshal is eventually forced to admit that his usual methods are not enough. Whether he likes it or not, he has to feel his way into the case, constantly trying to predict Kimble's next move. Eventually he has no choice but to join forces with Kimble in the search for the real murderers.

The audience's attention gradually shifts away from Kimble's escape as his intelligence and creativity increasingly impress the police and awaken the marshal's sense of justice, until eventually their joint efforts to find the real criminals become the central focus of the movie. Everything leads back to Kimble's original workplace at the hospital and to his influential friends. The movie ends with the discovery of a network of intrigue so exciting it can do without the scenes of violence featured in most action films.

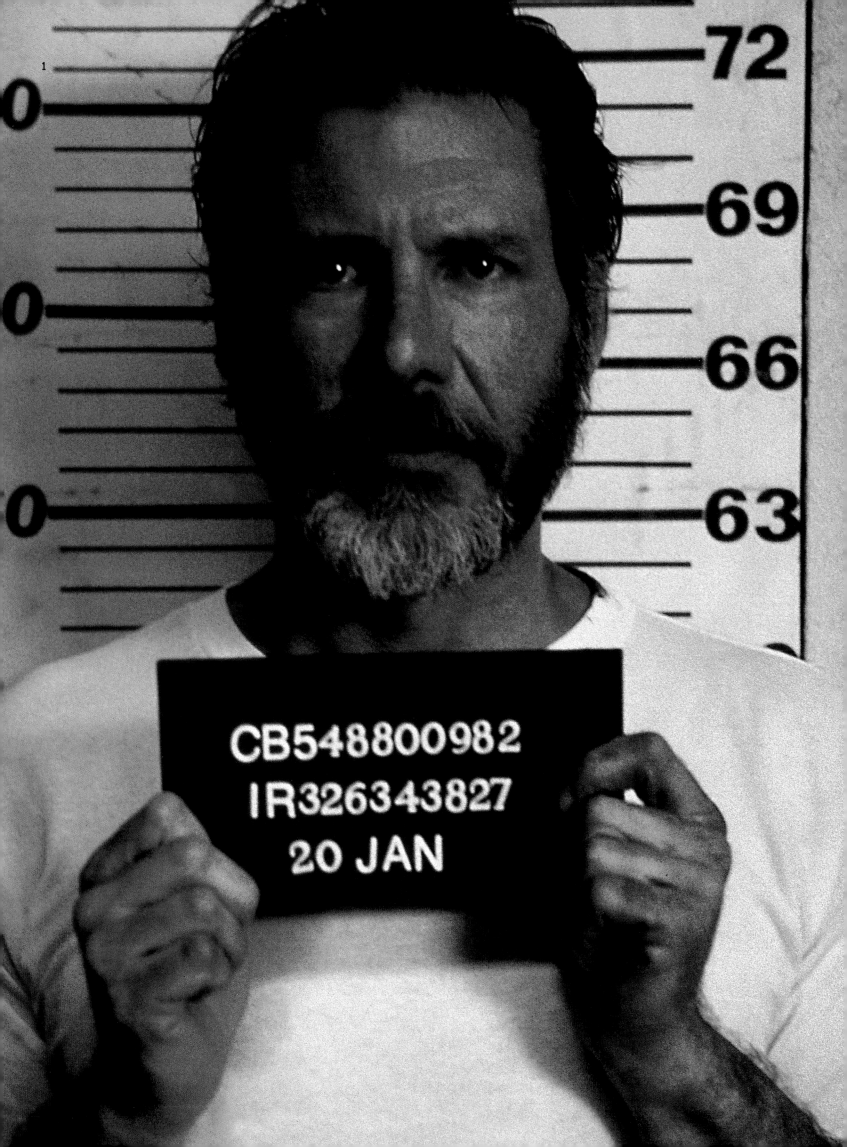

"The way in which Tommy Lee Jones extracts
a proper person from a stereotype role, overbearing,
lightning quick, cunning, and cold ... is a minor
work of art." *Der Spiegel*

HARRISON FORD Harrison Ford trained as a carpenter and, had some film producers got their way, he would still be hammering and sawing. Born in Chicago in 1942, he is not spectacularly good looking; he has never been an angry young man, an intellectual, or a sporty type. But he doesn't shy away from controversial films like *The Mosquito Coast* (1986), and he doesn't try to hide his age. He has also become the actor whose movies have earned the most money: the first *Star Wars* trilogy (1977, 1980, 1983), the four parts of the *Indiana Jones* franchise (1981, 1984, 1989, 2008), and the Tom Clancy adaptations *Patriot Games* (1992) and *Clear and Present Danger* (1994). Yet his filmography includes not just action movies and thrillers, but also comedies like *Morning Glory* (2010) in which he happily plays the grumpy guy.

1   Strange things are afoot: Harrison Ford as
    Dr. Richard Kimble with a criminal record.

2   An unusual hero who knows how to defend himself.

3   A final attempt to kill: Dr. Charles Nichols (Jeroen
    Krabbé) tries to escape arrest.

4   On the run: Dr. Kimble manages to escape the
    police time and again.

5   A false ID card: Samuel Gerard (Tommy Lee Jones)
    tracking down clues. Dr. Kimble has managed to
    gain access to the hospital archives.

SHORT CUTS

1993 – USA – 188 MIN. – DRAMA, EPISODIC FILM
DIRECTOR ROBERT ALTMANN (*1925)
SCREENPLAY ROBERT ALTMAN, FRANK BARHYDT, based on short
stories by RAYMOND CARVER DIRECTOR OF PHOTOGRAPHY WALT LLOYD
EDITING SUZY ELMIGER, GERALDINE PERONI MUSIC MARK ISHAM
PRODUCTION CARY BROKAW for AVENUE ENTERTAINMENT, FINE LINE
FEATURES, SPELLING FILMS
STARRING ANDIE MACDOWELL (Ann Finnigan), BRUCE DAVISON
(Howard Finnigan), JACK LEMMON (Paul Finnigan),
MATTHEW MODINE (Dr. Ralph Wyman), JULIANNE MOORE
(Marian Wyman), ANNE ARCHER (Claire Kane), FRED WARD
(Stuart Kane), JENNIFER JASON LEIGH (Lois Kaiser), CHRIS PENN
(Jerry Kaiser), ROBERT DOWNEY JR. (Bill Bush),
MADELEINE STOWE (Sheri Shepard), TIM ROBBINS (Gene Shepard),
LILY TOMLIN (Doreen Piggott), TOM WAITS (Earl Piggott),
LILI TAYLOR (Honey Bush), FRANCES MCDORMAND
(Betty Weathers), PETER GALLAGHER (Stormy Weathers),
LORI SINGER (Zoe Trainer), LYLE LOVETT (Andy Bitkower),
HUEY LEWIS (Vern Miller)

"Is this a war which can be won?"

A movie usually tells the story of one person, or maybe several. This is what
we're used to. We get to know them, we understand them, we suffer and
rejoice with them, and at the end we join them in overcoming some kind of
final challenge. Robert Altman's Short Cuts is different. The plot seems to lose
itself in an endless chain of different stories and characters, there is no time
to get to know the protagonists, and we are immediately confronted with
closed scenarios. The brevity of the episodes stops us from identifying with
the characters, and we can do nothing other than sit back and watch as they
lead their unhappy, depraved, and solitary lives.

    Their fates are shown in such fragmentary fashion that it seems impos-
sible to discover the real motivations for their actions, But the abiding impression is still one of precise observation, coupled with a laconic attitude which
Altman has preserved from Raymond Carver's brilliant short stories

From the very beginning we find ourselves in the midst of the action.
The Shephards are having another in a series of family arguments. Gene (Tim
Robbins) is a bad-tempered redneck, a motorbike policeman who hates dogs.
He is lying to his wife Sheri (Madeleine Stowe), telling her hypocritical tales
of late hours at work and secret investigations. The truth is that he has a lover
Betty Weathers (Frances McDormand), it's her birthday and she is waiting for
him. Betty's husband Stormy (Peter Gallagher) promised to pick up their son
but instead he too is making a scene. Television anchorman Howard Finnigan
(Bruce Davison) and his wife Ann (Andie MacDowell) are lying in bed watching his program. Cellist Zoe Trainer (Lori Singer) is giving a concert, while
painter Marian Wyman (Julianne Moore) and her husband Ralph (Matthew
Modine), a pediatric surgeon, are in the audience. They make friends with
their neighbors and hold a barbecue together with unemployed sales rep-

2

1   An American family (Madeleine Stowe and Tim Robbins): the only thing missing from this idyllic scene is a dog.

2   It's a strange world: the child needs oral satisfaction, and so do the clients on the other end of the phone (Jennifer Jason Leigh).

3   In Altman's films, only drink provides moments of happiness (Lily Tomlin and Tom Waits).

"One feels that the film can never end, that here we will stay in the company of these ten families that we have learnt to recognize on sight, who enact beneath our eyes their lives of petty frustrations and intimate betrayals." *Le Monde*

Stuart Kane (Fred Ward) and his wife Claire (Anne Archer) who works as a clown at children's birthday parties.

Lois Kaiser (Jennifer Jason Leigh) helps pay the family bills by working for a telephone sex line. While she fakes oral and anal intercourse for her client on the other end of the line, she changes her baby's diaper and makes obscene gestures to her husband Jerry (Chris Penn) which leave us in no doubt as to what she thinks of him. Doreen Piggott (Lily Tomlin) works as a waitress in a coffee shop. Stuart Kane and his friends start off from the coffee shop on a fishing expedition. When they find a naked woman's body in the river they decide to tie it up so they can get on with their fishing undisturbed.

One episode follows another and the audience is permitted brief glances into the lives of the 22 figures. Altman never uses longer sequences to tell us more about the couples he introduces and very few of the scenes are directly connected. The various plot strands are all heading straight for some sort of crisis or disaster. Gene Shepard is trying to give up smoking, his nerves are raw, and he secretly kidnaps his children's dog and abandons it in another part of town. The Finnigans' son is run over on his way to school by Doreen. Although she is very concerned and tries her hardest to take care of him, he simply won't let her as he has been told not to speak to strangers. Once home he passes out and his mother has to rush him to the hospital.

Despite its fragmentary nature, *Short Cuts* is more genuine and more tragic than a conventional melodrama could ever be, as it transforms chance and banality, those two poles of human life, into an artistic form. The tragic dimension of the film comes not from its presentation of a number of tragic existences, but rather from the way the sum of its scenes illustrates humanity's lovelessness. The characters' lives seem to be ruled by blind chance. Altman nonetheless manages to avoid any exaggeration or misplaced sentimentality. In this plot without classic story lines or tension, seemingly without any dramatic structure, there can be no heroes and no surprising revelations; the audience may hope for a happy ending, but those hopes are dashed

when the Finnigans' son dies and Zoe Trainer commits suicide. The stories continue without interruption and we see a family picnic. Bill Bush (Robert Downey Jr.) and Jerry Kaiser leave the party to go behind the bushes with two women they have just met. Kaiser, in a moment of madness, beats one of them to death.

As so often in Los Angeles, there is an earthquake, but this is no catastrophe of Biblical proportions and afterwards everything is much as it was before. At the end of the film we're not looking into a brighter future with different conditions and better people. Instead these fragments from the lives of so many different characters show us the difficulties of life itself.   SL

"Old Master Robert Altman appears to have no difficulty at all in giving us an understanding of the stories of twenty-two protagonists using a highly unusual narrative style." *Fischer Film Almanach*

EPISODIC FILMS Episodic narration means that many storylines can exist alongside each other; only occasionally may they be brought together in a common plot. Cinema has always been fascinated with parallels and simultaneous plot strands. In the '70s, directors tried to represent simultaneous action by dividing the screen into four or more parts, in a technique known as "split screen." Robert Altman uses a different method. *Short Cuts* (1993) gives the audience only brief glimpses of the lives of his numerous protagonists; when their paths coincide in hot, summery Los Angeles, these meetings have tragic, if not fatal, consequences. This type of screenplay developed by Altman has influenced many films. Well known examples are *Pulp Fiction* (1994), *Playing by Heart* (1998), and *Magnolia* (1999). Examples of episodic films that consist of separate juxtaposed episodes rather than parallel plot strands are *Night on Earth* (1991) and *Amores Perros* (2000).

4   Does this baker (Lyle Lovett) look like a happy man?

5   That's all we needed: Daddy (Jack Lemmon).

6   Men and their habits (Fred Ward, center): a study in headwear . . .

7   Gene lies every time he opens his mouth. But it matters little, as nobody (Betty, Frances McDormand) believes him anymore.

FORREST GUMP ♟♟♟♟♟♟

1994 – USA – 142 MIN. – COMEDY
DIRECTOR ROBERT ZEMECKIS (*1952)
SCREENPLAY ERIC ROTH, based on the novel of the same name by WINSTON GROOM
DIRECTOR OF PHOTOGRAPHY DON BURGESS EDITING ARTHUR SCHMIDT MUSIC ALAN SILVESTRI
PRODUCTION WENDY FINERMAN, STEVE TISCH, STEVE STARKEY, CHARLES NEWIRTH for
PARAMOUNT
STARRING TOM HANKS (Forrest Gump), ROBIN WRIGHT (Jenny Curran), GARY SINISE
(Lt. Dan Taylor), SALLY FIELD (Mrs. Gump), MYKELTI WILLIAMSON (Benjamin Buford
"Bubba" Blue), MICHAEL CONNER HUMPHREYS (Forrest as a boy), HANNA HALL
(Jenny as a girl), TIFFANY SALERNO (Carla), MARLA SUCHARETZA (Lenore),
HALEY JOEL OSMENT (Forrest Junior)
ACADEMY AWARDS 1995 OSCARS for BEST PICTURE, BEST ACTOR (Tom Hanks), BEST DIRECTOR
(Robert Zemeckis), BEST VISUAL EFFECTS (Allen Hall, George Murphy, Ken Ralston,
Stephen Rosenbaum), BEST FILM EDITING (Arthur Schmidt), and BEST ADAPTED
SCREENPLAY (Eric Roth)

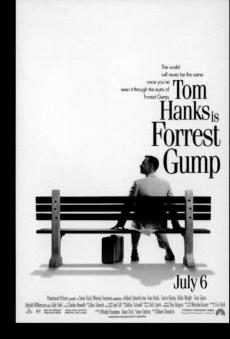

"Shit happens!"

A bus stop in Savannah, Georgia. A man with the facial expression of a child sits on the bench, a small suitcase next to him and a box of chocolates in his hand. While he is waiting for the bus, he tells the story of his life to the others sitting around him.

The story begins sometime in the 1950s in a place called Greenbow in Alabama. Here Forrest Gump (Michael Conner Humphreys), a young boy named after a hero from the Civil War, is growing up without a father. He is different from the other children: his IQ of 75 is way below average, and as his mother (Sally Field) says, his spine is as bent as a politician's morals. But his mother is a strong-willed woman, and she manages to balance out these defects. She makes her boy wear leg braces and although she's prepared to use her body to convince the headmaster that Forrest doesn't need to go to a special school, she teaches her son morals: "Dumb folks are folks who act dumb," being one of the many pearls of wisdom from her rich repertoire.

Forrest, who is friendly and unsuspecting, doesn't have an easy life. No one wants to sit next to him on the school bus, apart from Jenny (Hanna Hall), who soon becomes his only friend. When Forrest is being teased by his school mates for the thousandth time, she tells him to run away. Forrest always does what people tell him, and suddenly he discovers hidden gifts like speed and endurance. The leg braces shatter, and with them the limitations of his simple mind fall away. Swifter than the wind, Forrest runs and runs and runs through his youth.

Years later, when he's almost an adult, Forrest is running away from his schoolmates again and by mistake ends up on a football field. Simple-minded Forrest is offered a college scholarship and a place on an All-American football team.

"Life is like a box of chocolates. You never know what you're gonna get" – another gem from Mrs. Gump's treasury. There's a lot in this for Forrest. Thanks to his knack for being in the right place at the right time, his football career is followed by military service and the Vietnam War, where he becomes not only a war hero but also a first-class table tennis player. After the war he fulfills a promise he made to Bubba (Mykelti Williamson), his friend and comrade in arms, and he makes his fortune as the captain of a shrimping boat.

He becomes even richer when he invests his millions in what he believes to be a fruit firm by the name of "Apple."

Forrest Gump's life is a 40-year long-distance run through American postwar history. He shakes hands with Presidents Kennedy and Nixon, shows Elvis Presley the hip thrust, and inspires John Lennon's song "Imagine." He invents the smiley face as well as the "Shit happens" sticker. By pure chance his finger is always on the pulse of the times. He gets mixed up in a protest action for racial integration, in a demonstration against the Vietnam War, and accidentally witnesses the Watergate Affair.

Just as Forrest's career and his experiences of American history are unintentional, his meetings with the love of his life, Jenny (Robin Wright),

"Hanks is a kid again in director Robert Zemeckis' Forrest Gump. Slow-witted and likeable, Forrest races through the rubble of the '50s, '60s and '70s." *Time Magazine*

1 As simple as they come: Forrest Gump (Tom Hanks) fulfills the American dream in his own way.

2 A safe seat: one of his mother's sayings was "Dumb folks are folks who act dumb" and this stays with him all his life.

3 Jenny (Hanna Hall) is Forrest's (Michael Conner Humphreys) only friend. She sticks by him, even though everybody teases him because he is so slow physically and mentally.

4 A woman's wiles: Forrest's single mother (Sally Field) uses everything in her power, even her own body, to ensure that her son leads a normal life.

3

4

are also unplanned. Instead of fulfilling her dream and becoming a folksinger she has ended up a junkie hanging around the hippie scene, singing in a third-rate nightclub. When his mother dies, Forrest moves back to Greenbow, where he has a short but unsuccessful affair with Jenny. Once more, Forrest tries to run away from his destiny and he runs through America for three years without a concrete destination, accompanied by a growing band of followers.

Director Robert Zemeckis is known for being a specialist in technically demanding entertainment movies. He literally turned Meryl Streep's head in *Death Becomes Her* (1992), and his *Back to the Future* trilogy suggests that he has a weakness for time travel (*Back to the Future I-III*, 1985, 1989, 1990).

Forrest Gump, adapted by Eric Roth from the novel of the same name by Winston Groom, is also a strange journey into the past.

With the help of George Lucas's special effects firm Industrial Light & Magic (ILM), Zemeckis uses sophisticated visual tricks and original film footage to create the illusion that Forrest was actually present at various historical occasions. For the scene where Forrest shakes hands with President Kennedy in the Oval Office, the digital technicians of ILM used archive material with the real people cut out and a superimposed image of Forrest Gump. Tom Hanks was filmed in front of a blue screen and this was combined with the archive film by computer. Computer technology is present throughout *Forrest Gump*, though audiences are unlikely to notice it. With its help, a

"Throughout, Forrest carries a flame for Jenny, a childhood sweetheart who was raised by a sexually abusive father and is doomed to a troubled life. The character's a bit obvious: Jenny is clearly Forrest's shadow – darkness and self-destruction played against his lightness and simplicity." *San Francisco Chronicle*

thousand real extras were transformed into a hundred thousand simulated demonstrators.

The naive boy-next-door image which Tom Hanks had developed else-where made him the ideal actor for this part, which one critic described as "Charlie Chaplin meets Lawrence of Arabia." His Forrest Gump is the coun-terpart of Josh Baskin, the twelve-year-old who grows into the body of a man overnight in Penny Marshall's comedy *Big* (1988).

Forrest Gump is not a direct reflection of contemporary history, but it does reflect a distinctly American mentality. History is personalized and shown as a series of coincidences. The moral of the movie is as simple as

BLUE/GREEN SCREEN Blue/green screen is a process by which moving silhouettes can be combined with a picture background. The actors, figures, or objects are first filmed in front of a blue screen. Then two versions of the movie are made: in the first, all the colors are filtered out of the background; in the second, only the silhouettes of the actors remain on a white background. The layers can be amalgamated either in an optical printer or digitally. The computer process, known as compositing, was used in films including *Jurassic Park* (1993), *Godzilla* (1997), and *Gladiator* (2000).

5   Love, Peace, and Happiness? Jenny (Robin Wright) resorts to drugs while running away from herself.

6   An inspired move: Forrest Gump owes a large part of its authentic feel to the special effects of Industrial Light & Magic. These lead the viewer to think that Forrest really did meet President Nixon.

7   A promise with consequences: Forrest promises his dying friend Bubba (Mykelti Williamson) that he will fulfill their shared dream of going shrimp fishing.

the sayings of Forrest's mother. Everything is possible – you just have to want something to happen, or be at the right place at the right time, even if you hardly realize what is going on and don't take an active part in events. International moviegoers loved the unique and entertaining worldview of this simple soul from Alabama, underscored by a soundtrack which is a musical cross section of the whole century. The movie made 330 million dollars in the USA, and almost doubled that sum worldwide. It was awarded six Oscars in 1995, and suddenly smiley faces were in fashion again and everyone went around saying "Shit happens!" Winston Groom's novel and Bubba's shrimp cookbook stood on many bookshelves. *Forrest Gump* is somewhat

reminiscent of Hal Ashby's comedy *Being There* (1979), where Peter Sellers plays a simple gardener who only knows the world from his television. Ashby's movie is an intelligent and sometimes highly comic satire, but *Forrest Gump* didn't take that opportunity, or didn't want it: it's pure entertainment which only pretends to reflect on modern history. That combination of historical reproduction and conventional Hollywood plot links *Forrest Gump* to Steven Spielberg's *Schindler's List* (1993): the audience flips through the movie like a photo album, they reassure themselves about their own past and leave the movie theater two hours later, satisfied and by no means unpleasantly moved.

APO

CHUNGKING EXPRESS
CHONGQING SENLIN

994 – HONG KONG – 97 MIN. – DRAMA
DIRECTOR WONG KAR-WAI [WANG JIAWEI] (*1958)
SCREENPLAY WONG KAR-WAI **DIRECTOR OF PHOTOGRAPHY** CHRISTOPHER DOYLE,
ANDREW LAU [LIU WEIQIANG] **EDITING** WILLIAM CHANG, KAI KIT-WAI,
KWONG CHI-LEUNG **MUSIC** ROEL A. GARCIA, FRANKIE CHAN
[CHEN SHUNQI] **PRODUCTION** CHAN YI-KAN [CHEN YIJIN] for
JET TONE PRODUCTIONS
STARRING BRIGITTE LIN [Lin Qingxia] (Woman with the blond wig),
TAKESHI KANESHIRO [He Qiwu] (# 223), TONY LEUNG
[Liang Chaowei] (# 663), FAYE WONG [Wang Jinwen] (Faye),
VALERIE CHOW [Shou Jialing] (Stewardess), "PIGGY" CHAN
[Chen Jinquan], GUAN LINA, HUANG ZHIMING, ZHEN LIANG,
ZUO SONGSHEN

"California Dreamin'"

To begin with, *Chungking Express* was just occupational therapy for Wong Kar-Wai: he had a couple of months' break in the middle of a big production called *Ashes of Time* (*Dung che sai duk*, 1992 –94) and he wanted to fill it in by knocking out a short movie. He started out with little more than a couple of clearly defined characters and locations to go with them. The internal links and the plot, were all to be found in the process of filming.

April 30, 1994. A woman (Brigitte Lin) in a garish blond wig and enormous sunglasses has to pass on a packet of drugs, but she loses it and has to go and look for it. At the same time policeman He Qiwu – officer no. 223 – sits in a snack bar drowning his sorrows, as his girlfriend left him exactly a month ago. Since then he has survived on cans of pineapple whose sell-by date is today, symbolizing the end of his love. Gloomily he gets more and more drunk and empties his last can of pineapple. To cap it all, today is his 25th birthday. He decides to fall in love with the first woman who comes into the snack bar. Enter the blonde with the sunglasses, worn out from a

Another policeman – officer no. 663 – has also split up with his girlfriend, a stewardess. She has left her key to his apartment in his regular bar with Faye the waitress, who constantly listens to the promises of "California Dreamin'." Faye has secretly been in love with the policeman for a long time and has absolutely no intention of passing on the keys. She starts creeping into his apartment every day. Sometimes she simply cleans up, often she plays some kind of trick, swaps labels on tin cans, dissolves sleeping pills in drinks, or puts new fish in his aquarium. One day she finds a message from the policeman: he wants to meet her and arranges a date in the Restaurant California.

The particular conditions of the movie's production, meant that Wong had to fight not only with his inspiration but also with the plans of his film team, who were booked up for months ahead. Apparently the set was the scene of the most extraordinary comings and goings as both the actors and the technicians were constantly disappearing off to other film sets.

contained, as it was unclear how the scenes would fit together at the end. Despite the movie's transitory character, this gives every moment a high degree of concentration. Wong withdrew to the editing room with the piecemeal material and two months later, *Chungking Express* was finished.

The movie became Wong Kar-Wai's greatest international success, the blonde with the sunglasses the icon of a whole generation and Chris Doyle one of the most important cameramen of the '90s. Wong Kar-Wai became a style. Wong Kar-Wai came to mean loose plots structured like poems, eccentric voice-overs, bright colors, spectacular handheld camera work, and outlandish picture composition: an urbane cinema of memories, where romance is only possible in retrospect, set in a city which is constantly changing, which denies its pasts and which will soon cease to exist.   OM

"It's beautiful, simple, funny, and smart. I wish more films were like it." *Le Monde*

CHRISTOPHER DOYLE Christopher Doyle was born in Sydney in 1952. His work with director Wong Kar-Wai, whose movies he filmed from *Days of Being Wild* (*A Fei zhengzhuan*, 1990) onward, made him into one of the most imitated cameramen of the '90s. His sensitive approach to color combined with precise handheld camera work came to express the melancholy of the period's fin-de-siècle school of international art films. Doyle, who speaks fluent Mandarin and Cantonese, moved to Hong Kong and then adopted a Chinese name: Duk Ke-feng (lord, master, like the wind). From 1998 onward, Doyle has worked as director of photography on English-language productions like *Liberty Heights* (1999), *The Quiet American* (2002), and *Ondine* (2009).

1   "[I'm the] DJ of my own films."
    Wong Kar-Wai

2   Self-reflection, Hong Kong style: Cantonese pop superstar Faye Wong [Wang Jinwen] as Faye in a typical Wong game with the identities of his actors.

3   Another icon of 1990s cinema: Asian hit woman Brigitte Lin [Lin Qingxia] in a blonde wig.

4   "There is so little space in Hong Kong that you would have no chance with a fixed camera. You have to work with a handheld camera."
    Cameraman Christopher Doyle

5   "The scenes in *Chungking Express* [...] are set in places that he [Wong Kar-Wai] himself frequents, such as the 'Midnight-Express' fast-food stand in the Lan Kwai Fong district."
    Production Manager & Chief Editor William Chang

LÉON / THE PROFESSIONAL

1994 – FRANCE / USA – 110 MIN. – ACTION FILM, DRAMA
DIRECTOR LUC BESSON (*1959)
SCREENPLAY LUC BESSON **DIRECTOR OF PHOTOGRAPHY** THIERRY ARBOGAST **EDITING** SYLVIE LANDRA
MUSIC ERIC SERRA **PRODUCTION** CLAUDE BESSON, LUC BESSON for GAUMONT, LES FILMS DU DAUPHIN
STARRING JEAN RENO (Léon), GARY OLDMAN (Norman Stansfield), NATALIE PORTMAN (Mathilda), DANNY AIELLO (Tony), PETER APPEL (Malky), MICHAEL BADALUCCO (Mathilda's father), ELLEN GREENE (Mathilda's mother), ELIZABETH REGEN (Mathilda's sister), CARL J. MATUSOVICH (Mathilda's brother), LUCIUS WYATT "CHEROKEE" (Tonto)

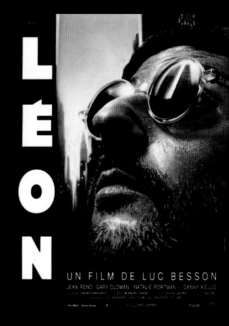

UN FILM DE LUC BESSON

"No women, no kids, that's the rule."

In the virtuoso opening scene to Luc Besson's movie *Léon / The Professional* the camera "swings" from a starry night sky to daylight. From a bird's-eye view, it glides over trees until the skyline of New York fills the viewfinder. It then dives into the valleys of the city's long streets and finally comes to a standstill in front of an Italian restaurant. Inside two men are sitting opposite each other. One of them is Tony (Danny Aiello), a respectable member of society, while the other, Léon (Jean Reno), lives outside of any community. Léon doesn't say much – he prefers his pistol to do the talking. He is a "cleaner", the best professional killer of his kind. Apart from the orders that he receives from Tony, which he invariably carries out with clockwork precision, Léon has nothing: he has no friends, no women, no hobbies, and no money. His only companion is a pot plant that he cares for with the same thoroughness he demonstrates in his work. Mathilda (Natalie Portman), a 12-year-old child-woman, lives in the same house as Léon and often has to take refuge from her violent father on the stairs. One day when she comes home from shopping, she finds that a corrupt team of plainclothes cops from the drug squad under the command of psychopath Norman Stansfield (Gary Oldman) has murdered her entire family. The camera shows the seemingly endless hallway that Mathilda walks down, past the corpse of her father and his murderers, up to Léon who is watching everything through the peephole in his door. Only after hesitating for a long time does Léon open the door to his apartment and to his life. When the girl discovers that Léon is a killer, she wants to avenge her little brother, and she convinces Léon to teach her his profession.

Léon would like to get rid of the girl, but he doesn't know how – "no women, no kids" is his professional watchword. The two stay together and start to learn from each other. Léon shows Mathilda how to clean a gun, she teaches him to read and write; he teaches her about death, and she teaches him about life.

This French/American coproduction unites many opposites. The introverted, principled professional killer, Léon, is a good contrast to Stansfield, the lunatic drug cop who kills in a haze of bloodlust and amphetamines, and Léon, a child in the body of a man is played off against Mathilda, a woman in the body of a child. Eric Serra's atmospheric music contrasts with Thierry Arbogast's cool and effective camera work and the impressive choreographed action scenes form a fine contrast to what is after all a moving love story.

The main characters in Luc Besson movies are often outsiders who find it difficult to fit into society, but they have strong moral integrity and live by their own rules.

Léon / The Professional is like a continuation by other means of *Nikita* (1990), a previous Besson movie. In *Nikita*, Jean Reno also plays a "cleaner," and a taste for murderous women is common to both movies: Nikita has been sentenced to death and can only save her skin by agreeing to kill for the government.

In 1996 the "Version intégrale" (Director's Cut) of *Léon / The Professional* was re-released in France. This longer version contains 26 minutes cut after disastrous US screenings. Not only do those missing minutes allow viewers to form a clearer picture of the unusual relationship between Léon and Mathilda, they also transform the whole nature of the movie – and what appeared to be basically an action film became a drama with action elements. APO

2

"What Léon does is kill people – cleanly, efficiently and without the slightest trace of remorse. From all appearances, there is nothing else in his life. No friends, no hobbies, no distractions."

The Washington Post

3

4

"**"She's something like the Jodie Foster character in *Taxi Driver*, old for her years. Yet her references are mostly to movies: 'Bonnie and Clyde didn't work alone,' she tells him. 'Thelma and Louise didn't work alone. And they were the best.'"** *Chicago Sun-Times*

SCREENING Unfinished versions of high-budget movies are often given trial theater showings to an audience (target group) which has been selected according to particular criteria. After the showing, the audience is asked for its opinion, usually in the form of voting slips. The results of this survey are then used to produce the version of the movie to be released to movie theaters. After bad screenings, screenplays are often reworked, whole parts of the movie filmed again or edited differently to ensure as large an audience as possible upon release.

1 A killer with the heart of a child: Léon (Jean Reno), kept as a childlike protégé by a Mafia godfather, doesn't grow up until the young girl Mathilda puts her life in his hands.

2 To arms: Léon teaches his bright young pupil Mathilda (Natalie Portman) the basic principles of his deadly trade.

3 A man like a loaded gun: Gary Oldman takes his role as drug-addicted cop Norman Stansfield to the very limit. He acts as if drunk: his character is unnerving and teeters constantly on the edge of hysteria.

4 Reformed: once Léon has given up his life for Mathilda, thus atoning for the death of her brother, the girl realizes that from now on she will have to find her own path.

ED WOOD ♟♟

1994 – USA – 126 MIN. – COMEDY
DIRECTOR TIM BURTON (*1958)
SCREENPLAY SCOTT ALEXANDER, LARRY KARASZEWSKI, based on the biographical novel
NIGHTMARE OF ECSTASY: THE LIFE AND ART OF EDWARD D. WOOD JR. by
RUDOLPH GREY **DIRECTOR OF PHOTOGRAPHY** STEFAN CZAPSKY **EDITING** CHRIS LEBENZON
MUSIC HOWARD SHORE **PRODUCTION** DENISE DINOVI, TIM BURTON for
BURTON/DINOVI PRODUCTIONS (for TOUCHSTONE)
STARRING JOHNNY DEPP (Ed Wood), MARTIN LANDAU (Bela Lugosi),
SARAH JESSICA PARKER (Dolores Fuller), PATRICIA ARQUETTE (Kathy O'Hara),
JEFFREY JONES (Criswell), BILL MURRAY (Bunny Breckinridge), G. D. SPRADLIN
(Reverend Lemon), VINCENT D'ONOFRIO (Orson Welles), LISA MARIE (Vampira),
MIKE STARR (Georgie Weiss)
ACADEMY AWARDS 1995 OSCARS for BEST SUPPORTING ACTOR (Martin Landau), and
FOR BEST MAKEUP (Ve Neill, Rick Baker, Yolanda Toussieng)

"Cut!!! Perfect!!!"

Ed Wood enjoys the doubtful but wonderfully marketable reputation of being the worst director of all time. Tim Burton's movie is a monument to a colleague who more than deserves it. Burton may have immeasurably more talent as a filmmaker, but he still feels that there is a spiritual link between his work and that of Wood, who was a tireless maker of cheap movies in the '50s. Accordingly, his homage always maintains a certain level of respect: even at his funniest and most absurd moments, Ed Wood is never made to look ridiculous.

Hollywood has always perpetuated its own myth by celebrating its heroes and legends. This movie is something of an exception as it turns its attention to one of tinsel town's hopeless losers. To prevent Ed Wood (Johnny Depp) from appearing an amiable but hopelessly incompetent idiot, Burton almost overdoes the thematic links between his career and that of Orson Welles (Vincent D'Onofrio). Like Wood, Welles was the epitome of the all-American filmmaker, who tried to realize his cinematic vision by being a

writer, producer, director, and leading actor all rolled into one. He is now considered to be the embodiment of the uncompromising artist doomed to failure by a refusal to bow to the production conditions of a capitalist film industry.

The dimensions of their failures may have been different, but in a key scene of the movie, Ed and Orson are shown drowning their sorrows together as victims of the same system. Ironically, Burton himself was not free from the constraints of the industry, despite enjoying a wunderkind reputation in the mid '90s: as he wanted to give the movie the flatness of a '50s B movie and make it in black and white, he had to do without Columbia's financial backing and make *Ed Wood* as an independent production.

What Wood as director lacked in artistic talent and financial resources, he made up for with boundless enthusiasm and the noble art of improvisation. His absolute lack of (self-)irony gives his movies their unmistakable touch. Everything was meant absolutely seriously, and one of Wood's greatest

problems was that he was even more naïve than the audience he hoped to bring flooding to the movie theaters. Johnny Depp plays Wood like a child who, even with the most unlikely-looking toys, is able to simply ignore reality and disappear into the fairy-tale world of his own imagination.

Plots are so crude they seem out of this world, dialogue is unintentionally comic, a color-blind cameraman uses the same light for every scene regardless of whether it is day or night, special effects look as if they were made in a kindergarten, and staggeringly untalented actors, all friends of the director, are constantly falling over the scenery. As one of Wood's actresses said, "His carelessness in technical matters is only surpassed by his com-

plete lack of concern in showing his amateurism." But Wood was far too wrapped up in himself and his work to be bothered with such details. He wasn't careless out of disrespect for his audience, it was just that his thoughts were always way ahead of the scene he was working on.

His problem was that he always saw things as a whole, as a complete vision, just like his great colleague Orson Welles. After every first take, Depp shouts, "Cut!!! That was perfect!!!" and opens his eyes as wide as they'll go to demonstrate his absolute abandonment to his own crazy ideas: this is Burton biting back any suggestion of cynicism, and it is exactly the attitude that gives the movie its human integrity.   UE

4

5

1   Look at me: Ed Wood (Johnny Depp) and Bela Lugosi (Martin Landau) try their hand at long-distance hypnosis.

2   Strange passion: is Wood in love with his wife Dolores (Sarah Jessica Parker) or just with her angora jumper?

3   The director in discussion with his hero. On the wall are posters of films he used as models.

4   Wood's *Plan 9 From Outer Space* is considered to be one of the worst films of all time.

5   Wood's working principle: the first take is always the best.

"A moving, dreamlike homage to a monstrous, childish form, *Ed Wood* is also a paean to the way love of film gets passed down." *Cahiers du cinéma*

ED WOOD Edward D. Wood Jr. (1924–1978) belonged to a long-gone age when Hollywood directors were not mass-produced in film schools, but came from all walks of life and based their work on their own experiences. He was both a veteran of the war in the Pacific and a self-confessed transvestite (something which took great courage at the time) with a particular weakness for cuddly angora pullovers. He exposed his personal obsessions to the outside world without any regard for their effect in his very first movie, *Glen or Glenda?* (1952), a pseudo-religious, superficial horror film about a sex change. Audiences were outraged, alienated, and way out of their depth. Later he preferred to indulge himself primarily in the genres of horror and science fiction. *Plan 9 From Outer Space* (1959), his most infamous movie, was a tale of alien grave robbers. Around that time Wood met Bela Lugosi, the original movie *Dracula*, who had long been cast off by official Hollywood and left for dead. With his practically non-existent means, Wood tried to save the great actor from oblivion and give him the sort of send-off that he deserved. This touching act of humanity makes the quality of the movies they made together seem almost irrelevant. The fact that the only Oscar *Ed Wood* won was best supporting actor for Martin Landau as Lugosi speaks volumes about the treatment of men and myths in Hollywood.

THE SHAWSHANK REDEMPTION

1994 – USA – 142 MIN. – PRISON FILM, DRAMA
DIRECTOR FRANK DARABONT (*1959)
SCREENPLAY FRANK DARABONT, based on the short novel *RITA HAYWORTH AND THE SHAWSHANK REDEMPTION* by STEPHEN KING DIRECTOR OF PHOTOGRAPHY ROGER DEAKINS
EDITING RICHARD FRANCIS-BRUCE MUSIC THOMAS NEWMAN PRODUCTION NIKI MARVIN for CASTLE ROCK ENTERTAINMENT
STARRING TIM ROBBINS (Andy Dufresne), MORGAN FREEMAN (Ellis Boyd "Red" Redding), BOB GUNTON (Prison Director Norton), WILLIAM SADLER (Heywood), JAMES WHITMORE (Brooks Hatlen), CLANCY BROWN (Captain Byron Hadley), GIL BELLOWS (Tommy), MARK ROLSTON (Bogs Diamond), LARRY BRANDENBURG (Skeet), NEIL GIUNTOLI (Jigger)

"Fear can make you prisoner. Hope can set you free."

In 1947 bank clerk Andy Dufresne (Tim Robbins) is given two life sentences for the murder of his wife and her lover. Although he insists he is innocent in court, all the evidence seems to point to his guilt.

When the prisoner transport van passes through the gates of the Shawshank prison, the inmates press their faces against their cell doors and yell, "Fresh fish! fresh fish!" Not a lot happens in Shawshank, and the bets as to which of the newcomers will break down and cry during his first night in jail make a pleasant change. Prisoner Red (Morgan Freeman) bets two packets of cigarettes, the prison's currency, on Andy Dufresne. He loses his bet.

Red is a lifer, like Andy Dufresne. He acts as a small-business man inside the prison walls and he can get hold of everything from cigarettes to movie posters. He is the first to notice Andy's behavior when he saunters around the yard during exercise like a man "without a care in the world, like he's wearing an invisible coat that protects him from this place." At first Andy stays aloof from his fellow inmates and they know nothing about him or about what keeps him going. All they see is that the warders' hassling doesn't get him down, and neither do the repeated brutal rapes by the other prisoners. As first-person narrator and observer, Red is the central figure in *The Shawshank Redemption*. In the course of the movie he befriends the new prisoner and through his eyes we can at least observe Andy Dufresne, even if we don't know what's going on in his head.

The endless time can't pass slowly enough for Andy; who carves chess pieces with immense composure, writes petitions, and over the years builds up an amazing library. He uses his professional training to climb up the prison pecking order: he starts off as tax advisor for all of the prison staff, later

3

"Exactly the same kind of enigmatic smile is written all over the face of Tim Robbins in his role of the lifer, that Stephen King must have had in mind: a kind of inner light, where otherwise there is only darkness and hopelessness."

Frankfurter Allgemeine Zeitung

1 Hope with its back to the wall: his friendship with Andy Dufresne (Tim Robbins, left) teaches Red (Morgan Freeman) that you can break free of your chains if you manage to preserve your inner freedom.

2 Initiation: when Andy is assigned to special work with other prisoners, this sets the course for his rise in the prison hierarchy.

3 Andy Dufresne plays things close to his chest. He wears a mask as impenetrable as the prison walls, behind which he conceals an indomitable character who knows that revenge is not only sweet, but tastes best when served cold.

he gets a desk in the director's office and keeps the accounts of his illegal dealings. When Andy manages to escape without anyone noticing in 1975 after 30 years of careful planning, he has not just feathered his own nest but also exacted an extremely subtle revenge: not with hot blood and burning sword, but in the manner of an accountant who "redeems" a debt.

The Shawshank Redemption, based on Stephen King's short novel *Rita Hayworth and the Shawshank Redemption* is no conventional prison movie, even if it does include motifs typical of the genre. It nods to other prison movies by seeing the prison as a closed system with immutable, often illogical rules that turn people into numbers, and mean that opposition to the warders is the only means of self-definition available to the inmates. Darabont has an economical touch, and cleverly emphasizes only vital things. The movie posters in Andy's cell for example (Rita Hayworth, Marilyn Monroe, Raquel Welch) are not just an indication of the passing of time, but also symbols for cinema as a window onto life. *The Shawshank Redemption* is a great movie about time, patience, and above all, hope. "Hope can drive a man mad," Red says at the beginning of the film. But he doesn't allow that to happen. Every ten years he has to appear before the probation board who ask him if he is fit for life in society. Although he confirms this every time (with conviction that decreases with the passing of the years) he is never pardoned. But when Andy Dufresne finally regains his freedom because he never lost either hope or patience, Red also dares to hope again. Hope sets him free, at least inwardly.

APO

GOOFS One of the great pleasures of many regular cinemagoers is looking out for "goofs" or mistakes in the movies. These include anachronisms, like someone using a cell phone in the Middle Ages. They also include continuity mistakes, as when a actor wears a tie in a particular scene or shot, but no longer has it on in the next. Factual errors also count as goofs, as would be the case for a movie set in Los Angeles, where the audience could see the Statue of Liberty. Technical mistakes also count, like visible microphones or members of the crew who suddenly wander into shot.

4 Life sentence: Red also knows ways of preventing the never-changing prison routine from wearing him down.

5 The insignia of power: prison is an enclosed system where the guards represent the authority of the state.

6 Victim of circumstantial evidence: everything points to the fact that Andy Dufresne murdered his wife.

NATURAL BORN KILLERS

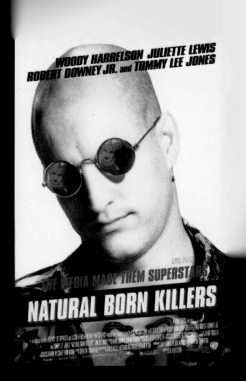

1994 – USA – 119 MIN. – ROAD MOVIE, SATIRE

DIRECTOR OLIVER STONE (*1946)

SCREENPLAY DAVID VELOZ, RICHARD RUTOWSKI, OLIVER STONE, based on a story by QUENTIN TARANTINO DIRECTOR OF PHOTOGRAPHY ROBERT RICHARDSON EDITING BRIAN BERDAN, HANK CORWIN MUSIC Various songs PRODUCTION JANE HAMSHER, DON MURPHY, CLAYTON TOWNSEND for IXTLAN, NEW REGENCY, J. D. PRODUCTIONS

STARRING WOODY HARRELSON (Mickey Knox), JULIETTE LEWIS (Mallory Knox), ROBERT DOWNEY JR. (Wayne Gale), TOMMY LEE JONES (Dwight McCluskey), TOM SIZEMORE (Jack Scagnetti), EDIE MCCLURG (Mallory's mother), RODNEY DANGERFIELD (Mallory's father), BALTHAZAR GETTY (Gas station attendant), RICHARD LINEBACK (Sonny), LANNY FLAHERTY (Earl)

FF VENICE 1994 SPECIAL JURY PRIZE (Oliver Stone)

"We got the road to hell in front of us."

Natural Born Killers begins on a desert highway with a close-up of a hissing snake, accompanied by Leonard Cohen singing "Waiting for a Miracle" – a hypnotic introduction, which makes the scenes that follow all the more shocking. Mickey and Mallory (Woody Harrelson and Juliette Lewis) are letting off steam in a diner. While Mickey calmly finishes his piece of cake, his ethereal girlfriend brutally beats up a young redneck. A blues song floats out from the jukebox. Later, the pair of them kill almost all the other diners. Mickey and Mallory are a nightmare couple: they are Bonnie and Clyde or Sid and Nancy, but most of all they are the natural born killers of Oliver Stone's title. During their odyssey through Southwest America they randomly kill 52 people and only spare witnesses who will report deeds. Mickey and Mallory

are a gift for the TV nation which quickly styles the two serial killers as TV superstars. They are pursued not only by the police but by the media too, who hope to profit from their fame. In many of his films, from *Salvador* (1986) and *The Doors* (1991) to *Any Given Sunday* (1999), Oliver Stone has worked on the contradictions and myths of modern America. *Natural Born Killers*, based on a story written by Quentin Tarantino, combines Stone's favorite themes – violence, capitalism, the media, pop culture – in a dark, satirical tour-de-force about the obsessions of the American media. The movie breaks the bounds of classic narrative cinema, polarizing and disturbing its audiences, disappointing their expectations before leaving them in a state of breathless astonishment. To do that Stone makes use of practically all of the cinema's

technical possibilities, changing the cameras and the film and video formats, using all the color and effect filters imaginable, and blending in back projections and archive material. He underscores Robert Richardson's hyperactive camera work and the occasionally hysterical editing with an eclectic soundtrack including everything from Orff's "Carmina Burana," Bob Dylan and Patsy Cline to Nine Inch Nails and Dr. Dre. Stone claimed to have used over 100 different pieces of music in the movie. The music often acts as a counterpoint to the action on screen, as in "I love Mallory," a scene filmed in the style of an American sitcom, where instead of wholesome family life the opposite is shown. Stone adds canned laughter and applause to the verbal and physical beating which Mallory's vile father deals out to his wife and daughter.

Stone knows full well that he is throwing a stone at the media glass house where he himself lives. When Mickey and Mallory have sex in front of a hostage, the window of their motel shows some explosive archive material: in between the reptiles and insects and the images of Hitler and Mussolini are scenes from *The Wild Bunch* (1969) and *Midnight Express*, the movie whose screenplay won Stone his first Oscar in 1978.

Does art imitate life or life art? Can images cause real violence? Stone's fiction was certainly overtaken by reality. One of Mickey and Mallory's admirers in the movie remarks that if he were a mass murderer he'd want to be just like them. Years later, Stone was still answering charges that his movie had inspired countless copycat crimes.

APO

1 Totally cracked up: Mickey Knox (Woody Harrelson) doesn't let anything stand in his way on his deadly journey towards media stardom.

2 Director Oliver Stone uses unusual visual devices like super-imposition and color effects to convey his message to the general public.

3 Corpses litter their path: the cute little scorpion that Mallory (Juliette Lewis) has symbolically tattooed on her belly inflicts a deadly sting. Mickey and Mallory are just as dangerous and unpredictable, a nightmare made flesh on a death-dealing trip through the USA.

4 Look back in anger: Mallory's past is like a soap opera of brutality where the laughter of the band drowned out her father's physical and verbal beatings.

4

"Visually, the film is a sensation, resembling a demonically clever light show at a late '60s rock concert. The narrative is related in color 35 mm, black-and-white 8 mm, and video, and at different speeds." *Variety*

5   Prison director Dwight McCluskey (Tommy Lee Jones) is as fanatical as he is hungry for media attention. He later falls victim to the hell that he himself has created.

6   Messianic: in prison Mickey provokes a riot when he tells his interviewer about the cleansing power of killing

INTERVIEW WITH THE VAMPIRE: THE VAMPIRE CHRONICLES

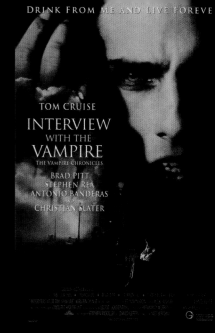

1994 – USA – 122 MIN. – HORROR FILM, DRAMA
DIRECTOR NEIL JORDAN (*1950)
SCREENPLAY ANNE RICE, based on her novel of the same name
DIRECTOR OF PHOTOGRAPHY PHILIPPE ROUSSELOT EDITING MICK AUDSLEY, JOKE VAN WIJK
MUSIC ELLIOT GOLDENTHAL PRODUCTION DAVID GEFFEN, STEPHEN WOOLEY for
GEFFEN PICTURES (for WARNER BROS.)
STARRING BRAD PITT (Louis), TOM CRUISE (Lestat), KIRSTEN DUNST (Claudia),
CHRISTIAN SLATER (Malloy), STEPHEN REA (Santiago), ANTONIO BANDERAS
(Armand), VIRGINIA MCCOLLAM (Prostitute on the riverbank), MIKE SEELIG (Pimp),
SARA STOCKBRIDGE (Estelle), THANDIE NEWTON (Yvette)

"The world changes, we do not, and there lies the irony that finally kills us."

San Francisco. Two men sit in a hotel room high over the gloomy streets. One of them, Malloy (Christian Slater), is a journalist and he is here to take down the life story of the other. It's a fascinating, incredible story that begins two hundred years previously in New Orleans in 1791, when Louis (Brad Pitt) first became a vampire. When his wife dies in childbirth, the young widower is beside himself with grief and no longer capable of looking after his plantation. Searching for oblivion and death he spends his nights in the town's dives, and his sorrow drives him into the arms of prostitutes and to the gambling table – and he is constantly on the lookout for a fatal fight to end his torment. But however much he longs for death, his wishes are never granted. One night Louis meets the vampire Lestat (Tom Cruise), who tells him of eternal youth and an existence without grief. Louis then makes a fateful decision that he will later regret.

Neil Jordan's vampires have very little to do with the traditional mythology presented in innumerable movies and books. Rather, they are descended in a direct line from Friedrich Wilhelm Murnau's *Nosferatu* (1921), although they are considerably better looking. Being a vampire is no fun, and there is no escape except through crucifixes or silver bullets. Vampires are people – but they are forced to live as outcasts.

After his transformation into a vampire, Louis's grief is replaced by melancholy and solitude when he learns about the less appetizing sides of a vampire's existence. He doesn't want to kill anybody and instead feeds on rats and other small animals. Lestat on the other hand is a bloodsucker who goes by the book. In haunts of low repute and at intoxicating balls he searches for his victims, handsome young men and women mostly, kills them and drinking their blood with the same carelessness with which he indulges his passion for the hunt.

One night Louis kill a little girl called Claudia (Kirsten Dunst), and to bind Louis to himself, Lestat turns her into a vampire. At first, the relationship between Louis, Lestat, and their adopted daughter seems a happy ménage à trois, but before long things turn sour and it becomes a living hell for all three of them. Only Lestat seems to enjoy being undead. Louis longs for the life which Lestat has taken from him, and the child-woman Claudia dreams of a life which she will never know.

The movie is based on Anne Rice's best-selling novel *Interview with the Vampire* and is Neil Jordan's second adaptation of fantasy literature. In 1984 he made the Red Riding Hood story *The Company of Wolves* based on a book by Angela Carter. In both movies there is a similar mixture of sensual

1   A vampire with Style: Lestat (Tom Cruise) lives off the blood of his victims.

2   The reporter Malloy (Christian Slater) listens to an incredible story …

3   … Louis (Brad Pitt) tells him about his life as a vampire.

4   Louis is being destroyed by the paradox of his blood-sucking existence. He has to kill in order to live.

"The initial meeting between Louis and Lestat takes the form of a seduction; the vampire seems to be courting the young man, and there is a strong element of homo-eroticism in the way the neck is bared and the blood is engorged." *Chicago Sun-Times*

and the supernatural, and hints of homoeroticism, incest, and pedophilia, although these elements are mostly latent in *Interview with the Vampire*, where they are concealed in looks and fatal embraces.

The opulent images of the film and the emotions they inspire are far more impressive than with the coherency of the plot. Dante Ferretti, the set designer, creates a visually overwhelming and uncanny vampire world that reaches from the swamps of Louisiana all the way to the catacombs of Paris. Cameraman Philippe Rousselot (*Diva*, 1981) uses colors which seem overlain with black velvet, as though to illustrate what Louis has lost: Louis has to wait a hundred years before he can see a glorious dawn again like the one he saw before his transformation: and when he sees it, it's in a black-and-white movie, in Murnau's silent classic *Sunrise* from 1927.   APO

VAMPIRE FILMS The first known vampire movie was called *Le Manoir du Diable* (*The Devil's Manor*) and was produced by Georges Méliès in 1896. Vampire films are all about the ways in which plants, aliens, or beings either living or dead rob victims of their vital juices, mostly blood. Many vampire films, including F. W. Murnau's classic *Nosferatu* (1921), take their themes from Bram Stoker's novel *Dracula*. Vampire movies have been made in a wide variety of genres, including comedies, thrillers, and westerns.

When he's on the prowl, Cruise likes to seduce young women before exacting his dark red sustenance. With alarming swiftness, the victims swift from sexual excitement to outright horror, as Cruise's purpose becomes clear." *The Washington Post*

5 The picture of haughtiness. Lestat relishes his life as a vampire, and he is completely devoid of scruples.

6 The vampire Armand (Antonio Banderas) satisfies his blood lust on the stage.

7 Neither wife nor daughter: Claudia (Kirsten Dunst) becomes Louis's companion.

PULP FICTION ♟

1994 – USA – 154 MIN. – GANGSTER FILM
DIRECTOR QUENTIN TARANTINO (*1963)
SCREENPLAY QUENTIN TARANTINO, ROGER AVARY DIRECTOR OF PHOTOGRAPHY ANDRZEJ SEKULA
EDITING SALLY MENKE MUSIC Various songs PRODUCTION LAWRENCE BENDER for
JERSEY FILMS, A BAND APART (for MIRAMAX)
STARRING JOHN TRAVOLTA (Vincent Vega), SAMUEL L. JACKSON (Jules Winnfield),
UMA THURMAN (Mia Wallace), HARVEY KEITEL (Winston Wolf), VING RHAMES
(Marsellus Wallace), ROSANNA ARQUETTE (Jody), ERIC STOLTZ (Lance),
QUENTIN TARANTINO (Jimmie), BRUCE WILLIS (Butch Coolidge), MARIA DE MEDEIROS
(Fabienne), CHRISTOPHER WALKEN (Koons), TIM ROTH (Ringo / Pumpkin),
AMANDA PLUMMER (Yolanda / Honey Bunny)
IFF CANNES 1994 GOLDEN PALM
ACADEMY AWARDS 1995 OSCAR for BEST ORIGINAL SCREENPLAY (Quentin Tarantino,
Roger Roberts Avary)

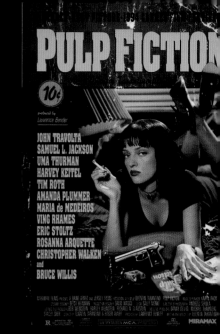

"Zed's dead, baby. Zed's dead."

After his amazing directorial debut, *Reservoir Dogs* (1991), Quentin Tarantino had a lot to live up to. The bloody studio piece was essentially a purely cinematic challenge, and such an unusual movie seemed difficult to beat. But Tarantino surpassed himself with *Pulp Fiction*, a deeply black gangster comedy. Tarantino had previously written the screenplay for Tony Scott's uninspired gangster movie *True Romance* (1993) and the original script to Oliver Stone's *Natural Born Killers* (1994). At the beginning of his own movie, he presents us with another potential killer couple. Ringo and Yolanda (Tim Roth and Amanda Plummer), who lovingly call each other Pumpkin and Honey Bunny, are sitting having breakfast in a diner and making plans for their future together. They are fed up of robbing liquor stores whose multi-cultural owners don't even understand simple orders like "Hand over the cash!" The next step in their career plan is to expand into diners – why not start straight away with this one? This sequence, which opens and concludes *Pulp Fiction*, serves a framework for the movie's other three inter-woven stories, which overlap and move in and out of chronological se-quence. One of the protagonists is killed in the middle of the movie, only to appear alive and well in the final scene, and we only understand how the

The first story is "Vincent Vega and Marsellus Wallace's Wife." Vin and Jules (John Travolta and Samuel L. Jackson), are professional assas on their way to carry out an order. Their boss Marsellus Wallace (Ving Rham wants them to bring him back a mysterious briefcase. A routine job, as can tell from their nonchalant chitchat. Their black suits make them loo if they have stepped out of a '40s *film noir*. Vincent is not entirely happy he has been given the job of looking after Marsellus's wife Mia (Uma Thurm when the boss is away. In gangster circles, rumor has it that Vincent's pre cessor was thrown out of a window on the fourth floor – apparently for c nothing more than massaging Mia's feet.

"The Golden Watch," the second story in the film, is the stor has-been boxer Butch Coolidge (Bruce Willis). He too is one of Marsell "niggers," as the gangster boss calls all those who depend on him. Butch accepted a bribe and agreed to take a dive after the fifth round in his fight. At the last minute, he decides to win instead and to run away with money and his French girlfriend Fabienne (Maria de Medeiros).

In the third story, "The Bonnie Situation," a couple of loose narra strands are tied together. Jules and Vincent have done their job. Howeve

2

"Hoodlums Travolta and Jackson – like modern-day Beckett characters – discuss foot massages, cunnilingus and cheeseburgers on their way to a routine killing job.
The recently traveled Travolta informs Jackson that at the McDonald's in Paris, the Quarter Pounder is known as 'Le Royal.' However a Big Mac's a Big Mac, but they call it 'Le Big Mac.'"

The Washington Post

back of the car. The bloody car and its occupants have to get off the street as soon as possible. The two killers hide at Jimmie's (Quentin Tarantino), although his wife Bonnie is about to get back from work at any moment, so they have to get rid of the evidence as quickly as possible. Luckily they can call upon the services of The Wolf (Harvey Keitel), the quickest and most efficient cleaner there is.

To like *Pulp Fiction*, you have to have a weakness for pop culture, which this film constantly uses and parodies, although it never simply ridicules the source of its inspiration. Quentin Tarantino must have seen enormous quantities of movies before he became a director. The inside of his head must be

like the restaurant where Vincent takes Mia: the tables are like '50s Cabrios, the waiters and waitresses are pop icon doubles: Marilyn Monroe, James Dean, Mamie van Doren, and Buddy Holly (Steve Buscemi in a cameo appearance). Vincent and Mia take part in a Twist competition. The way the saggy-cheeked, aging John Travolta dances is a brilliant homage to his early career and *Saturday Night Fever* (1977).

With his tongue-in-cheek allusions to pop and film culture, Tarantino often verges on bad taste: in one scene from "The Golden Watch," a former prisoner of war and Vietnam veteran (Christopher Walken) arrives at a children's home to give the little Butch his father's golden watch. The scene begins like a kitsch scene from any Vietnam movie, but quickly deteriorates into the scatological and absurd when Walken tells the boy in great detail about the dark place where his father hid the watch in the prison camp for so many years.

Tarantino has an excellent feel for dialogue. His protagonists' conversations are as banal as in real life, they talk about everything and nothing, about potbellies, embarrassing silences, or piercings. He also lays great value on those little details which really make the stories, for example the toaster, which together with Vincent's habit of long sessions in the bathroom will cost him his life – as he prefers to take a detective story rather than a pistol into the lavatory.

Tarantino's treatment of violence is a theme unto itself. It is constantly present in the movie, but is seldomly explicitly shown. The weapon is more important than the victim. In a conventional action movie, the scene where Jules and Vincent go down a long corridor to the apartment where they will kill several people would have been used to build up the suspense, but in Tarantino's film Vincent and Jules talk about trivial things instead, like two office colleagues on the way to the cafeteria.

One of the movie's most brutal scenes comes after Vincent and Mia's restaurant visit. The pair of them are in Mia's apartment, Vincent as ever in the bathroom, where he is meditating on loyalty and his desire to massage Mia's feet. In the meantime Mia discovers his supply of heroin, thinks it is cocaine and snorts an overdose. Vincent is then forced to get physical with her, but not in the way he imagined. To bring her back to life, he has to plant an enormous adrenaline jab in her heart.

Pulp Fiction also shows Tarantino to be a master of casting. All the roles are carried by their actors' larger-than-life presence. They are all "cool": Samuel L. Jackson as an Old-Testament-quoting killer, and Uma Thurman in a black wig as an enchanting, dippy gangster's moll. Bruce Willis drops his habitual grin and is totally convincing as an aging boxer who refuses to give up. Craggy, jowly John Travolta plays the most harmless and good-natured assassin imaginable. If *Pulp Fiction* has a central theme running through it, then it's the "moral" which is present in each of the three stories. Butch doesn't run away when he has the opportunity but stays and saves his boss's life. Vincent and Jules live according to strict rules and principles and are very moral in their immoral actions. Vincent is so loyal that it finally costs him his life. Jules's moment of revelation comes when the bullets aimed at him miraculously miss. Coincidence or fate? Jules, who misquotes a Bible passage from Ezekiel before each of the murders he commits, decides that henceforth he will walk the path of righteousness. In the last scene when Ringo and Honey Bunny rob the diner, Ringo tries to take the mysterious shiny briefcase. He fails to spot Jules draw his gun and under normal circumstances he would be a dead man. But Jules, who has decided to turn over a new leaf, has mercy on both of them – and that's not normal circumstances.

APO

4

"Tarantino's guilty secret is that his films are cultural hybrids. The blood and gore, the cheeky patter, the taunting mise-en-scene are all very American — the old studios at their snazziest." *Time Magazine*

1 Do Mia's (Uma Thurman) foot massages turn into an erotic experience?

2 The Lord moves in mysterious ways: Jules (Samuel L. Jackson) is a killer who knows his Bible by heart.

3 Completely covered in blood: Vincent (John Travolta) after his little accident.

4 Everything's under control: as The Wolf, the "cleaner" (Harvey Keitel), takes care of any dirty work that comes up.

5 Echoes of *Saturday Night Fever:* Mia and Vincent risk a little dance.

6 In his role as Major Koons Christopher Walken plays an ex-Vietnam prisoner of war as he did in *The Deer Hunter.*

7

> **"Split into three distinct sections, the tale zips back and forth in time and space, meaning that the final shot is of a character we've seen being killed 50 minutes ago."** *Empire*

PULP Cheap novels in magazine format, especially popular in the '30s and '40s, owing their name to the cheap, soft paper they were printed on. The themes and genres of these mostly illustrated serial novels and short stories ranged from comics to science fiction to detective stories. The first pulp stories appeared in the 1880s in the magazine *The Argosy*. In the 1930s there were several hundred pulp titles available, but by 1954 they had all disappeared – pulp was replaced by the cinema, the radio, and above all, the new paperback book.

7 Will his pride desert him? Boxer Butch (Bruce Willis) gets paid every time he loses in the ring.

8 You gotta change your life! Jules and Vincent talk about chance and predestiny.

9 Hand over the cash! Yolanda (Amanda Plummer) carries out …

10 … the plan that she and Ringo (Tim Roth) hatched a few moments before.

8

QUEEN MARGOT
LA REINE MARGOT

1994 – FRANCE / ITALY / GERMANY – 144 MIN. – HISTORICAL FILM, DRAMA
DIRECTOR PATRICE CHÉREAU (*1944)
SCREENPLAY DANIÈLE THOMPSON, PATRICE CHÉREAU, based on the novel of the same name by ALEXANDRE DUMAS THE ELDER **DIRECTOR OF PHOTOGRAPHY** PHILIPPE ROUSSELOT
EDITING FRANÇOIS GÉDIGIER, HÉLÈNE VIARD **MUSIC** GORAN BREGOVIC
PRODUCTION CLAUDE BERRI for RENN PRODUCTIONS, FRANCE 2 CINÉMA, D. A. FILMS, RCS FILMS & TV, NEF FILMPRODUKTION, DEGETO
STARRING ISABELLE ADJANI (Marguerite de Valois / Margot), DANIEL AUTEUIL (Henri de Navarre), JEAN-HUGUES ANGLADE (Charles IX), VINCENT PEREZ (La Môle), VIRNA LISI (Catherine de Medici), PASCAL GREGGORY (Henri III), CLAUDIO AMENDOLA (Coconnas), MIGUEL BOSÉ (Guise), ASIA ARGENTO (Charlotte de Sauve), JEAN-CLAUDE BRIALY (Coligny), ULRICH WILDGRUBER (René)
IFF CANNES 1994 BEST ACTRESS (Virna Lisi), JURY PRIZE (Patrice Chéreau)

"But what fortunes await me tonight? A knife in my stomach, a cup of poison ...?"

In 1572, thousands of Protestant Huguenots travel to Paris to celebrate the marriage of Marguerite de Valois (Isabelle Adjani), sister of the French king Charles IX (Jean-Hugues Anglade), to the Protestant Henri de Navarre (Daniel Auteuil). Charles is officially head of state, but he is a weak man, and in reality France is ruled by Catherine de Medici (Virna Lisi), the king's mother, who is an expert in diplomatic intrigue. The marriage was her idea, and it is taking place against her daughter's wishes, with the intention of putting an end to years of conflict between the Protestants and the ruling Catholics. To consolidate her own power and the future of her three sons, she also arranges the assassination of Coligny (Jean-Claude Brialy), her son's closest advisor. When the murder attempt fails and the Huguenots threaten revenge, she decides to rid France of them altogether. On the night of August 23–24, 1572, which went down in history as the "St. Bartholomew's Day Massacre" she had thousands of Huguenots slaughtered in Paris and the surrounding provinces. Patrice Chéreau's movie is based on Alexandre Dumas's 1845 novel *La Reine Margot*, a tale first published in serial form. It was produced by Claude Berri, and between them, they created a cinematic opera with a cast which is excellent all the way down to the minor roles. Virna Lisi was pronounced best actress at the Cannes International Film Festival for her portrayal of the power-obsessed queen mother who rules her family like a Mafia godfather, and indeed Chéreau named Francis Ford Coppola's three-part epic *The Godfather* (1971, 1974, 1990) as an important model for his film. She remains cool and calculating even when her son Charles is on his deathbed sweating blood as the result of a bungled poisoning carried out on her orders. Instead of going into mourning, she has heads roll.

Patrice Chéreau comes from a theatrical background – among other things, he once directed Wagner's *Ring* in Bayreuth – and this is very evident in the movie. Henri de Navarre and Margot are held captives in the Louvre

3

> # "The seat of power is laid waste, and the people are desolate."
>
> *Frankfurter Allgemeine Zeitung*

4

1   The king with his sister and lover: Isabelle Adjani and Vincent Perez in an intimate embrace.

2   A political marriage: Roman Catholic Margot has to marry Protestant Henri (Daniel Auteuil), in an effort to bring the Wars of Religion to an end.

3   Cornered: the Protestant La Môle fends off his attackers.

4   Director Patrice Chéreau shows the unbelievable cruelty of the Wars of Religion.

5   Decadence and life at court: a scene at the royal palace.

after the massacre and this becomes his stage. But he still uses all the conventional expressive means of the cinema. The camera is never still, and restlessly follows the corridors which are as twisted, cramped, and dark as the protagonists' thoughts. Behind secret doors, on narrow stairs, and in halls lit only by candles, Chéreau presents the customs and atmosphere of a courtly society where the wrong word at the wrong time could cost your head, and a kiss might be punished with death. Anyone who shows feelings here is lost. Henri de Navarre has to learn this – but the statuesquely beautiful Margot, played by Isabelle Adjani, seems to have absorbed that with her mother's milk. Outwardly she is a plaything, abused by her mother and brothers in various ways. But secretly she has a relationship with the Protestant La Môle (Vincent Perez), who she picked up on her wedding night and saves from the massacre only a few days later. Outwardly she supports her husband right to the end when she follows Henri to Navarre. But in her lap lies the head of her lover.

Queen Margot is a bloody, brutal, and naturalistic picture of another age. When the camera closes in on the faces and the long, unkempt hair of the men, when it registers the endless series of murdered Protestants, the audience doesn't just see the terrors of the Counter-Reformation, it has their stench in its nose. One unforgettable scene shows that Chéreau wanted to make more than a historical drama: when hundreds of lifeless bodies are shoveled into a mass grave, there is more than a premonition of the Holocaust – there is a distant echo of all the massacres in history.

APC

HISTORICAL FILMS An umbrella term for various kinds of fictional movies that portray clearly defined periods of time or particular historical events. Filmmakers have been recreating the past with the camera and the help of costumes and dialogue since the silent era, in films like D. W. Griffith's *Birth of a Nation* (1915). Within the genre there are various subgenres, including adventure movies, where the historical elements serve above all as background settings. Costume dramas, movies about myths and legends, and big-budget spectaculars are other types of film often included within the genre.

DISCLOSURE

1994 – USA – 128 MIN. – EROTIC THRILLER

DIRECTOR BARRY LEVINSON (*1942)

SCREENPLAY PAUL ATTANASIO, based on the novel of the same name by MICHAEL CRICHTON

DIRECTOR OF PHOTOGRAPHY ANTHONY PIERCE-ROBERTS **EDITING** STU LINDER **MUSIC** ENNIO MORRICONE

PRODUCTION BARRY LEVINSON, MICHAEL CRICHTON for BALTIMORE PICTURES

STARRING MICHAEL DOUGLAS (Tom Sanders), DEMI MOORE (Meredith Johnson), DONALD SUTHERLAND (Bob Garvin), CAROLINE GOODALL (Susan Hendler), ROMA MAFFIA (Catherine Alvarez), DYLAN BAKER (Philip Blackburn), ROSEMARY FORSYTH (Stephanie Kaplan), DENNIS MILLER (Marc Lewyn), ALLAN RICH (Ben Heller), NICHOLAS SADLER (Don Cherry)

"Sex is power."

Tom Sanders (Michael Douglas) is the proud owner of a dream house and the mild-mannered head of a picture-book family. His domestic paradise is on a small island just outside the booming metropolis of Seattle and every morning he leaves with the ferry to cross over into the real world. There a battle rages of which Sanders is as yet completely unaware, even though he himself is one of the combatants. He works at DigiCom, a computer technology firm which despite being a market leader lacks capital, and is on the verge of being taken over. Although he is one of the company's most creative executives, his lack of power instinct means he is not very high up in the pecking order.

On the day Sanders expects to be promoted to vice president, the ill-omened toothpaste fleck on his tie is not the only shadow which falls over his paradise. Sanders is cheated out of his reward for the pioneer work he put into the company by an intrigue which has clearly been developing for some time. He is passed over in favor of Meredith Johnson (Demi Moore), an ex-lover from his wilder days, who becomes his new boss under his very nose. Johnson is a power-dressing career woman, and she enjoys the protection of the company's founder Garvin (Donald Sutherland). At their very first meeting, she tries to exercise her new power by lighting up the sparks of the old relationship, and Sanders, whose knowledge of human nature isn't quite on a level with his expertise in bits and chips, falls blindly into the trap. However, the model father and family man is overcome by moral scruples halfway. In the face of the full frontal erotic attack launched with brute force by Demi Moore, he flees in a chaotic retreat which naturally serves only to get him into deeper trouble.

After this rebuff, the new vice president uses every means at her disposal to accuse Sanders of what amounts to attempted rape, to try and force him out of the company. Up to this point, Tom Sanders has fit into conventional role clichés: in a conversation on bringing up children he asks what is wrong with Barbie dolls, he pats his secretary on the behind, and laughs at his colleagues' sexist jokes without a second thought. Suddenly forced onto the defensive, he develops unsuspected insights and fighting capacities.

In other hands this would be enough material for a dialogue-based courtroom drama, and for a few scenes *Disclosure* becomes precisely that. But the movie has a second, more wide-ranging theme that turns it into an exciting thriller: the career woman overestimates her own influence and is eventually disposed of in her turn as part of the global players' treacherous intrigues.

The movie is highly successful in creating an atmosphere full of latent threat. Although the company's office block seems welcoming with its open stairwells, hanging walkways, and expanses of glass, what it really represents is a climate of permanent surveillance. *Disclosure* questions the computer age utopia where it is claimed that race and sex fade into the background in the face of new technology, and that the human race is freed from its physical existence as though from an unnecessary evil. A key scene in this respect is the fight between Meredith and Tom in cyberspace. It may not be sensationally new to show how every means is permissible to get rid of the competition, especially in the computer industry, where company culture is so demonstratively casual, but *Disclosure*'s sophisticated and rigorously logical exploration of its themes guarantees genuine suspense and perfect entertainment. JM

1 Sex at the office. Tom Sanders's (Michael Douglas) female boss starts making advances.

2 Rejected, Meredith Johnson (Demi Moore) plans revenge.

3 The network of conspirators draws ever tighter. Bob Garvin (Donald Sutherland) is another colleague who proves disloyal to Sanders.

4 The struggle continues in cyberspace. Sanders's opponent attempts to manipulate the truth in her favor.

5 The computer as instrument of power. Sanders receives mysterious e-mails.

"*Disclosure* seems a very calculated attempt to tap the zeitgeist." *Sight and Sound*

MICHAEL DOUGLAS Michael Douglas has always had a feel for quality. Even when he was still appearing in TV series, he produced one of the cult movies of the '70s – *One Flew Over the Cuckoo's Nest* (1975). Endowed with a chin almost as impressive as that of his famous father, Michael can play both brutal and reckless or dumb and servile. As a result, he is just as convincing as a ruthless neo-liberal trader in *Wall Street* (1987) and the sequel *Wall Street: Money Never Sleeps* (2010) as he is as the office slave who takes the law into his own hands in *Falling Down* (1993). His looks mean that he fits perfectly into the wealthy, upper-crust settings that form the backdrop to many of his movies, as in *A Perfect Murder* (1997). In *The Game* (1997), his upper-class character is given the appropriate hobby of human game hunting. His rare excursions into comedy include *Wonder Boys* (2000) – a sublime performance as a permanently stoned professor – and *It Runs in the Family* (2003), in which he appears with father Kirk and two other family members.

MAYBE ... MAYBE NOT
DER BEWEGTE MANN

1994 – GERMANY – 93 MIN. – COMEDY
DIRECTOR SÖNKE WORTMANN (*1959)
SCREENPLAY SÖNKE WORTMANN, based on the comics *DER BEWEGTE MANN and PRETTY BABY* by RALF KÖNIG **DIRECTOR OF PHOTOGRAPHY** GERNOT ROLL **EDITING** UELI CHRISTEN
MUSIC TORSTEN BREUER **PRODUCTION** BERND EICHINGER for NEUE CONSTANTIN FILM, OLGA FILM GMBH
STARRING TIL SCHWEIGER (Axel Feldheim), KATJA RIEMANN (Doro Feldheim), JOACHIM KRÓL (Norbert Brommer), RUFUS BECK (Walter/"Waltraut"), ARMIN ROHDE (Butcher), NICO VAN DER KNAAP (Fränzchen), ANTONIA LANG (Elke Schmitt), MARTINA GEDECK (Jutta), JUDITH REINARTZ (Claudia), KAI WIESINGER (Gunnar)

"I think I'd better go now!"

The young waitress, secretly puffing away at a cigarette in the bathroom during her break, hears groans of pleasure from next door and grins. The grin fades quickly however when she discovers that the man in the next cubicle enjoying himself with another woman is her boyfriend. Or rather, was: Axel (Til Schweiger) gets his marching orders. Although his address book is full of telephone numbers from his past affairs, none of his old flames want to take him in. Eventually he finds a place to stay with Norbert (Joachim Król) of all people, perhaps the saddest but most caring man in the world. The bourgeois gay worrier and the self-confident, high-powered golden boy make the strangest pair of housemates since Jack Lemmon and Walter Matthau in *The Odd Couple* (1967). They are not only divided by their differing opinions on cleanliness and housekeeping, but also by a purely one-sided attraction.

Norbert falls hopelessly in love with Axel, cooking for him and mothering him, and hoping against hope that one day the robust hetero will have a

moment of weakness. But all his efforts are in vain. "After all," wrote one critic, "this is a German movie, not a French one." An erotic high point is reached when the two of them lie naked in bed looking through holiday slides, and a nude picture of Axel has got mixed up with the sandy beaches and palm trees. But with impeccable timing, Doro (Katja Riemann), Axel's ex arrives. Norbert hides in a cupboard and when she finds him there, they are both horrified. Norbert, the shy little man with the big button eyes, collects his clothes and takes his leave with an unforgettable "I think I'd better go now," and suddenly the audience knows who will fall by the wayside in this ménage à trois. When Axel discovers that Doro is pregnant with his child there is only one possible solution for him. It's the high road to bourgeois contentment – home to his sweetheart, and time to found a little family, even though there is still plenty of hormonal confusion before the final happy ending, including a hilarious scene where he is found crouching naked on a '50s style kidney-shaped table.

Sönke Wortmann took stories from *Der bewegte Mann* and *Pretty Baby*, two comics by Ralf König, to make this comedy about relationships. Unlike the hard-liners who criticized the cinema version as a soft soap version that pandered to the masses, the cartoonist himself did not seem bothered that some of his characters' spicier or more provocative moments were lost on screen. For even if the movie tones down König's swollen-nosed fairies, queens, gays, and dykes to loveable mainstream sinners, it does not become less amusing or sharp-witted. Axel, the hetero hunk, may never doubt his sexuality, in contrast to the comic hero, but Wortmann sticks to the quick, clever, and dry dialogue of his model and resists the temptation to create a couple of model gays.

Wicked, pointed, and filled with mockery, *Maybe … Maybe Not* is an ironic kaleidoscope of vanities. The only downside is the portrayal of women, who seem like one-dimensional paper cutouts, so that the relationship between Axel and Doro is a dud. There was never any talk of a new German movie dream couple. It was clear that Riemann-Schweiger was never going to be the dream couple that saved German movie comedy, but the movie itself did herald something of a renaissance. The movie's success (over six million viewers, the Bambi prize, the Federal Film Prize, and the Ernst Lubitsch Prize) was followed by a long-lasting boom in German comedies about relationships. AK

"Germany's funniest film in years ..." *Variety*

1 Into the closet! Although the lovestruck Norbert (Joachim Król) never gets his way, he's still pushed into the classic hiding place.

2 A sight that most women would prefer not to see: their boyfriend being entertained by a strange woman in the ladies' toilet.

3 Axel (Til Schweiger) is less than pleased when Waltraut (Rufus Beck) and the other queens turn up unexpectedly at his wedding.

4 Bernd Eichinger's productions frequently owed part of their success to the excellent cast. In Til Schweiger and Katja Riemann he picked two stars of the new German cinema boom.

5 Til Schweiger, the sexiest man German cinema has produced in decades, as an object of lust. Straight guy Axel is thunderstruck when a gay man doesn't hesitate to show him his "prize exhibit" as a come-on.

SÖNKE WORTMANN Sönke Wortmann was born in 1959 and his movies lit the fuse for an explosion in new German comedy. At the beginning of the '90s, he hit a nerve with *Allein unter Frauen* (*Alone among Women*, 1991) and *Kleine Haie* (*Little Sharks*, 1992), and played an important part in changing the image of German cinema, which had come to be associated with auteur films and academic introversion. Wortmann first drew attention to himself during his studies at the Munich Academy for Film and Television, when his graduation work *Drei D* (*Three Ds*, 1988) was nominated for a student movie Oscar. *Kleine Haie* is a sensitive comedy about three young men who want to go to acting school and meet up time after time as they travel from audition to audition across the German Republic. It was awarded the Federal Film Prize as well as the prize for best first film at the Montreal Film Festival. "The film shows many things which I experienced as a student," Wortmann once explained. His definitive breakthrough came with the comic adaptation *Der bewegte Mann* (*Maybe... Maybe Not*, 1994). Literary adaptations feature prominently in Wortmann's later output, including *The Hollywood Sign* (2000) – from Leon de Winter's *Der Himmel von Hollywood* – and sports movies like *Das Wunder von Bern* (*The Miracle of Bern*, 2003).

SPEED ⚆⚆

1994 – USA – 116 MIN. – ACTION FILM
DIRECTOR JAN DE BONT (*1943)
SCREENPLAY GRAHAM YOST DIRECTOR OF PHOTOGRAPHY ANDRZEJ BARTKOWIAK EDITING JOHN WRIGHT
MUSIC MARK MANCINA PRODUCTION MARK GORDON for 20TH CENTURY FOX
STARRING KEANU REEVES (Jack Traven), DENNIS HOPPER (Howard Payne),
SANDRA BULLOCK (Annie), JOE MORTON (Captain McMahon), JEFF DANIELS
(Harry Temple), ALAN RUCK (Stephens), GLENN PLUMMER (Jaguar driver),
RICHARD LINEBACK (Norwood), BETH GRANT (Helen), JAMES HAWTHORNE (Sam)
ACADEMY AWARDS 1995 OSCARS for BEST SOUND (Bob Beemer, Gregg Landaker, David MacMillan,
Steve Maslow) and BEST EFFECTS, SOUND EFFECTS EDITING (Stephen Hunter Flick)

"Miss, can you handle this bus?" – "Oh sure. It's just like driving a really big Pinto."

Jack Traven (Keanu Reeves) and his partner Harry Temple (Jeff Daniels) work in the Anti-Terrorist Unit of the Los Angeles Police Department. When the film opens, they are trying to free some hostages who are trapped in an elevator in one of the city's skyscrapers. The kidnapper is demanding a ransom of three million dollars, without which a bomb will explode killing all the hostages. In the last second, Jack and Harry manage to get the captives to safety. In a normal movie, a moment's relaxation would follow. But in Jan de Bont's action spectacle *Speed,* what would normally be enough material for a whole evening's entertainment is merely the curtain-raiser to a racing roller coaster ride in three acts which grips the audience from beginning to end.

The next morning, while Harry Temple is still sleeping off his hangover after the celebrations, Jack sets off for work. Suddenly a bus explodes a few meters away, and a public telephone rings at the same moment. It is Howard Payne (Dennis Hopper), the bomber they had believed dead. This time he wants 3.7 million dollars – but the personal revenge is more important than the money. He sets Jack the task of finding a bus which is driving through Los Angeles full of passengers. On board is a bomb that will explode as soon as the

bus goes faster than 50 miles an hour. However, the bomb will also explode should the bus drop its speed below 50 miles an hour. Jack manages to find the bus, and to clamber on board. While he feverishly attempts to defuse the bomb, the bus driver is shot by one of the passengers. Annie (Sandra Bullock), another passenger, takes the wheel – and isn't about to let go of it again in a hurry. During the hellish ride that follows she steers the heavy bus at breakneck speed along congested freeways and through red lights.

At the last moment Jack manages to get all the passengers out of the exploding bus, which they have driven onto the runway of a nearby airport. Jack and Annie fall into each other's arms. In a normal film, we might expect that to be the end of the story. But Jan de Bont has yet another surprise in store: in the third act he has Annie covered in dynamite like a gift-wrapped present, racing towards certain death in an out-of-control subway train accompanied by Payne and Jack.

Before his debut as a director with *Speed*, Dutchman Jan de Bont was a cameraman on many big-budget action films. He obviously paid great attention to the directing on the sets of movies like *Die Hard* (1987), *The*

"Rarely is cinema so exclusively focused, without handicaps from other art forms or borrowed aims."

Frankfurter Allgemeine Zeitung

3

4

Hunt for Red October (1990), or *Lethal Weapon 3* (1992). *Speed*, his first movie, is the condensed essence of all action films, freed from all unnecessary ballast: with one exception, there are no senselessly violent scenes or mindless destruction. Minor figures are kept in the background, and we learn nothing about their previous lives. The terse dialogue isn't used for reasoning or moralizing, it simply advances the plot or gives the audience a split-second pause to draw breath. De Bont tells his story almost exclusively with pictures, and the racing images alone create an almost unbearable tension. The focal point of *Speed* really is speed; and like the bus, the movie maintains its tempo without flagging from the first to the last. Its timing is as precise as the clockwork mechanism of Payne's bomb.   APO

TYPECASTING If actors play several similar roles in quick succession, their future career is often determined by this stereotype. A particular type of character, like a villain, becomes identified with an actor's face, and thereafter they may only be offered roles that correspond to that image. One of the most famous examples is Edward G. Robinson who played many different roles, but will always be remembered as a gangster.

---

1   Fasten your seatbelts: police officer Jack (Keanu Reeves) next to reluctant bus driver Annie (Sandra Bullock).

2   Other directors make cars fly, with action specialist Jan de Bont it's buses.

3   Yet another psychopath: Dennis Hopper plays the part of terrorist bomber Howard Payne.

4   Mind the gap: a dangerous initiative to save lives.

5   The psychopath means business: the explosion at the start of the film shows how dangerous an opponent he is.

6   Like Annie, viewers are held captive right up to the very last minute.

THE LION KING ♙♙

1994 – USA – 88 MIN. – ANIMATION
DIRECTOR ROGER ALLERS (*1949), ROB MINKOFF (*1962)
SCREENPLAY JIM CAPOBIANCO, IRENE MECCHI **EDITNG** IVAN BILANCIO **MUSIC** HANS ZIMMER
PRODUCTION DON HAHN, SARAH MCARTHUR, THOMAS SCHUMACHER, CLAYTON TOWNSEND
for WALT DISNEY PICTURES
VOICES JAMES EARL JONES (Mufasa), MATTHEW BRODERICK (Simba), JEREMY IRONS
(Scar), WHOOPI GOLDBERG (Shenzi), ROWAN ATKINSON (Zazu), MOIRA KELLY (Nala),
CHEECH MARIN (Banzai)
ACADEMY AWARDS 1995 OSCARS for BEST MUSIC (Hans Zimmer), BEST SONG (Elton John,
Tim Rice, "Can You Feel The Love Tonight")

"Remember who you are.
You are my son and the one true king."

The story begins on Pride Rock, a cliff in the middle of the vast empire of Mufasa, the ruling king of the lions. Proudly he presents to his people the little prince Simba, his son and heir.

However, Mufasa's power-hungry brother Scar sees the baby prince as a threat to his chances of ruling and forges a deadly plan, and Mufasa dies saving his son's life. Simba is plagued by feelings of guilt and runs away into the jungle, where he grows up with his faithful companions Timon the meerkat and Pumbaa the warthog. This carefree life comes to an end when Simba meets his old friend Nala again. She convinces him that if he really wants to grow up, he must face the demons of the past and take on his responsibilities.

Whereas Disney's previous movies *Aladdin* (1992), *Beauty and the Beast* (1991), and *The Little Mermaid* (1989) focused on love stories between unequal partners, the romance between Simba and Nala is not the main story line. Instead, Disney's 32nd animated movie *The Lion King* is like a jungle version of Shakespeare's *Hamlet*, although it is the first animated movie in Disney's history not to be based on a literary model or story. This tragic tale of guilt and atonement, of to be or not to be – or rather to eat or be eaten – tells of intrigues at court and the power of blood ties, but has a happy ending.

Naturally, *The Lion King* also has comic moments, mostly thanks to the repartees handed out by Timon and Pumbaa. But it remains a somewhat gloomy and moralizing movie about growing up and how to deal with guilt

3

1 Group portrait in the savannah: the King of the Lions and his subjects.

2 Zebras form a guard of honor: Simba and Nala are as yet relatively untouched by the burden of kingship.

3 Simba listens reverently to his father's instruction.

4 Walt Disney's Africa is enchantingly beautiful.

5 Hounded out of his kingdom, Simba finds two loyal friends in exile: Timon the meerkat and Pumbaa the warthog.

WALT DISNEY Walt Disney, creator of Mickey Mouse and king of the animated movie, was born in Chicago in 1901. He sold his first drawings at the age of 7, but his career did not begin in earnest until 1923, when he set off for Hollywood with $40 in his pocket. In 1932 he was awarded the first of a total of 32 personal Academy Awards for *Flowers and Trees*. In the following years he created such animated classics as *Pinocchio* (1940), *Dumbo* (1941), and *Bambi* (1942). In 1940 Disney opened his studio in Burbank, where he employed over 1000 artists and technicians. He planned the Disney theme park in Florida, but it was first opened by his brother Roy in 1971, five years after Walt Disney's death.

"Music can break hearts and make the Top 40. But a cartoon's narrative imagination is first and finally in the images. Animation is a supple form; it can be as free as free verse, as fanciful as a Bosch landscape."

me Magazine

...d fear. Death and violence are not taboo and the audience is not presen-...d with a perfect world. These elements put the movie back in the tradition ...earlier Disney movies, which were often based on moral fables. The first-...ass detailed animation of *The Lion King* was produced by hundreds of ...tists and is one of the main reasons why the movie is the most successful ...ature-length cartoon of all time to date. With glowing colors and fine ...ushstrokes Disney's cartoonists brought the African steppe and its inhabi-...nts to life.

Since the film music to *The Little Mermaid* (1989) won two Oscars, the ...usical element of Disney movies has become just as important as their visual side. *The Lion King*'s symphonic soundtrack with its colorful African elements was written by Hans Zimmer and the successful Broadway team Alan Menken and Howard Ashcroft created the songs which are performed by Elton John and Tim Rice.

As in all cartoon movies, pictures and music are used to evoke strong emotions. But the movie also contains a political element. When the hyenas march to the dissonant song "Be Prepared" we are forcibly reminded of Leni Riefenstahl's film *Triumph des Willens* (*The Triumph of the Will*, 1935). Rather than a historical quotation from film, the pictures of the hyenas marching in step are an implied critique of totalitarian rule. APC

5

TRUE LIES

1994 – USA – 141 MIN. – ACTION FILM, COMEDY, REMAKE
DIRECTOR JAMES CAMERON (*1954)
SCREENPLAY JAMES CAMERON **DIRECTOR OF PHOTOGRAPHY** RUSSELL CARPENTER **EDITING** CONRAD BUFF,
MARK GOLDBLATT, RICHARD A. HARRIS, JAMES CAMERON **MUSIC** BRAD FIEDEL
PRODUCTION JAMES CAMERON, STEPHANIE AUSTIN for LIGHTSTORM ENTERTAINMENT
(for 20TH CENTURY FOX)
STARRING ARNOLD SCHWARZENEGGER (Harry Tasker), JAMIE LEE CURTIS (Helen Tasker),
TOM ARNOLD (Gib), BILL PAXTON (Simon), TIA CARRERE (Juno Skinner), ELIZA DUSHKU
(Dana), ART MALIK (Salim Abu Aziz), GRANT HESLOV (Faisil), MARSHALL MANESH
(Jamal Khaled), JAMES ALLEN (Colonel)

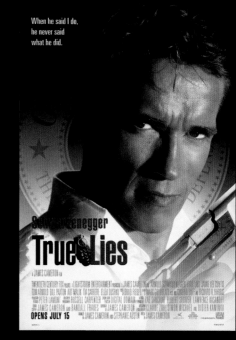

When he said I do,
he never said
what he did.

"Ask me a question I would normally lie to."

"If I can't sleep, I simply ask Harry how his day was. After six seconds I'm fast asleep." Helen Tasker (Jamie Lee Curtis) really loves her husband (Arnold Schwarzenegger), but it's not a barrel of laughs being married to a computer salesman who can't even get home on time on his own birthday. It's not surprising then that she has secret meetings with a spy called Simon (Bill Paxton) who may not be the physical equal of her husband, but who has a definite advantage. He needs her – supposedly to be able to travel to Europe without arousing suspicion.

Helen doesn't realize that her husband's job is nothing but a (perfect) façade, behind which he really leads the kind of excitement-filled life that she constantly dreams of. Harry, in actual fact, is a secret agent for the government's Omega Sector, and is a kind of super James Bond who regularly saves the world – with the same blasé attitude others develop selling computers or insurance policies.

While Helen is sitting at home bored, Harry infiltrates a group of fanatical Arab terrorists who are planning a nuclear attack on the USA, speaks fluent Arabic and French, and shows he can dance the tango as well as he can handle his huge arsenal of weapons. Machine guns and Dobermans can't hold him back but no matter how good he is as a top agent, he is a complete failure as a husband. When he realizes his wife has gone, he sets off to find her, and he soon discovers that she is with Simon, who turns out to be a second-hand car salesman. But instead of confronting her and agreeing to stop neglecting his duties as a husband, he uses all the tricks of his spying profession instead. Harry Tasker is in his element when he humiliates Helen by interrogating her using voice distortion and one-way mirrors, and he even calls in a SWAT team to break up Helen and Simon's tête-à-tête in a caravan.

James Cameron's movie is based on ideas taken from Claude Zidi's French comedy movie *La Totale!* (1991) and it breaks all the rules of the genre. It was made with a budget of 100 million dollars, which was gigantic to the standards of the time. That said, Cameron's *Titanic*, filmed only six years later in 1997, cost twice that amount.

True Lies is a fantastic action movie with breathtaking stunts, innumerable dead bodies, and terrific chase scenes like the police horse that gallops through a hotel lobby. It was Schwarzenegger's third movie together with Cameron, with whom he had previously made the two *Terminator* films, and to some extent Cameron is Frankenstein and Schwarzenegger the monster he has created. In the seven years between *Terminator* (1984) and *Terminator 2: Judgment Day* (1991), Arnie was transformed from a cyborg to a machine with almost human features. In *True Lies* Cameron didn't simply content himself with putting any number of pyrotechnics into Schwarenegger's hands and having him rescue his teenage daughter Dana (Eliza Dushku) with a Harrier jump jet, he also gave him a heart to go with the muscles. Like his earlier movie *The Abyss* (1989), *True Lies* tells the story of a couple who grow apart but are brought back together again by exceptional circumstances. Of course, *True Lies* is also a comedy, and its punch lines are as well aimed as Harry Tasker's machine gun salvos: "You're fired!" he shouts at the terrorist Malik (Salim Abu Aziz) as he fires the rocket which Malik is clinging to for dear life under the wing of his Harrier jet. It's also a homage to James Bond, and it uses technical and thematic set pieces straight out of the 007 adventures, and there is no shortage of unlikely but imaginative episodes involving groups of international terrorists, elegant parties, and a female villain who is as beautiful as she is evil.

APO

"Schwarzenegger tackles patching up his marriage with the same macho attitude as saving the world ..." *Frankfurter Allgemeine Zeitung*

1 At last Helen (Jamie Lee Curtis) realizes that her husband Harry (Arnold Schwarzenegger) is no couch potato.

2 Firing on all cylinders as usual: Schwarzenegger has everything under control.

3 Like something out of a James Bond movie: resourceful, elegant, and professional, just like Her Majesty's Secret Agent 007, Harry knows how to keep his head in any situation.

4 "You're fired!" was the line just before he fired the rocket on the terrorists.

5 This is perhaps a little more adventure than Helen might have wished for.

REMAKE Remakes, which are new versions of movies that already exist, are produced to bring out new aspects of old stories. Sometimes they develop different elements of the original idea, while at other times they are simply an attempt to penetrate new markets. Remakes are common after technical advances, as when silent films became talkies and black and white became color. Today most remakes are made in the USA, as foreign language movies are not dubbed in America, and subtitles are unpopular with US cinema audiences.

4

"There is one image in the midst of all the commotion, which gives an insight into the film's essence: the woman drops the machine gun, which somersaults down a flight of steps firing

5

shots that finish off at least as many opponents as Arnie himself. The out of control weapon, which can take the place of any person, is this film's true heart, a soulless pacemaker." *Süddeutsche Zeitung*

APOLLO 13 ♟♟

APOLLO 13

1995 – USA – 139 MIN. – ADVENTURE FILM
DIRECTOR RON HOWARD (*1954)
SCREENPLAY WILLIAM BROYLES JR., AL REINERT, based on the book *LOST MOON* by
JIM LOVELL, JEFFREY KLUGER **DIRECTOR OF PHOTOGRAPHY** DEAN CUNDEY **EDITING** DANIEL P. HANLEY,
MIKE HILL **MUSIC** JAMES HORNER **PRODUCTION** BRIAN GRAZER, TODD HALLOWELL for
IMAGINE ENTERTAINMENT
STARRING TOM HANKS (Jim Lovell), BILL PAXTON (Fred Haise), KEVIN BACON (Jack Swigert),
GARY SINISE (Ken Mattingly), ED HARRIS (Gene Kranz), KATHLEEN QUINLAN
(Marilyn Lovell), MARY KATE SCHELLHARDT (Barbara Lovell), EMILY ANN LLOYD
(Susan Lovell), MIKO HUGHES (Jeffrey Lovell), MAX ELLIOTT SLADE (Jay Lovell)
ACADEMY AWARDS 1996 OSCARS for BEST SOUND (Rick Dior, Steve Pederson, Scott Millan,
David MacMillan) and BEST FILM EDITING (Daniel P. Hanley, Mike Hill)

"Houston, we have a problem."

In May 1961, President Kennedy promised that an American would land on the moon before the decade was out. This was his answer to Russia's head start in the space race, which had been an unpleasant surprise for America. The first spacecraft to orbit the earth was a Russian Sputnik and a Russian cosmonaut was the first man to travel in space. Although the official reason for the space race was scientific research, in actual fact it was a prestige duel between the super powers. The astronauts were old fashioned explorers rather than servants of science.

However, after only two successful moon landings, mankind's final heroic chapter came to a shuddering halt. The third lunar mission Apollo 13 started on April 11, 1970. It seemed routine until five words uttered by Commander Jim Lovell (Tom Hanks) instantly entered everyday speech and

tore the nation and the watching world out of its complacency: "Houston, we have a problem." What Lovell meant by this heroic understatement worthy of Hemingway was that the oxygen tank vital to the astronauts' survival had exploded. Apollo 13 then suffered a whole series of related problems and there followed dramatic, drawn-out rescue attempts to bring back the three astronauts adrift in space. Like every modern American fairy tale, the crisis brought together the potent combination of highly developed technology and the tried and tested virtues of a pioneer nation: inventiveness, pragmatism, and selfless teamwork.

Apollo 13's dramatic handicap is that virtually every viewer knows from the very beginning that the story has a happy ending. However, Ron Howard set out to write a simple heroic epic – and succeeded in being just as cool,

1 On the way to the moon. Apollo 13's journey gets off to an encouraging start.

2 The astronauts' wives watch the rocket take off.

3 A legendary place: in the Houston control room engineers work together to save the astronauts' lives.

4 Fear eats the soul (Kevin Bacon, center): several systems aboard the space module have failed, making the return journey extremely hazardous.

aconic, and unsentimental as Lovell's report of the near fatal disaster from 200,000 miles away. All the characters are in the same boat, they all put their personal problems aside and do their bit for the happy ending. That goes for the three astronauts themselves as much as for the colleague dropped from the mission shortly before the start with suspected measles, who goes over and over the most incredible rescue maneuvers in the flight simulator. It also includes national hero Neil Armstrong, who reassures Lovell's mother in a nursing home, and goes right down to the most insignificant employee of the Texas mission control center.

Movies that exalt supposed national virtues and claim as American the capacity to make impossible things possible by sheer force of will may seem naive or even dangerous. Manned space travel also has its critics, and the genre ingredients used here to create emotional effect have all been seen once too often. Nevertheless, as Apollo 13 approaches splashdown at the end of the movie and the entire mission control center breaks out in shouts and cheers, it's a hard-baked and cynical viewer who begrudges them some sort of approving remark.

UE

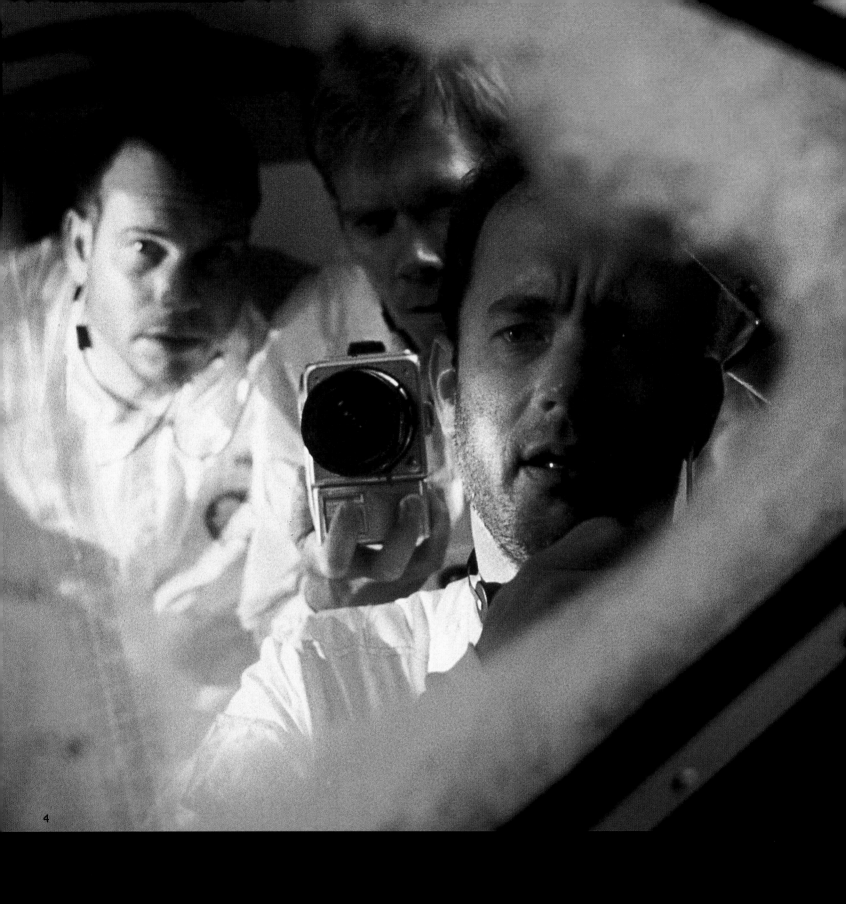

4

SPACE TRAVEL IN THE CINEMA Manned space travel was promoted in the '60s as mankind's last great adventure. The crude fantasies of armies of SF authors aside, the real space race for the moon and stars features astonishingly seldom in Hollywood feature films. Strictly speaking, there are only two movies on the subject that can be considered anything like a masterpiece. The first is *The Right Stuff* (1983), Philip Kaufman's partly mythical, partly tongue-in-cheek adaptation of Tom Wolfe's reportage novel of the same name, describing the transition period when the first astronauts took over from the old test pilots and proclaimed themselves to be the true heroes of the modern-day Wild West. Clint Eastwood's late work *Space Cowboys* (2000), whose brilliant title says it all, would have to be the second: a laconic yet wry movie with a touch of melancholy, it tells the story of the forgotten pioneers of the first hour who are called upon to get Houston out of a tight spot. An old-fashioned satellite is out of control and the old-timers are the only ones who still know how it works. Their mission is a success and they finally receive the fame that is their due.

5

6

"In the summer Apollo 13 shot like a rocket to the top of the US box office. President Clinton had it shown to him at the White House, and the Speaker of the House and science fiction writer Newt Gingrich declared the film quite simply

7

8

9

HATE
LA HAINE

1995 – FRANCE – 98 MIN. – DRAMA, SOCIAL STUDY
DIRECTOR MATHIEU KASSOVITZ (*1967)
SCREENPLAY MATHIEU KASSOVITZ DIRECTOR OF PHOTOGRAPHY PIERRE AÏM EDITING MATHIEU KASSOVITZ,
SCOTT STEVENSON MUSIC BOB MARLEY, ISAAC HAYES, ZAPP AND ROGER, etc.
PRODUCTION CHRISTOPHE ROSSIGNON for LES PRODUCTIONS LAZENNEC
STARRING VINCENT CASSEL (Vinz), HUBERT KOUNDÉ (Hubert), SAÏD TAGHMAOUI (Saïd),
KARIM BELKHADRA (Samir), EDOUARD MONTOUTÉ (Darty), FRANÇOIS LEVANTAL
(Asterix), SOLO DIKKO (Santo), MARC DURET (Inspector "Notre Dame"),
HÉLOÏSE RAUTH (Sarah), RYWKA WAJSBROT (Vinz's Grandmother)
IFF CANNES 1995 PRIZE for BEST DIRECTOR

"Okay so far."

An Arab, a Black African, and a Jew, all of them outsiders, underdogs, and socially disadvantaged. They're only 20, but they're already used to staring into a bleak future and fighting for survival from one day to the next. The large families they come from have no fathers. They spent most of their school days as truants and their school burnt down in one of the riots that break out whenever the neighborhood needs to work off its pent-up rage. The three of them are ready to take on the world, and they certainly won the hearts of cinema audiences, but with attitudes like that they had no hope of success in the world as portrayed in the film.

That world is a cheerless Paris suburb, where social dynamite seems to have become part of the architecture. In the opening sequence we see a single, fire-red lightning flash that is clearly meant to tell us that this world will soon be reduced to ruins and ashes – perhaps at the end of the movie, perhaps just a little later. The movie contents itself with telling the story of a 24-hour period in cold, high-contrast black and white, a visual style totally appropriate for the subject of the film.

The title is also a clue to the movie's contents. *Hate* begins where other teen films leave off, and is a radical presentation of what in more enlightened times was known as structural violence. Despite the best hopes of starry-eyed film critics, director Mathieu Kassovitz is no genius ghetto kid, and neither is his film the result of a wish granted by a passing fairy godmother. It may look chaotic, but it's an integral part of the cultural scene. Kassovitz himself was clever enough to know that it was mostly chance that set off the powder keg. The plot of the movie is as tight as a straitjacket. – In the course of one of the many street battles with the police, a 16-year-old acquaintance of Saïd (Saïd Taghmaoui), Hubert (Hubert Koundé), and Vinz (Vincent Cassel) was arrested and beaten in the interrogation that followed. Now he lies in hospital fighting for his life. Vinz finds the duty weapon that the policeman lost in the heat of the fight, and swears revenge should the boy die. The audience realize from the very beginning that this is inevitable. What they don't know is where and how Vinz will unleash his rage, or whether one of the other two will beat him to it.

"This bloke falls from the 50th floor of a tower block. As he falls, he says to himself as he passes each floor, 'Okay so far. Okay so far. Okay so far. Okay so far.' The moral of the story is: It doesn't matter how you fall, but how you land."

The joke that is told at the beginning and end of the film.

Before the movie's violent climax Kassovitz uses the remaining 98 minutes to take a racy, sometimes hopeless, depressing, but constantly witty and affectionate look at his characters and their milieu. He is well aware that realism is the audience's only yardstick for this kind of cinema, and that every look, word, and gesture has to be right. The director sticks close to the protagonists and accompanies them everywhere with his restless handheld camera. Sometimes they hang around bored, at other times they are driven by crazy energy, ricocheting off the walls of the concrete estates and trying their luck as touchingly amateurish petty criminals. Kassovitz draws us into an anonymous, senseless urban environment with straightforward natural-ism, neither preaching nor wallowing with the eyes of an outsider in ill-placed "ghetto chic." Here every stock phrase and every lie about why things are as they are has been heard at least once too often. The conventional explanations and solutions are no longer enough. Never for a moment does the director use the wedge of pop-psychology to divorce the characters from their awful world, and so we never really get to know them: Saïd constantly spouts verbal rubbish, Hubert dreams of a boxing career but is really just a child, and Vinz retreats ever further behind a protective shield of hate. We never get to know them very well, but we never really forget them once we've seen the film.

UB

CINÉMA BEUR *Beur* is the slang term for French-born second-generation immigrants from the Maghreb in North Africa, predominantly from the former French colonies of Algeria and Morocco. *Cinéma Beur* discusses the problems of this ethnic minority, who are easily the largest minority in France. It portrays the day-to-day racism that the immigrants have to deal with, and shows the tricks of survival and the conformist strategies that the immigrants' children have been forced to adopt. In the mid '80s the growth of Jean-Marie Le Pen's Front National made it even more difficult to break down racist stereotypes and fight for a separate cultural identity.
Movies of many different genres are counted as part of the Cinéma Beur movement, from crime movies like Francis Girod's *The Big Brother* (*Le Grand Frère*, 1982) and *Tchao Pantin* (1983) by Claude Berri to comedies like *L'Œil au beur(re) noir* (1987) by Serge Maynard, which takes an ironic look at the social problems caused by housing deficits in big cities. This is as much part of Cinéma Beur as the touching, tongue-in-cheek youth drama *Le Thé au harem d'Archimède* (1985) by Mehdi Charef, the best known filmmaker of this French minority group.

1   A sworn alliance: Saïd (Saïd Taghmaoui), Hubert (Hubert Koundé), and Vinz (Vincent Cassel) live in a bleak suburb of Paris.

2   Being cool: can the hero's actions be transferred from screen to real life?

3   A vicious circle: violence breeds violence.

4   Fit for the cold hard world: Hubert after boxing training.

BRAVEHEART ♟♟♟♟♟

1995 – USA – 177 MIN. – HISTORICAL FILM
DIRECTOR MEL GIBSON (*1956)
SCREENPLAY RANDALL WALLACE DIRECTOR OF PHOTOGRAPHY JOHN TOLL EDITING STEVEN ROSENBLUM
MUSIC JAMES HORNER PRODUCTION MEL GIBSON, ALAN LADD JR., BRUCE DAVEY for ICON,
LADD PRODUCTIONS
STARRING MEL GIBSON (William Wallace), SOPHIE MARCEAU (Princess Isabelle),
PATRICK MCGOOHAN (King Edward I), CATHERINE MCCORMACK (Murron),
BRENDAN GLEESON (Hamish), JAMES COSMO (Campbell), DAVID O'HARA (Stephen),
ANGUS MCFAYDEN (Robert the Bruce), PETER HANLY (Prince Edward),
JAMES ROBINSON (William as a boy)
ACADEMY AWARDS 1996 OSCARS for BEST PICTURE, BEST DIRECTOR (Mel Gibson),
BEST CINEMATOGRAPHY (John Toll), BEST SOUND EFFECTS EDITING (Lon Bender,
Per Hallberg) and BEST MAKEUP (Peter Frampton, Paul Pattison, Lois Burwell)

"Your heart is free.
Have the courage to follow it."

"They fought like warrior bards. They fought like Scotsmen." After a long, but never dull 177 minutes, these two lines don't just bring the audience back from the Middle Ages to the present, but also from the sort of lavish, epic historical spectacle that most people assumed to have died out with *Lawrence of Arabia* (1962). Not least because of its return to a classic narrative style, *Braveheart* was a welcome and highly acclaimed exception at a time when most movies were non-committal, derivative, and made only with reference to each other. As that medieval Scottish chronicler notes, *Braveheart* is a story of war, and as critics were quick to point out on its release, it brought a new dimension to the war movie genre. But it's also a movie filled with poetic moments and it tells us more about Scotland and its people than we would normally expect from a historical film. William Wallace is a mythical figure – Scotland's greatest folk hero, more popular than Rod Stewart, Sean Connery, and Jock Stein put together. A simple man of the people who fought valiantly for the freedom of his fellow Scots against an arrogant, all-powerful enemy, who was prevented from achieving his aim by treachery from within his own ranks. He was a passionate patriot, a strategic genius, and a social revolution-

ary à la Robin Hood. He seems made for Hollywood, and it's surprising that there was no cinematic monument to him before Mel Gibson decided to try out his directorial skills.

Kevin Costner's sensational success with *Dances With Wolves* (1990) led to a host of other star actors taking over the director's chair, and that was the main reason why Gibson was able to attempt a 70 million dollar project after the flop of his previous effort, *The Man Without a Face* (1993). Australian by choice, Gibson is best known to the public for his action hero role in the *Lethal Weapon* movies (1986, 1988, 1992, 1997). He approached the risky business of *Braveheart* with admirable calm, trusting to his star qualities. The story unfolds with tantalizing slowness. The first half hour tells of the youth of William Wallace (James Robinson), and Gibson skillfully uses tried and tested genre conventions to introduce both sides of the coming conflict and to win the audience's sympathies for his hero.

From the very first frame, the leisurely pace seems to mirror the rhythm of life of a much slower age, making the later fight scenes even more impressive and dramatic. Gibson sketches in the social milieu with a few

"At last: a costume drama that wears its costumes with pride, a period drama that has the courage of its convictions." *Sunday Times*

muddy-colored, dimly lit sequences. The Scottish nobility want to maintain their material privileges and are prepared to compromise with the English whereas the peasants, who have been deprived of their rights, are spoiling for a fight and have literally nothing to lose but their lives.

The movie has its fair share of folklore clichés and features to tempt the modern palate. The hearty rough-and-tumble that leads to the firm friendship between William and his faithful vassal Hamish (Brendan Gleeson) is a little too reminiscent of Robin Hood and Little John. But, *Braveheart* is generally successful in transporting its audience back in time without too much visible effort.

A single ingenious but gruesome scene is all that is needed in the brilliant opening section to establish the perfidiousness of Edward I (played by that ever reliable "Prisoner" Patrick McGoohan), when dozens of good-natured and unarmed Scottish landowners are invited to negotiate with the English, only to be hung in a barn by the king's henchmen. William's father is one of the victims of this terror tactic, which does nothing to deter the freedom fighters: "The problem with Scotland is that it is full of Scots," comments the king. He then introduces the *jus primae noctis*, reasoning that if they can't throw the Scots out, they can at least outbreed them. This in turn leads to the murder of William's beautiful bride Murron (Catherine McCormack), adding

1   The camera produces a hero. A low-angle shot sets off William Wallace (Mel Gibson), leader of the Scottish rebels.

2   The Scottish warriors try to defend themselves with powerful lances against the army of English knights.

3   "Warrior poets" in full war paint.

4   Caught between love and reasons of state: French princess Isabelle (Sophie Marceau) is married to the English heir to the throne.

5   English king Edward I (Patrick McGoohan) rules with a rod of iron and puts down the Scottish uprisings.

6   The French princess at the English court. The young woman manages to defy the king's demands repeatedly.

personal vengeance to patriotic duty as his motives for the fight. At first, William resists the seemingly all-powerful enemy with just a handful of determined comrades, but following his first unexpected military successes, the local revolt soon becomes a rebellion which spreads through the whole of the North of Britain and even over to Ireland.

Braveheart's best moments are without a doubt the fight sequences. Seldom in the history of cinema has the horror of war been presented so grippingly, and the carefully planned attacks of cavalry, archers, and infantry seem nothing more than random clashes between two huge masses of men, who hack and slash wildly. King Edward is forced onto the defensive despite his efforts to involve his daughter-in-law, the French princess Isabelle (Sophie

Marceau), and the crafty tricks he plays on the Scottish nobility. William Wallace becomes a legend in his own lifetime, the focus of all Scotland's dreams of national liberation. The beautiful Isabelle sides with the uncompromising rebel and the movie's second love story develops. However, Robert the Bruce (Angus McFayden), the best of the aristocrats, is a fickle ally who in the end cannot bring himself to go against the interests of his own class. His betrayal seals the rebels' fate. It only remains for Robert to fulfill the shameful task of recounting the heroic saga of William Wallace: "English historians will call me a liar. But history is written by those who hang the heroes."

UB

8

7 Forbidden love. The people's hero and the French princess.

8 Resolutely he rides off on a new mission. This is how the hero will be remembered.

MEL GIBSON In 1979, the first part of the *Mad Max* trilogy was a new aesthetic departure in film and quickly became a cult movie. Born in the USA in 1956 and raised in Australia, Mel Gibson was a complete unknown when he played the title role, but with his bright blue eyes and physical presence it was clear that he had what it took to become a star. His two greatest successes were both filmed in the first half of the '80s: *Gallipoli* (1981) and *The Year of Living Dangerously* (1982). Perhaps his best work was with the director Richard Donner, with whom he made the *Lethal Weapon* series (1986, 1988, 1992, 1997) and most recently *Conspiracy Theory* (1997). Gibson attracted renewed attention when he began directing his own films in the mid-'90s. His second movie, *Braveheart* (1995), brought him two Oscars, for Best Director and Best Film. The excessive violence of his Biblical film *The Passion of the Christ* (2004) and the Mayan civilization drama *Apocalypto* (2006) ensured he hit the headlines, but they were not box-office successes. He received brilliant reviews for his acting in *The Beaver* (2011), directed by Jodie Foster, in which he plays a man with a psychological illness.

BABE, THE GALLANT PIG (Australia) BABE (USA) 🏆

1995 – AUSTRALIA – 92 MIN. – COMEDY
DIRECTOR CHRIS NOONAN (*1952)
SCREENPLAY CHRIS NOONAN, GEORGE MILLER, based on the book *THE SHEEP-PIG* by
DICK KING-SMITH DIRECTOR OF PHOTOGRAPHY ANDREW LESNIE EDITING MARCUS D'ARCY,
JAY FRIEDKIN MUSIC NIGEL WESTLAKE PRODUCTION GEORGE MILLER, DOUG MITCHELL,
BILL MILLER for KENNEDY MILLER PRODUCTIONS
STARRING JAMES CROMWELL (Farmer Arthur Hoggett), MAGDA SZUBANSKI (Esme Hoggett),
ZOE BURTON (Daughter), PAUL GODDARD (Son-in-law), WADE HAYWARD (Grandson),
BRITTANY BYRNES (Granddaughter), MARY ACRES (Valda), DAVID WEBB (Vet),
MARSHALL NAPIER (Presiding Judge)
ACADEMY AWARDS 1996 OSCAR for BEST VISUAL EFFECTS (Scott E. Anderson, Charles Gibson,
Neal Scanlan, John Cox)

"Christmas? Christmas means dinner, dinner means death! Death means carnage; Christmas means carnage!"

From the very beginning of this movie, the images have a fairy-tale, unrealistic shimmer, making us fear one of those sugary celluloid feasts offered up as family entertainment in the run-up to Christmas. The only clue that this is a movie which will not gloss over the hard facts of life is the fact that its coauthor is of all people George Miller, the man who gave us the *Mad Max* trilogy.

Babe, the Gallant Pig is as uncompromising as it is moving. Based on the popular Australian children's book *The Sheep-Pig* by Dick King-Smith, this is a real movie in sheep's clothing, as it were. It tells the tale of a comical piglet who by chance (a chance almost as unlikely as winning the national

lottery and being struck by lightning on the same day) manages to escape being turbo-fattened and ends up in the idyllic farmyard of Farmer Hoggett (James Cromwell). Farmer Hoggett has all kinds of animals, but a strict pecking order is presided over by his fat wife, who is faced with the tricky task of deciding between duck or delicious roast pork for Christmas dinner. The movie's suspense comes from little Babe's efforts to escape the oven; he is of course incredibly plucky, has a heart of gold, and does everything in his power to avoid ending up as crackling and pork scratchings.

Two basic elements are used to ensure that his fight for survival tugs at the audience's heartstrings. All the animal figures are given human

ANIMALS AS PEOPLE *Babe*'s most obvious model is the George Orwell novel *Animal Farm*, although not just because pigs and sheep are among its main protagonists. Orwell's text is a bitterly satirical critique of totalitarian government, a parable about the world during the Cold War and a subtle description of the powerful mechanisms of self-destruction inherent in all revolutions. *Babe* is a movie about individual self-fulfillment, and about the solidarity, friendship, and courage we need to survive in a world which does not seem to have provided all its creatures with their own place or purpose.

characteristics and can talk to each other, although the humans in the movie don't realize this, and as in a fable, the animals' behavior is a perfect reflection of the relations between human beings. As a strategy, that can be moving or comic, but it also runs the risk of being merely irritating.

The piglet's only hope is to prove that he is useful, or better still, indispensable – an idea that he gets from the duck, his rival in the fight not to end up as the Christmas dinner. The duck decides to take over the job of the somewhat lazy rooster and gives bloodcurdling wake-up calls every morning, but his plan is foiled when Hoggett buys an alarm clock instead. For want of a better alternative, Babe dedicates himself to the long-term task of infiltrating the domain of the sheepdogs, the animals who up until that point have been his only protectors. He tries to help looking after the herds of sheep that are the main source of income for the farm. And because movies of this kind always have a happy ending, not only does he manage to do this after various ups and downs, but he also manages to win the trophy his owner has long coveted, as an unusual competitor in the sheep dog trials.

As far as the film craft is concerned, the story is told in vivid images which skillfully combine the acting talents of real, meticulously trained animals with computer-animated models. This is a technique originally pioneered by Disney, and it is known as "animatronics." UE

1 A pig that thinks he's a dog. Babe and his "master" Arthur Hoggett (James Cromwell) at a sheepdog competition.

2 The film depicts a rural idyll in picturesque images, but also brings across the hardships of living off the land.

3 At first the sheep are Babe the pig's opponents, but gradually he manages to win them over.

4 An unusual friendship. In the end the farmer considers Babe to be his best sheepdog.

5 Four watchful eyes: Babe learns from the dogs how to keep watch over a flock of sheep.

6 A hilarious trio: musical rats in concert.

SE7EN

1995 – USA – 125 MIN. – THRILLER
DIRECTOR DAVID FINCHER (*1964)
SCREENPLAY ANDREW KEVIN WALKER **DIRECTOR OF PHOTOGRAPHY** DARIUS KHONDJI
EDITING RICHARD FRANCIS-BRUCE **MUSIC** HOWARD SHORE **PRODUCTION** ARNOLD KOPELSON,
PHYLLIS CARLYLE for ARNOLD KOPELSON PRODUCTIONS (for NEW LINE CINEMA)
STARRING MORGAN FREEMAN (William Somerset), BRAD PITT (David Mills), KEVIN SPACEY
(John Doe), GWYNETH PALTROW (Tracy Mills), JOHN C. MCGINLEY (California),
RICHARD ROUNDTREE (Talbot), R. LEE ERMEY (Chief of Police), JULIE ARASKOG
(Mrs. Gould), REGINALD E. CATHEY (Dr. Santiago), JOHN CASSINI (Officer Davis)

"Detective, the only reason that I'm here right now is that I wanted to be."

One cop tries to pit his idea of order against the chaos of the world. After 34 years of service, disillusioned Detective William Somerset (Morgan Freeman) is about to retire but he is still not hardened to the job. He fights against decay and decadence with pedantry: the coffee jug is always rinsed out before he goes to work and his utensils for the endless grind in the urban jungle are tidily arrayed on the chest of drawers. The first ritual actions we see in this movie are Somerset carefully tying his tie and picking a piece of fluff off his jacket, but before long the movie is dominated by rituals of quite a different kind. When the first corpse of the day is found, Somerset registers the circumstances of the crime with a mixture of routine efficiency and mute fatalism.

Despite his outward appearance, Somerset's new colleague David Mills (Brad Pitt) is not made out of such stern stuff. The newcomer is shown the ropes as he is to be Somerset's successor. Pitt plays Mills with concentrated energy, giving us a character as an apparently confident go-getter. But Mills is soon forced to admit that both his older colleague and the murderer are his superiors. The audience also soon realizes that the new arrival in this anonymous, permanently rainy city is not as clever as he makes out; the elevated train rumbles every quarter of an hour over the apartment he has been talked into taking. Tracy (Gwyneth Paltrow), is waiting for him there. She has been with him since high school.

This uneven pair, familiar from innumerable police films, the wise old veteran and the enthusiastic greenhorn, have to catch a serial killer who commits appalling crimes with missionary zeal, taking gluttony, greed, sloth, lust, pride, envy, and anger – the seven deadly sins – as his pattern. The self-appointed avenger is also a familiar figure of the genre; he believes he has been chosen by a higher power to turn the sins of the world against the sinners. But there is more at stake in *Se7en* than simple character studies.

The killer (Kevin Spacey) works under the nom de guerre of John Doe – the name American authorities routinely give to unidentified male corpses. His readings in the great works of Western literature (Thomas Aquinas, Dante Alighieri, Geoffrey Chaucer) have inspired him to send a warning to the world. The first deadly sin he punishes is that of gluttony, when he forces a hugely fat man to literally eat himself to death. This extraordinary opening crime begins a series of murders which all feature sophisticated hidden hints left for the investigating cops. The indispensable minimum of shock effects and horrific images needed in a serial killer movie is delivered in an almost offhand manner during the fat man's autopsy as if to fulfill an unavoidable obligation.

It soon becomes clear that director David Fincher is only marginally interested in the usual thrills and kicks, and that he is not concerned at all with any kind of guessing game as to who has committed the bizarre murders.

"If you want people to listen to you, tapping them on the shoulder isn't enough. You have to hit them with a sledgehammer."

John Doe in *Se7en*

5

DAVID FINCHER When the dark third part of the *Alien* series was released in 1991, it left both critics and audiences puzzled. It seemed that the Hollywood career of music video and commercial director David Fincher had ended before it had properly begun. But *Se7en* (1995) marked quite a comeback. His manhunt thriller *The Game* (1997) and satire on capitalism *Fight Club* (1999) also reveal a profoundly pessimistic world view. Fincher's films are often extremely impressive visually; he uses apocalyptic settings to tell stories so dark they would probably have been unthinkable ten years before. *Zodiac* (2007), the biopic about a serial killer, and the adaptation of Stieg Larsson's *The Girl with the Dragon Tattoo* (2011) were also marked by the same gloomy Fincher atmosphere. Born in 1962, Fincher moved into lighter territory on two occasions, with literary epic *The Curious Case of Benjamin Button* (2008) and Facebook drama *The Social Network* (2010).

Fincher has a message to proclaim, like his diabolically precise and brutal killer. It is delivered with shattering clarity and goes like this: the urban spaces of our civilization are in dangerous decline. In this miserable setting, the murderer's crimes are merely the culmination of the general fear and alienation which creeps like a poison through the movie's stylized images from the very first moment. We see random pictures of a gloomy, dirty gray cityscape, where the constant rain can't wash away the filth, and people slink between the houses, bowed, anxious, and filled with latent aggression that threatens to break out into violence at every moment.

Although the visual aspects of *Se7en* are often compared to Ridley Scott's *Blade Runner* (1982), Fincher's movie is a far cry from the overloaded metaphorical structure of that earlier movie with its visual symbols of a mythical past and a threatening future. Everything that happens here in the way of hidden codes and numbers serves almost exclusively to further the development of the plot.

The clues written in blood that the killer leaves at the second crime scene leave the cops no doubt as to the serial nature of the murders. They are on the defensive and feel helpless, as all they know is that they can expect five further corpses in as many days. As the two detectives put together the first pieces of the fiendish mosaic and, in keeping with the rules of the genre, quickly become friends in the process, their methods and thoughts become inextricably intertwined with those of the killer. Early on, we begin to suspect that the finale will be a personal affair. However, when John Doe saunters into the police headquarters after the fifth murder has been discovered and gives himself up, the chase comes to an abrupt end thereby breaking all the conventions of the genre.

Se7en's main quality is its meditation on cultural pessimism. All three of the protagonists have failed in the face of modern civilization, in the long tradition of archetypal American (anti)heroes, and they all touch a raw nerve in our souls. Somerset is bowed with age and at odds with society, he wants to escape but he doesn't know where to, while his youthful partner barely hides his violent tendencies behind the rules of his job. The serial killer, that familiar institution in popular culture, escapes from his identity crisis and the perversion and madness of the world in a closed, cruelly logical system of thought and action but in the end wants only to die. *Se7en* is full of striking images. The opening sequence has become famous, and is visually so revolutionary that it is often copied in commercials.

UB

1   Cop David Mills (Brad Pitt) tries to uncover a system behind the murders. But common sense isn't enough to understand the psychopath's atrocities.

2   A gruesome discovery. The investigators catch their breath at the scene of the crime.

3   Seeking reassurance. Mills shortly before the final confrontation.

4   Nerve-racking police work. Somerset and Mills study photos of the crime scenes.

5   A rare moment of happiness. Mills and his wife (Gwyneth Paltrow) have invited his colleague to dinner.

DEAD MAN WALKING ⚊

1995 – USA – 122 MIN. – MELODRAMA, PRISON FILM
DIRECTOR TIM ROBBINS (*1958)
SCREENPLAY TIM ROBBINS, based on SISTER HELEN PREJEAN'S autobiography of the same name **DIRECTOR OF PHOTOGRAPHY** ROGER A. DEAKINS **EDITING** LISA ZENO CHURGIN, RAY HUBLEY
MUSIC DAVID ROBBINS **PRODUCTION** JON KILIK, TIM ROBBINS, RUDD SIMMONS for WORKING TITLE FILMS, HAVOC PRODUCTIONS
STARRING SEAN PENN (Matthew Poncelet), SUSAN SARANDON (Sister Helen Prejean), ROBERT PROSKY (Hilton Barber), RAYMOND J. BARRY (Earl Delacroix), R. LEE ERMEY (Clyde Percy), CELIA WESTON (Mary Beth Percy), LOIS SMITH (Helen's mother), SCOTT WILSON (Farley), ROBERTA MAXWELL (Lucille Poncelet), MARGO MARTINDALE (Sister Colleen)
ACADEMY AWARDS 1996 OSCAR for BEST ACTRESS (Susan Sarandon)
IFF BERLIN 1996 SILVER BEAR for BEST ACTOR (Sean Penn)

"I want the last face you see in this world to be the face of love, so you look at me when they do this thing."

Never for a moment does this movie doubt the guilt of the condemned man, and the title makes it clear from the beginning that the execution will be carried out. Matthew Poncelet (Sean Penn), a vain, showy, shabby piece of white trash is to pay with his own messed-up life for the double murder of a pair of young lovers, symbol of America's hopes for a purer and better future.

Tim Robbins's second movie intentionally avoids the effects generally used in conventional prison thrillers to create suspense and win the audience's sympathy. There is no wrongly accused innocent saved at the last minute in a dramatic race against time, and no one pulls the condemned man's head out of the noose at the last moment. The movie does not set out to appeal against the death penalty, but rather to describe the grinding machinery of death row, with its strictly observed rituals and its wheels that turn with such agonizing slowness.

Poncelet, the murderer in the film, has been waiting six years for his execution, while the national average is considerably more. He is not dragged to the gallows the way he would be in a Western or forced into the electric chair like in a classic gangster film, as modern-day Louisiana takes a far more clinical approach when it comes to deciding over the life and death of its citizens. Nevertheless, shortly before the injection machine begins to pump poison into Poncelet's veins, the table he is tied to is set in an upright position. The impression that a diseased animal is being released from its suffering and put to sleep is replaced by an image of the crucifixion. Here the deeply-rooted religious symbolism of American society is plain to see: through his crucifixion, God is with the sinner. This is however combined with a fundamentalist idea of revenge and retaliation, anchored in the Manichaean view of many American churches that only absolute good and absolute evil exist.

That conviction, and the cliché of America as a nation eternally wedded to violence are arguments that are often trotted out to make capital punishment seem acceptable even today in "God's own country." But the thinking is that even though evil must be rooted out mercilessly, the condemned

3 4

"As ... in lighting and set design, the film discards prison movie cliché: this jail is no shadowy gothic hellhole but institutionally dull, almost cosy in its way. *Sight and Sound*

1   It takes Sister Helen Prejean (Susan Sarandon) some time to win the trust of condemned murderer Matthew Poncelet (Sean Penn).

2   A courageous woman. Sister Helen does not desert the murderer on his final journey.

3   Love for her fellow man also means overcoming her

4   Even in the face of death there are happy moments. Laughter reaches across where words fail.

5   Poncelet only accepts responsibility for the crime a

5

should not be deprived of spiritual comfort. Poncelet writes to Helen Prejean (Susan Sarandon), a Catholic nun who is also a social worker in a ghetto, and asks her to visit him in prison. Sister Helen takes up his invitation and gets her first insight into the grim workings of the prison system, which both upsets her and inspires her decision to accompany the murderer on his way to death. The offensive, boasting, dishonest side of Poncelet breaks through again and again, and Sean Penn is magnificent in the way he constantly alienates the audience and thereby creates a wholly convincing criminal. By a huge act of will, Sister Helen eventually succeeds in building up a relationship of trust with Poncelet, a closeness the limits of which are subtly emphasized by the director's constant use of grids and dividing walls. Although there are no explicit hints of forgiveness or redemption, Sister Helen does nonetheless develop the beginnings of an understanding for this totally alien man.

According to her partner Robbins, Sarandon's character was intended to be the eyes of the audience. As we accompany this uncertain, doubt-rid-

den handmaid of the Lord, we see many other perspectives on Poncelet's case, all presented in an unsentimental and non-judgmental way. We see the victim's embittered families crying out for retribution, the self-sacrificing, dedicated but incompetent legal aid lawyer, the contemptuous prison officials who fulfill their duties so unwillingly, and the sympathy of hypocritical local politicians who are hopelessly constrained by the limitations of the system – and all of these figures are treated with the necessary respect. Like all good movies, *Dead Man Walking* takes its audience seriously and demands that it come to its own conclusions. The viewers themselves must decide whether, given the terrible conditions of the prisons, it is more humane to lock someone up for life without any prospect of early release (the only alternative to the death penalty in the USA), or to execute him straight away. It is no secret that the overwhelming majority of Americans are in favor of the latter, and *Dead Man Walking* is clever enough to avoid launching a direct attack on that conviction. UB

MOVIES AND THE DEATH PENALTY In real life, we may never get to see an execution. But films allows us to examine the process at our leisure, and American cinema in particular has been fascinated with showing the death penalty on screen since the early days of silent film. In 1938, when hardly anyone doubted that the death penalty was an effective deterrent, James Cagney played a courageous game with his own image in Michael Curtiz's *Angels With Dirty Faces.* As a salutary warning to other criminals and potential imitators, the hardest-boiled cinema gangster of all time is transformed into a coward, trembling with fear before the electric chair. Twenty years later, Robert Wise produced a stirring appeal against capital punishment with his film biography of executed murderess Barbara Graham; Susan Hayward won an Oscar for the role in *I Want to Live!* (1958). Similarly, the film *Monster* (2003) was inspired by the life of a real-life criminal – the first female serial killer in the USA to be executed – and also won an Oscar for the actress who played her, Charlize Theron. *The Life of David Gale* (2002), on the other hand, is a fictitious account about an opponent of capital punishment who finds himself on death row.

TOY STORY

1995 – USA – 81 MIN. – ANIMATION, COMEDY
DIRECTOR JOHN LASSETER (*1957)
SCREENPLAY JOSS WHEDON, ANDREW STANTON, JOEL COHEN, ALEC SOKOLOW
DIRECTOR OF PHOTOGRAPHY JULIE M. MCDONALD, LOUIS RIVERA EDITING ROBERT GORDON,
LEE UNKRICH MUSIC RANDY NEWMAN PRODUCTION RALPH GUGGENHEIM, BONNIE ARNOLD
for PIXAR ANIMATION STUDIOS (for WALT DISNEY PICTURES)
VOICES TOM HANKS (Woody), TIM ALLEN (Buzz Lightyear), DON RICKLES (Mr. Potato Head),
WALLACE SHAWN (Rex), JOHN RATZENBERGER (Hamm), JIM VARNEY (Slinky Dog),
ANNIE POTTS (Bo Peep), JOHN MORRIS (Andy), LAURIE METCALF (Mrs. Davis),
R. LEE ERMEY (Sergeant)

"You've got a friend in me."

Day breaks in Andy's playroom. After the boy has gone to school, it's time for his toys to stretch and scratch and sometimes even to fit themselves back together. Rex the neurotic dinosaur broadcasts his problems to the whole world, Mr. Potato Head gives a running sarcastic commentary, Slinky Dog slopes through the room in his friendly and melancholic way, and Woody, the cowboy doll, calmly watches over his herd. The toys live, they have feelings, and above all they have a fine sense of irony about their function, although the humans know nothing of all that.

One day the fine social balance that has developed in the playroom over the years is destroyed by the arrival of a newcomer. His name is Buzz Lightyear, his vocation is to save the universe, and he takes his mission seriously. Woody and the others recognize this childish fresh-out-of-the-packag-

ing syndrome right away and try to explain to Buzz that he is only a toy. To no avail. The situation is not improved by the fact that in no time at all Buzz is Andy's favorite toy, and he begins to neglect all his other old play partners. Woody is depressed and tries to win back his place in Andy's heart. If anything should upset Buzz Lightyear's electronics in the process, then so much the better.

Soon however a tricky situation comes about, and Woody, Buzz, and all the other toys have to pull together to solve it.

Even if the story weren't the little masterpiece that it is, this movie would still have a place in cinema history, for it was the first film ever to be made using only computer animation. Everything from the smallest blade of grass to the plastic army was developed inside a computer, from the earliest

"To rephrase Wittgenstein, for all the characters in *Toy Story*, technology is the limit of their world."

Sight and Sound

sketches to the three-dimensional finished object. Technical advances like that mean that some classic film jobs like camerawork can be simulated, although the eye of the cameraman, and above all his thinking are still vital to the project. *Toy Story* had its first contact with the outside world when the finished work was transferred from hard disk to 35 mm film. When its sequel appeared four years later, alternative methods of distribution were already available: *Toy Story 2* was the first film in the world which was shown in selected cinemas via beam projection. *Toy Story* is a great movie indepen-

dently of its technical innovations. It demonstrates a belief in traditional cinematic qualities which are often considered old-fashioned: the characters are well drawn and consistent, the plot is logical and beautifully constructed, and it's filled end to end with humor and suspense. The movie is also convincing in the way it works on different levels, and has something to offer for every age group. It is an exciting adventure for children which passes on values of friendship and trust. For adults it is an affectionate yet amazingly unsentimental homage to childhood and the difficulties of growing up.   OM

1 Woody sees to it that communal life is harmonious in Andy's playroom. The voice of Tom Hanks lends the windup cowboy a friendly, naïve soul.

2 Hamm the piggybank and Mr. Potato Head are compulsive cardplayers. One of many endearing pieces of fun in the world's first full-length animated feature film produced entirely using computer graphics.

3 Even a windup cowboy has feelings: Woody with Bo Peep, his beloved shepherdess doll.

4 Cosmic warrior Buzz Lightyear has an identity crisis. His role as Messiah to a race of three-eyed extra-terrestrials proves too much for him.

PIXAR ANIMATION STUDIOS Pixar Animation Studios originally belonged to George Lucas's Industrial Light and Magic (ILM). Pixar was therefore responsible for the computer generated pictures in Richard Marquand's *Return of the Jedi* (1982), as well as for Nicholas Meyer's *Star Trek – The Wrath of Khan* (1982) and Barry Levinson's *Young Sherlock Holmes* (1985). In 1986 Pixar became an independent company under Steve Jobs, the founder of Apple. It began to concentrate on the development of the software necessary for the creation of movies that were totally computer-animated. After the production of various short films, Pixar finally succeeded in making *Toy Story*, which was the first movie in the world to have been produced entirely in a computer, under the direction of the creative head of the studio, John Lasseter. In 2006, The Walt Disney Company acquired Pixar for 7.4 billion dollars. In 2010, Toy Story 3 arrived in theaters.

KIDS

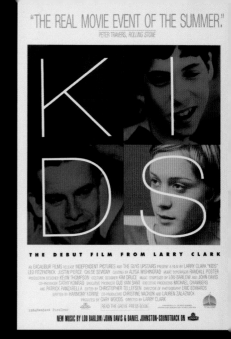

1995 – USA – 91 MIN. – DRAMA
DIRECTOR LARRY CLARK (*1943)
SCREENPLAY LARRY CLARK, HARMONY KORINE DIRECTOR OF PHOTOGRAPHY ERIC ALAN EDWARDS
EDITING CHRISTOPHER TELLEFSEN MUSIC LOU BARLOW, JOHN DAVIS PRODUCTION CARY WOODS
for INDEPENDENT PICTURES, MIRAMAX
STARRING CHLOË SEVIGNY (Jennie), LEO FITZPATRICK (Telly), JUSTIN PIERCE (Casper),
YAKIRU PEGUERO (Darcy), MICHELE LOCKWOOD (Kim), ROSARIO DAWSON (Ruby),
BILLY VALDES (Stanly), BILLY WALDEMAN (Zack), SARAH HENDERSON (Girl 1),
SAJAN BHAGAT (Paul)

"When you are young not much matters. When you find something you like, that's all you got."

New York: teenage boys sit together and talk loud and long about sex, especially Telly (Leo Fitzpatrick), who "specializes" in virgins. New York: girls sit together and talk – with only slightly more reserve – about sex. Both groups soon start to talk about AIDS, and the boys are determined not to let it spoil their fun. Two of the girls have just had an AIDS test, although Jennie (Chloë Sevigny) really only went to make it less embarrassing for Ruby (Rosario Dawson). But when they go to collect the results, Jennie turns out to be HIV positive. Telly is the only person she has ever slept with, and alone, she sets off to find him. He's on the streets with his friend Casper (Justin Pierce) buying grass with money that he has stolen from his mother. In the park they meet another couple of teenagers. Together they beat up a passerby who they suspect is gay, and all the while they talk uninterruptedly about sex. Telly keeps talking about how he going to "crack a virgin" that evening, as he did

in that morning. This time the lucky girl is 13-year-old Darcy (Yakiru Peguero). He picks her up with his friends, and after dark they all they break into a swimming pool. While the others start playing games in the water, Telly begins to tell Darcy tenderly of his love – just like he did with another girl in the opening sequence of the movie.

As she trails him around the city, Jennie keeps arriving just after Telly has left. She has to listen to a taxi driver telling her that she should just forget about the test result because when she laughs, she looks like a prom queen. In a disco where she hopes to find Telly a friend persuades her to pop a few pills of the latest "stuff." When she finally catches up with Telly she finds him ensconced in the parents' bedroom at a friend's party, in the midst of deflowering Darcy. Jennie has come too late. Horrified and half numbed by the drugs, she watches through the doorway as they have sex.

1 When Jennie (Chloë Sevigny) goes for an AIDS test to support her friend, she's the one who turns out to be HIV positive …

2 … while her friend Ruby (Rosario Dawson) had been worrying for nothing.

3 When looking for a suitable image, nothing beats dramatizing your sexuality and showing it off.

"I was trying to bring you into a reality that grownups just don't see. Think about what it's like to be a kid. How you're living for the moment. How you just want to have fun. How you're not thinking about tomorrow." Larry Clark, CNN

4   The young boys emulate the older ones and experiment with their bodies and the topic of sex.

5   For they know not what they do: Casper (Justin Pierce) and Telly (Leo Fitzpatrick) aren't wicked or stupid, they just want to have fun.

6   For Telly this is just a kind of warm-up routine: he declares his love to any girl he likes, in order to be able to tell his mates about his sexual adventures afterwards.

AMATEUR ACTORS   It is much easier to work with non-professional actors in a movie than it is on the stage. Camera work and editing both exercise a selection process which means that neither the overall effect of a performance nor its single elements are important, and that unclear articulation or an imperfect physique are much less of a problem than they would be on the stage. On the other hand, film sometimes uses non-professionals precisely because of some distinguishing physical feature, but that is mostly the case for supporting roles. Amateurs are sometimes used – although rarely – for an alienation effect, as in the movies of Straub/Huillet. Their clumsy performances are a deliberate effect to remind us that we are watching an artificial product. Amateur actors often appear in children's films and youth movies. Capturing their spontaneity requires extremely careful filming and directing however, and they cannot be simply put in front of the cameras. Some directors specialize in this, like the French director Jacques Doillon, who after years of working with children has developed his own special technique to avoid cuteness, which has the effect of making the kids in his movies appear as fully rounded characters.

Eventually, she sinks down onto a couch in the last free corner in the living room which is full of drunken and doped up kids who have all fallen asleep. Only Casper – the friendly ghost – is still wandering around, sipping all the half-empty bottles. He tries to wake Jennie but gives up, removes her pants and penetrates her on the creaking leather sofa. The following morning, the sun shines down on the parks of New York. Casper opens his eyes and mutters: "Sweet Jesus, what happened?"

The kids of the title curse, smoke, and have continual sex with each other (or at least talk about it) and yet the movie still manages to avoid shock effects and cheap thrills. Photographer Larry Clark gives us an impressive portrait of the kids in what was only his first movie. Despite what critics said when the movie first appeared, the kids are by no means clichéd monsters.

The simple images tell the story of a single day and the audience are forced observe the chaotic search for satisfaction without any moral yardstick. The mitigating factors which customarily appear in similar movies to explain the kids' extreme behavior are intentionally omitted here, and neither the social milieu nor ethnic conflicts have an important role to play. Clark dissects his kids with a surgeon's scalpel. The film succeeds partly because Clark worked with young amateurs, and the result was an enormous variety of faces and gestures the like of which is rarely seen in standardized Hollywood movies. He also resisted the temptation to make his kids into pop stars with music, clothes, and other outward signs of coolness. Nevertheless, Chloë Sevigny – who takes the role of Jennie – has since been much in demand as an actress and has appeared in other films like *Boys Don't Cry*.   MS

TWELVE MONKEYS

1995 – USA – 131 MIN. – SCIENCE FICTION
DIRECTOR TERRY GILLIAM (*1940)
SCREENPLAY DAVID PEOPLES, JANET PEOPLES, loosely based on CHRIS MARKER's movie *LA JETÉE* **DIRECTOR OF PHOTOGRAPHY** ROGER PRATT **EDITING** MICK AUDSLEY **MUSIC** PAUL BUCKMASTER
PRODUCTION CHARLES ROVEN for POLYGRAM, UNIVERSAL, CLASSICO, ATLAS
STARRING BRUCE WILLIS (James Cole), MADELEINE STOWE (Dr. Kathryn Railly), BRAD PITT
(Jeffrey Goines), CHRISTOPHER PLUMMER (Dr. Goines), JON SEDA (Jose),
JOSEPH MELITO (Cole as a young man), MICHAEL CHANCE (Scarface),
VERNON CAMPBELL (Tiny), FRED STROTHER (L. J. Washington), RICK WARNER (Dr. Casey)

"You know what crazy is?
Crazy is majority rules!"

In 1996 the world as we know it comes to an end, when a killer virus destroys almost all life on earth. A small number of people manage to survive by living in sewers and subway tunnels, where they start to build up a provisional culture. As the decades pass the survivors join together in a society based on mutual need, and they make it their aim to prevent the human race from dying out completely. Eventually scientists succeed in building a time travel machine, and it becomes possible to undo the apocalypse by preventing the unleashing of the virus. In 2035, a hardened criminal named James Cole (Bruce Willis) is sent on a journey back to the fateful year. He is chosen because society considers him dispensable and the journey is highly dangerous, but also because he is continually plagued by dreams of the virus catastrophe.

When he arrives in 1996 Cole is predictably put into a mental hospital, which is run by Dr. Kathryn Railly (Madeleine Stowe). The symbol of the "Army of the 12 Monkeys" is all over the old world, and that is the symbol that Cole associates with his dreams and with the catastrophe. The leader of that secret association is a psychotic by the name of Jeffrey Goines (Brad Pitt) whose father is a virologist. Cole meets Goines in the mental hospital, and Goines helps him escape.

Terry Gilliam, visionary and iconoclast, uses Chris Marker's philosophical science fiction photo story *La Jetée* (1962) as inspiration for *Twelve Monkeys*. Gilliam claimed that he did not know *La Jetée* and that he only saw it after he had finished his own work, but given the many pictorial quotations which run through the movie's dense texture like distant memories this

seems a little unlikely. It might perhaps be fairer to say that *La Jetée* served as a model, as a short film can hardly be anything more than a point of departure. The journey in time is an idea of Marker's, as is the dramatic finale when Cole sees himself as a child and witnesses the catastrophe both as active participant and as passive spectator.

The biggest problem of *Twelve Monkeys* is that it adds little to the original. Both movies are ruled by the idea of the inevitability of death, and death is a force which both pursues the characters and which they rush towards in indefinable, semiconscious fear. Gilliam's film is much less constrained in the means that it has at its disposal, whereas apart from a few animated moments, Marker's film consists entirely of static images given a narrative context by a combination of music and voiceover. There is a great simplicity in the images and the content of the shots. *La Jetée* is hardly a movie at all in the traditional sense, but more a work made up of gaps or intervals. By contrast, *Twelve Monkeys* overwhelms us with a flood of images. The audience is frequently left in the dark regarding the supposed reality of what is shown. We see sequences that we believe to be reality until the camera moves back and we discover we have been looking at a television screen all the while. Gilliam's film also borrows more than once from Hitchcock's *Vertigo* (1958), a film with which it shares a fundamentally elegiac mood.

Gilliam's film is about the paradox of the passage of time: its hero has his whole life in front of him but has already experienced everything. Like all travelers in time, James Cole pays a high price: he lives a life without a present, a life in which presentiment and memory destroy the moment.   OM

1   James Cole (Bruce Willis) has no idea that his assignment will turn out to be a metaphysical suicide mission.

2   A prime example of Terry Gilliam's unique fantasy world: a tense juxtaposition of early industrial architecture and a disturbingly realistic hospital interior.

3   Dr. Kathryn Railly (Madeleine Stowe) is James Cole's only ally in his fight against the Army of the 12 Monkeys.

4   The end of the world in his eyes: Jeffrey Goines (Brad Pitt) reveals himself to be head of the Army of the 12 Monkeys.

CHRIS MARKER   The author and filmmaker Chris Marker is a particularly mysterious figure associated with the Nouvelle Vague movement. He was born in 1921 as Christian François Boche-Villeneuve in Neuilly-sur-Seine, or perhaps in Belleville or, according to one telling, in Ulan Bator. Like the American author Thomas Pynchon, he never appears in public. Marker is a master of the discursive film, and his movies switch effortlessly between fiction and documentation. Together with *La Jetée,* his most famous works include the movies *Le Joli Mai* (1962) and *Le Fond de l'air est rouge* (*The Air is Red*, 1977), which take political developments in France in the '60s and '70s as their theme. *Sans soleil* (*Sunless*, 1982) and its continuation *Level Five* (1996) are two studies of Japan, otherness, and the search for the unfilmable self.

"It just seems that I have this German-Expressionistic-Destructivist-Russian-Constructivist view of the future."

Terry Gilliam in *Sight and Sound*

CASINO

1995 – USA – 178 MIN. – GANGSTER FILM, DRAMA
DIRECTOR MARTIN SCORSESE (*1942)
SCREENPLAY NICHOLAS PILEGGI, MARTIN SCORSESE, based on the novel of the same name
by NICHOLAS PILEGGI DIRECTOR OF PHOTOGRAPHY ROBERT RICHARDSON
EDITING THELMA SCHOONMAKER MUSIC ADVISOR ROBBIE ROBERTSON
PRODUCTION BARBARA DE FINA for SYALIS, LEGENDE, CAPPA (for UNIVERSAL)
STARRING ROBERT DE NIRO (Sam Rothstein), SHARON STONE (Ginger McKenna), JOE PESCI
(Nicky Santoro), JAMES WOODS (Lester Diamonds), DON RICKLES (Billy Sherbert),
ALAN KING (Andy Stone), KEVIN POLLAK (Phillip Green), L. Q. JONES (Pat Webb),
DICK SMOTHERS (Senator), FRANK VINCENT (Frank Marino)

"Anywhere else I would be arrested for what I'm doing. Here they're giving me awards."

Sam "Ace" Rothstein (Robert De Niro) is a genius bookie. All addicted gamblers wait until Sam has laid his bets so that they can copy him. His perfectionism is legendary. If a jockey has problems with his wife or if a horse is ill, Sam is the first to know. That's why the Mafia chooses him to manage Tangiers, their Las Vegas casino. Sam makes it his life's work and keeps the Mafia bosses happy by constantly increasing their profit margins. Nothing escapes his tireless eye.

The casino Scorsese shows us is a perfect system where everyone spies on everyone else. Everything goes perfectly until two newcomers suddenly upset the workings of Sam's life. To protect him adequately and presumably also to keep an eye on him, the Mafia sends Nicky Santoro (Joe Pesci) to Vegas. Santoro is a psychopath who will do any dirty work necessary, a little man with big ambitions, who is obsessed with power and devoid of scruples. Nicky immediately begins to build up his own gangster mob, and in no time at all they have won control of petty crime in Las Vegas.

Sam sees Ginger McKenna (Sharon Stone) for the first time through the peephole in the casino's false ceiling. A prostitute who is as hardened as she is beautiful, she finds her clients among the ecstatic winners at the gambling tables. Sam falls in love with her. The only thing Ginger loves is her own self, but she is not adverse to Sam's money and power. To complicate matters, Lester, her former pimp, is still on the scene, and he still has a powerful hold on her. Scorsese retells a familiar tale of rise and fall, of powerful men who overreach themselves and end up losing everything, and he elevates his gangsters to the level of tragic heroes. Rothstein wants to rule the world by organizing it perfectly and watching over it, and he ruthlessly uses everyone around him to his own immoral ends. But in the process, he unwittingly destroys his own happiness.

Nicky is intoxicated with Las Vegas, and he believes he can force his own rules on the city. He begins a brutal reign of terror at the bookmakers' and on the streets, only to fall victim of his own cycle of violence. Ginger, the third main figure, is unable to love and prefers to spend her life dependent on other people.

One of the great strengths of Scorsese's movies is they way they manage to present the Mafia and the underworld from constantly new and

"I'm what's real out here. Not your country clubs and your TV show. I'm what's real: the dirt, the gutter, and the blood. That's what it's all about." Nicky Santoro in *Casino*

"What interested me was the idea of excess, no limits. People become successful like in no other city."

Martin Scorsese in *Sight and Sound*

1 Expressions that speak volumes: the paths of Sam "Ace" Rothstein (Robert De Niro) and Nicky Santoro (Joe Pesci) are not leading in the same direction.

2 A ruler and his empire: Robert De Niro as Sam Rothstein in an inferno of light.

3 Heavy guys throw dark shadows (Frank Vincent as Frank Marino, left): Nicky Santoro already senses that further humiliation awaits him.

4 The artificial smile of the professional: Ginger McKenna (Sharon Stone) at her place of work. This is where Sam Rothstein sees her for the first time. Ginger's glittering appearance comes to embody what he imagines happiness to be.

different perspectives. *Goodfellas* (1991), for example, presents criminals in a casual, almost comic way, like the men next door. *Casino* takes a radically different track, as though Scorsese had resurrected figures from Shakespearean tragedy. The film forces us to feel sympathy for these heroes, and as soon as we fall into that trap, we are forced stand by and watch their downfall. Sam's megalomania gets him into trouble with local politicians and suddenly life gets much more complicated; Nicky thinks he can run the racket to his own advantage without the Mafia noticing, and even Ginger's brilliant beauty starts to fade when she agrees to marry Sam Rothstein, who buys her love with jewelry, money, and furs.

Casino is a searingly beautiful movie. It presents the audience with the characters' innermost desires and fears through its off-screen narration. It does far more than tell one story, but is a complex weave of tales relating how

love cannot be bought, and how friendship can be easily betrayed. Despite its tragic elements, the movie is witty in its depiction of the normal everyday life of the criminal fraternity. And Scorsese's special talent for allowing comedy tip over unexpectedly into violence makes the movie a real rollercoaster ride.

The story also reflects the rise and fall of Las Vegas itself. We see this from Sam and Nicky's perspective, reflected in the everyday routine of the casino, and the endless struggle against cheats and conmen, the constant search for new ways to evade taxation, and ever more effective means of controlling employees. The movie's discursive structure is mirrored in Robert Richardson's camera work; he swings and zooms, looking curiously here and there. Scorsese's Vegas is a hell of sound and fury. The world, as ever, is his stage.

OM

SAUL BASS We have the graphic designer and filmmaker Saul Bass (1920–1996) to thank for the fact that uninspiring opening credit sequences have now become artworks in their own right. His work with Otto Preminger, for who he made the credits, promotional material, and, above all, posters and adverts from the mid-'50s onwards, played a major part in his development. Bass cultivated a minimalist style, using a small number of colors and motifs to emphasize the main theme of a movie. Although Saul Bass had officially retired, Martin Scorsese managed to persuade him to work on his movies. From *Goodfellas* (1991) to *Casino* (1995) Saul made all the credits for Scorsese's movies with the help of his wife Elaine. Bass has also directed music videos and many prize-winning short films as well as the feature film *Phase 4* (1973).

5   They've made it. Sam and Ginger blithely adopt the status symbols of the wealthy and the beautiful, unaware that nothing can protect them from a precipitous fall.

6   A fatal ménage à trois: the husband and his wife, the ex-callgirl and her pimp. Lester Diamonds (James Woods) has a greater hold over Ginger than Sam ever will.

"When you love someone, you've got to trust them. You've got to give them the keys to everything that's yours."

Sam Rothstein in *Casino*

7 A dissolute icon of depravity: as Ginger McKenna Sharon Stone plays the most impressive role of her career.

8 A roll of the dice leads to deceptive success: Robert De Niro in his most complex Scorsese role to date.

9 Forbidden fruit: Nicky allows himself to be seduced by Ginger, in a relationship that will plunge him into oblivion.

8

DEAD MAN

1995 – USA / GERMANY – 120 MIN. – WESTERN
DIRECTOR JIM JARMUSCH (*1953)
SCREENPLAY JIM JARMUSCH DIRECTOR OF PHOTOGRAPHY ROBBY MÜLLER EDITING JAY RABINOWITZ
MUSIC NEIL YOUNG PRODUCTION DEMETRA J. MACBRIDE for 12-GAUGE PRODUCTIONS,
PANDORA FILM
STARRING JOHNNY DEPP (William Blake), GARY FARMER (Nobody), JOHN HURT
(John Scholfield), GABRIEL BYRNE (Charlie Dickinson), LANCE HENRIKSEN (Cole Wilson),
MICHAEL WINCOTT (Conway Twill), EUGENE BYRD (Johnny Pickett), ROBERT MITCHUM
(John Dickinson), ALFRED MOLINA (Missionary), IGGY POP (Salvatore "Sally" Jenko),
BILLY BOB THORNTON (Big George Drakoulious), JARED HARRIS (Benmont Tench)

"That weapon will replace your tongue. You will learn to speak through it, and your poetry will now be written with blood."

After *Night on Earth* (1991) Jim Jarmusch realized that his filmmaking was in danger of getting stuck in a dead end, and that he had better change as quickly as possible if he wanted to maintain his integrity as an artist. So it was that he made his greatest movie to date. In the guise of a ramshackle Western, *Dead Man* is a meditation on huge themes like the irony of all being and the idea of death as a final journey. In short: Jarmusch got serious.

America, somewhere in the West, sometime towards the end of the 19th century. With his last few dollars, William Blake (Johnny Depp) travels to Machine to take up a position at the metal company of the feared John Dickinson (Robert Mitchum). Machine turns out to be a desolate place bereft of morals, dignity, and decency. Unsurprisingly, when he gets there, William learns that his job has already been given to someone else. When he tries to complain to Mr. Dickinson in person, he is lucky to escape with his life. He

shoots Mr. Dickinson's son in self-defense more or less by accident and is forced to flee Machine, getting wounded in the process.

He awakes to find himself being tended by a peculiar Indian by the name of Nobody (Gary Farmer). Nobody is pleased that William Blake has killed a white man, but he is also convinced that his patient is a reincarnation of the mystic poet of the same name, who he greatly admires. Nobody spent part of his youth in England studying the "white man's" civilization, but when he returned and tried to tell his people about it, he was cast out and now wanders homeless through the forests. Mr. Dickinson meanwhile has set a gang of three bounty hunters on William's trail, but they seem mostly concerned with killing each other. As the last of them gets closer and closer to William, he gradually finds his way to the eternal waters. The path to his redemption is purified with the blood of countless corpses.

1   William Blake (Johnny Depp) changes from a
    harmless employee into an unwilling killer.

2   The capitalist and his portrait: John Dickinson
    (Robert Mitchum) emphatically demonstrates that
    the language of commerce matches that of war.

3   An American group portrait: cheerful psychopaths
    characterized by the attribute of the skull.

4   William Blake realizes that his flight is in
    reality a metaphysical journey into the realm of
    transformation.

Jarmusch's usual audiences were left with a knowing laugh stuck in their throats. The eccentric characters, the actors who seem self-critical and distant, the delayed-timing dry humor were the same as ever, as was the poetic black and white. But there was also a spiritual depth that no one expected from the director of *Down by Law* (1986).

Seldom do cinema characters die as unspectacularly as in *Dead Man*. They stare at each other and shoot and then one, if not both, fall over, as casually as a branch cracks on a forest walk. Jarmusch was criticized in his turn for making killing a joke – worried critics were still dealing with the conse-

quences of so-called "Tarantinoism." However, Jarmusch's abstract directing style counteracts any suggestion of pathos, and anyone who insists that *Dead Man* is in bad taste has completely failed to understand that killing and death here are part of a metaphysical joke called life. In this respect, although it is not thematized in the movie, *Dead Man* is spiritually close to a particular school of Buddhism, which believes that the souls of the murdered have a part to play in the redemption of their killers. *Dead Man* is a serene elegy, which glides along to Neil Young's hypnotic guitar phrases and blossoms in its glowing white and warm, intense black.   OM

JIM JARMUSCH Jim Jarmusch (*1953) is the epitome of an American independent filmmaker in the '80s and '90s. He made his debut in 1980 with New Wave influenced *Permanent Vacation,* but international success only came with *Stranger Than Paradise* (1984) and the television film *Down by Law* (1986). *Mystery Train* (1989) took his sense of the bizarre a step further and with *Night on Earth* (1991) it became his trademark. In *Dead Man* (1995), however, Jarmusch produced a masterpiece that lifted his work into a whole new dimension. After the brilliant concert documentary film for Neil Young entitled *Year of the Horse* (1997), Jarmusch made the philosophical gangster movie *Ghost Dog* (1999) and tragicomedy *Broken Flowers* (2005), the latter of which gave lead actor Bill Murray a superb showcase for his blend of comic talent and tragic depth.

"Don't let the sun burn a hole in your ass: rise now, and drive your cart and your plow over the bones of the dead."

Nobody based on one of Blake's "Proverbs of Hell"

THE BRIDGES OF MADISON COUNTY

1995 – USA – 135 MIN. – MELODRAMA

DIRECTOR CLINT EASTWOOD (*1930)
SCREENPLAY RICHARD LAGRAVENESE, based on the novel of the same name by
ROBERT JAMES WALLER DIRECTOR OF PHOTOGRAPHY JACK N. GREEN EDITING JOEL COX
MUSIC LENNIE NIEHAUS PRODUCTION CLINT EASTWOOD, KATHLEEN KENNEDY
for MALPASO PRODUCTIONS, AMBLIN ENTERTAINMENT
STARRING CLINT EASTWOOD (Robert Kincaid), MERYL STREEP (Francesca Johnson),
JIM HAYNIE (Richard Johnson), ANNIE CORLEY (Carolyn Johnson), VICTOR SLEZAK
(Michael Johnson), SARAH KATHRYN SCHMITT (Carolyn as a girl),
CHRISTOPHER KROON (Michael as a boy), PHYLLIS LYONS (Betty), DEBRA MONK
(Madge), MICHELLE BENES (Lucy Redfield)

"This kind of certainty comes but once in a lifetime."

Des Moines isn't Bari, which is why Italian war bride Francesca has never fulfilled the dreams of her youth. She earns a steady living at the side of her honest and upright husband, and lives a life of gentle boredom, until one day, when she is standing on the veranda of her farm house, a stranger appears in a cloud of dust on the horizon. Strangers are rare in this out-of-the-way corner of Iowa. The audience doesn't find out about Francesca's story until much later, as the movie has a gentle pace, but the fine nuances of Meryl Streep's acting make it clear from the start that she is torn between long suppressed hopes and the fear of losing the security of what she has. All the moral decisions in this melodrama have been taken before the movie begins and Francesca takes the first step; she offers to show the covered wooden bridge, which is the area's only attraction, to Robert Kincaid (Clint Eastwood), a widely traveled photographer who works for *National Geographic* magazine. The lonely globetrotter with his laconic, decorous macho charm and the late flowering prairie rose slowly come together. A relationship begins, reserved and fragile at first, but soon becoming increasingly passionate. It's no coincidence that Robert J. Waller's successful novel, on which the movie is based, is set in Iowa, whose rigorous state motto proclaims "our liberties we prize, and our rights we will maintain."

Francesca's children Michael and Carolyn discover the story of her

and therefore the happiness that could have lasted for the rest of two lives is limited to four days in 1965 when Francesca's husband and her two teenage children are at the cattle show in Illinois. Husband Richard Johnson (Jim Haynie) hardly makes an appearance, but the way of life he stands for dominates the movie. Eastwood's movie may indulge overwhelming emotion, but in the final instance, it pays tribute to people who do not run away from their responsibilities.

Although the time the lovers spend together is limited, that only serves to make the affair more intense. The acting, camera work, and music combine with the brief time span to make that rare thing in contemporary cinema: a believable adult love story in which every nuance rings true. The melodramatic figures that move us most are those who experience believable emotions and suffer in a way that we can understand. Doomed cinema romances enable audiences to enjoy the small victories and great defeats of the heart at one remove. This work by Clint Eastwood is particularly effective because it manages to avoid that scourge of modern Hollywood melodramas – the self-righteous invocation of supposedly sacred values (family, faithfulness, etc.) which are often nothing more than stifling Puritanism and naked possessiveness.

What remains are the girlish gestures of Meryl Streep and the uncer-

1 Robert Kincaid is on the road to photograph the famous bridges of Madison County.

2 Her melancholic expression reveals that Francesca (Meryl Streep) won't be able to give up her previous life.

"Eastwood is unique among American filmmakers today; no one else captures, with such concentrated intensity, a character's least breath, their least flicker of emotion." *Cahiers du cinéma*

3 The performances of both principal actors make even naive actions both convincing and sincere.

4 A symbolic moment. It's as if Kincaid and farmer's wife Francesca Johnson were meant for each other.

CLINT EASTWOOD No Hollywood star ever planned a career more intelligently than Clint Eastwood, although his early films meant that he was frequently underestimated. Born in 1930, Eastwood quickly developed a disarming self-irony that prepared his fans for the day when the action-packed days of spaghetti Westerns and Dirty Harry would come to a close. Then, in 1992, he resurrected the subgenre of the late Western with the unexpected highlight of *Unforgiven,* which won the Oscar for Best Film. In *The Bridges of Madison County* (1995), we saw him in heartrending form as a mature, romantic figure. From 2000 onward, Eastwood began to turn out a film every one or two years, most of which met with critical acclaim; they were also designed to show the world what a superb director the former spaghetti Western star had become. They included war movies such as *Flags of Our Fathers / Letters from Iwo Jima* (2006) and political biopics like *J. Edgar* (2011). In the drama *Gran Torino* (2008), Eastwood seemed to be tracing the same evolutionary path as his public persona: the main character he plays develops from racist to defender of the weak – just as Eastwood himself has blossomed from Dirty Harry the avenger into a respected director.

SENSE AND SENSIBILITY 🏆

1995 – USA – 140 MIN. – LITERATURE ADAPTATION, COSTUME FILM
DIRECTOR ANG LEE (*1954)
SCREENPLAY EMMA THOMPSON, based on the novel of the same name by JANE AUSTEN
DIRECTOR OF PHOTOGRAPHY MICHAEL COULTER **EDITING** TIM SQUYRES **MUSIC** PATRICK DOYLE
PRODUCTION LINDSAY DORAN for MIRAGE PRODUCTION, COLUMBIA PICTURES
STARRING EMMA THOMPSON (Elinor Dashwood), KATE WINSLET (Marianne Dashwood),
ALAN RICKMAN (Colonel Brandon), HUGH GRANT (Edward Ferrars), HARRIET WALTER
(Fanny Dashwood), EMILE FRANÇOIS (Margaret Dashwood), JAMES FLEET
(John Dashwood), TOM WILKINSON (Mr. Dashwood), GREG WISE (John Willoughby),
GEMMA JONES (Mrs. Dashwood), IMOGEN STUBBS (Lucy Steele)
IFF BERLIN 1996 GOLDEN BEAR
ACADEMY AWARDS 1996 OSCAR for BEST ADAPTED SCREENPLAY (Emma Thompson)

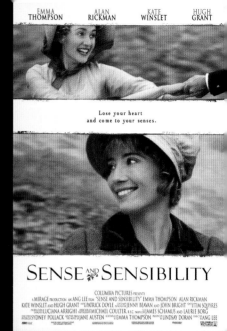

"Please don't say anything important till I come back."

England in the late 18th century: Mr. Dashwood, owner of Norland Park, has died suddenly. A son from his first marriage is declared his only heir, and he moves into the house with his wife. Mr. Dashwood's second wife is left penniless and together with her daughters Elinor (Emma Thompson), Marianne (Kate Winslet), and Margaret (Emile François) is forced to move into a tiny cottage given to her by a distant relative, where she must henceforth survive on an insignificant allowance.

Ang Lee's *Sense and Sensibility* is one of several popular adaptations of Jane Austen novels that appeared in the second half of the 1990s. With its combination of lighthearted and sober stylistic elements – in keeping with the fashion of the times – director Ang Lee resurrected the Regency with great success. The emotional confusion of its characters is counterbalanced by the patiently observed, timelessly classic style of the production, which contains

the sort of wisdom that the characters have to learn in the course of the movie.

Like all Jane Austen's novels, *Sense and Sensibility* focuses on a young woman whose intelligence and calm contradict the stereotype of her times and force her to go her own way in family matters, in society, and above all in love in order to find true happiness.

In Ang Lee's literature adaption, Elinor is played by Emma Thompson who fulfilled a long-held ambition with this intelligent and fresh interpretation of a classic novel. In life and love, Elinor corresponds exactly to the image of the clever, self-confident woman that Emma Thompson has cultivated throughout her acting career.

Before the second Dashwood family is forced to move to their new abode, Elinor happens to meet the clumsy yet loveable brother of the new

1   There is as much good sense as emotion in Elinor Dashwood's (Emma Thompson) polite smile.

2   Edward Ferrars (Hugh Grant) in a bitter moment of inner contemplation. Hugh Grant knows how to add dimension to the fairly one-sided character created by Jane Austin.

3   A typical example of the Flemish lighting that director Ang Lee and cameraman Michael Coulter were aiming for. The composition is based on a Vermeer.

4   The lightness and transparency of the Regency spirit are perfectly captured in the film's sets.

EMMA THOMPSON Emma Thompson first became known outside the UK as wife of the British theater and movie prodigy Kenneth Branagh. Her first successes were in stage plays, television, and finally in movies as a comedian, for example in *The Tall Guy* (1989). She later delivered brilliant performances in serious roles: for example, in James Ivory's *The Remains of the Day* (1993), *Sense and Sensibility* (1995), and as artist Dora Carrington in Christopher Hampton's film biography *Carrington* (1995). She won the Best Actress Oscar in 1993 for her leading role in *Howards End*. Thompson also writes screenplays, receiving a second Academy Award for her adaptation of *Sense and Sensibility*. She made guest appearances in three *Harry* Potter films (2004, 2007, 2011) and starred alongside Dustin Hoffman in the romantic movie *Last Chance Harvey* (2008). Her best acting achievement to date, however, must be her performance as a terminally-ill intellectual still full of the joys of life in Mike Nichols's television movie *Wit* (2001).

mistress of Norland Park, Edward Ferrars (Hugh Grant) – and they fall in love at first sight. However, Edward's sister keeps a jealous eye on the proceedings, eager to ensure that her brother does not waste himself on a poor relative but looks for an advantageous match instead. She makes sure that he returns to London as quickly as possible. Elinor hides her unhappiness, and only later, she discovers that Edward has been secretly engaged for years.

There is no lack of amorous excitement in the life of Marianne (Kate Winslet), her younger sister. She is wooed by two suitors: the moody Colonel Brandon, whom life has not always treated well, and Willoughby (Greg Wise), a man of the world who is as dashing as he is fickle. After a stormy courtship, Marianne falls for the latter, who then suddenly disappears and leaves for London under mysterious circumstances.

For weeks, Marianne waits in vain for a message from her lover and then together with Elinor she is invited to London by a wealthy relative. Both Dashwood sisters set off with high hopes, one to fetch the love of her life, the other to find out who the love of her life really is.

At first glance, *Sense and Sensibility* seems a rather unlikely project for Ang Lee who had previously made a name for himself as a precise chronicler of contemporary Chinese family and love relationships with movies like *The Wedding Banquet* (*Hsi yen*, 1993) and *Eat Drink Man Woman* (*Yin shi nan nou*, 1994). But with the benefit of hindsight, *Sense and Sensibility* appears as a kind of liberating work where Lee freed himself from his cultural background for the first time without abandoning his interest in complex family and love relationships.

OM

"Ang Lee [said that] he had Vermeer in mind, and indeed the creamily lit interiors and the close-ups bursting with pensive longing do recall the Dutch master." *Film Comment*

7

5   Thrown on their own resources: three of the four Dashwood ladies (Emma Thompson, Kate Winslet, Gemma Jones).

6   Love in the time of quill pens. Another striking example of Michael Coulter's skill with a camera using Flemish lighting.

7   A moment of profound solitude, when reason struggles despairingly with emotion. Ang Lee is fond of filming his subjects discreetly from behind in moments of high drama.

8   The naturally spontaneous Marianne Dashwood has to learn to love not only with her heart but also with her head.

9   Marianne's zest for life is revealed during a country dance.

"*Sense and Sensibility* is a happy accident, the happy union of happy souls." *Film Comment*

8

9

LEAVING LAS VEGAS ♗

1995 – USA – 112 MIN. – DRAMA

DIRECTOR MIKE FIGGIS (*1948)

SCREENPLAY MIKE FIGGIS, based on the novel of the same name by JOHN O'BRIEN

DIRECTOR OF PHOTOGRAPHY DECLAN QUINN **EDITING** JOHN SMITH **MUSIC** MIKE FIGGIS

PRODUCTION ANNIE STEWART, LILA CAZES for INITIAL PRODUCTIONS

STARRING ELISABETH SHUE (Sera), NICOLAS CAGE (Ben), JULIAN SANDS (Yuri), RICHARD LEWIS (Peter), STEVEN WEBER (Marc Nussbaum), KIM ADAMS (Sheila), EMILY PROCTOR (Debbie), VALERIA GOLINO (Terri), LAURIE METCALF (Landlady), DAVID BRISBIN (Landlord)

ACADEMY AWARDS 1996 OSCAR for BEST ACTOR (Nicolas Cage)

"I realized we didn't have much time, and I accepted him for what he was."

Ben (Nicolas Cage) is an alcoholic. He is so tired of life that he can't even bear it when he is completely drunk. When he loses his job, he takes it as a sign and decides to use his severance pay as a way of funding his alcohol consumption to the bitter end. As a failed scriptwriter, he feels that Las Vegas will be an appropriate setting for his intentions, as the bars in the city are open round the clock. On his way into town, he nearly runs over Sera (Elisabeth Shue), a young prostitute. She too is an addict, in her way: she is dependent on Yuri (Julian Sands), her Latvian pimp, who uses a knife on her whenever she disobeys. She has run away to Las Vegas in an attempt to regain control over her life, but Yuri has already tracked her down.

The next day, Ben and Sera meet again in a bar. Although Ben has been impotent for a long time, he takes her with him to his room. They get to know each other better. When Yuri finds out, he attacks Sera, as he has no patience with useless extras like emotional involvement. Luckily, it's for the last time:

a Mafia organization from the former Soviet Union has a problem with Yuri and solves it by getting rid of him.

Sera likes Ben and decides to help him with his plan. She continues to earn on the streets and when she has time, she takes care of him.

One evening when Sera is at work, Ben goes to a casino, has an unexpected run of luck, and in a good mood hires a prostitute who happens to be free and takes her to Sera's apartment. When Sera returns home she finds them both there and, beside herself with jealousy and rage, she goes to the room of three college boys who rape her and beat her up. When she returns home completely distraught, Ben rings from a flophouse. The end is near.

In the psychology of Ben and Sera's relationship there is no room for helper syndrome, so there is no need to fear sentimental last-minute rescue scenes in the final act. Ben is serious, and that could have been a real dramatic problem: when the audience knows from the very beginning how the

movie will end, there is not much room left for suspense. Moreover, Yuri's forced exit from the scene removes the only unpredictable element from the constellation comparatively quickly. Mike Figgis uses this narrative stagnation to give his characters space to develop emotionally, and he gives his actors the chance to exercise their improvisation skills. This approach is emphasized by his much-discussed decision to film the movie on super 16, although in fact that was partly a budget decision. This method uses a compact, light camera and cheap, high sensitivity film. Although it had long been the material of choice for documentary filmmakers, it lost its place in the market when digital video appeared. As a material DV is even less expensive, and it quickly grabbed everyone's attention. It also inspired Figgis to make *Time Code* (2000), his most experimental film up to that time, a not entirely successful attempt at non-linear narration.

Technical aspects aside, *Leaving Las Vegas* is a movie truly remarkable for the honesty with which Figgis presents emotions it portrays. Occasionally he may be a little heavy on the Freud in the analysis of Ben and Sera – but it's their souls that remain his central concern.

OM

ALCOHOLISM IN CINEMA Drugs have always been an important theme in feature films. Alcohol especially is a central motif, whether as the hard man's trademark or as a source of inspiration for writers and artists. The fatal consequences of alcohol consumption have often been dealt with as well: a life dragged down by alcohol and memory loss. We only have to think of Billy Wilder's masterpiece *The Lost Weekend (*1945), Blake Edwards's *Days of Wine and Roses* (1962), John Huston's *Under the Volcano* (1984), or Ken Loach's *My Name is Joe* (1999). Memorable performances of alcoholics include Dean Martin as a drunken deputy sheriff in Howard Hawks's Western *Rio Bravo* (1959) and Mickey Rourke in the title role of Barbet Schroeder's Bukowski homage *Barfly* (1987). Seldom has alcoholism been so sexy.

1 Las Vegas: city of lights but no dreams, the collection of curios that is the American dream.

2 The alcoholic Ben (Nicolas Cage) realizes that there is still love even for the lost and fallen. Even if it manifests itself in the form of the prostitute Sera (Elisabeth Shue).

3 Sera at work: here she is part of the false veneer of happiness of Las Vegas.

4 Elisabeth Shue made a breakthrough as a serious actress with this portrayal of a woman on the brink of spiritual self-realization.

5 Mike Figgis's favorite supporting actor Julian Sands as Sera's pimp Yuri.

6 Ben and Sera find common ground in the weightless world of a motel swimming pool.

3

4

"**Are you some sort of angel visiting me in one of my drunk fantasies?**"

Ben in *Leaving Las Vegas*

5

6

HEAT

1995 – USA – 172 MIN. – GANGSTER FILM, POLICE FILM
DIRECTOR MICHAEL MANN (*1943)
SCREENPLAY MICHAEL MANN **DIRECTOR OF PHOTOGRAPHY** DANTE SPINOTTI **EDITING** PASQUALE BUBA,
WILLIAM GOLDENBERG, DOV HOENIG, TOM ROLF **MUSIC** ELLIOT GOLDENTHAL
PRODUCTION MICHAEL MANN, ART LINSON for FORWARD PASS PRODUCTION,
REGENCY ENTERPRISES, LION BRAND FILM
STARRING ROBERT DE NIRO (Neil McCauley), AMY BRENNEMAN (Eady), AL PACINO
(Vincent Hanna), DIANE VENORA (Justine Hanna), VAL KILMER (Chris Shiherlis),
ASHLEY JUDD (Charlene Shiherlis), JON VOIGHT (Nate), TOM SIZEMORE
(Michael Cheritto), MYKELTI WILLIAMSON (Drucker), WES STUDI (Casals),
KEVIN GAGE (Waingro)

"I'm alone, I'm not lonely."

Neil McCauley (Robert De Niro) and his team – Chris, Cheritto, and Trejo – are preparing their next strike. They need a fifth man to make sure it all goes smoothly. They take on a guy by the name of Waingro (Kevin Gage), who messes up the job. The team manages to escape with the loot but now they are wanted for robbery and murder, and the police are on their trails. Waingro shot one of the guards dead just for fun, and it's not too long till we realize that he is a psychopath and a serial killer too. When McCauley tries to get rid of him, he vanishes without trace.

Michael Mann depicts McCauley's gang as a close-knit group of conspirators who are absolute professionals at what they do. The armored car robbery is carried out with the utmost precision, and they use extreme brutality whenever it's necessary.

A new detective, Vincent Hanna (Al Pacino), is assigned to the investigation of the case. One tiny detail and a seemingly crazy story told by an informer put Hanna on the trail of gang member Cheritto, and he unwittingly leads him to the others. As he has no proof, he has all of them shadowed.

During a break-in, McCauley realizes he is being watched. He sets a trap for his pursuer to find out who he is up against. The team pretends to prepare a new heist and lead Hanna and his men to an abandoned part of the harbor where they make their escape and then observe their pursuers at their leisure.

In *Heat*, Michael Mann is concerned with much more than a simple game of cat and mouse. He shows us single combat between two equally matched opponents and does not shrink from drama and emotions in the depiction of his heroes.

Heat also tells the story of three relationships. McCauley falls in love with the shy graphic designer Eady, Vincent and Justine Hanna's marriage breaks down and almost destroys the life of their daughter Lauren, and Chris and Charlene Shiherlis's marriage is put to a test where there is no second chance. One of the most memorable and understated scenes is the McCauley team family dinner. It looks for all the world like a normal dinner party where couples enjoy sharing an evening with friends. This quiet moment forms a shocking contrast with the violence of the other side of their lives.

McCauley and his team want to carry out a last robbery with which they will make enough to be able to retire, even though they know that the police are hot on their heels.

Heat is great actors' cinema. McCauley and Hanna are outsiders. They live according to their own principles and follow their own code of honor. McCauley repeats over and over that he cannot afford to have any ties in his job, but his actions tell a different story. When he chooses to go back and avenge his friends rather than escape to safety at the

2

"We're sitting here like a coupla regular fellas.
You do what you do. I do what I gotta do." Vincent Hanna in *Heat*

1 Ready to take life as it comes: break-in specialist Neal McCauley (Robert De Niro) knows that plans can go wrong and that lives can be ruined.

2 A great moment in film history: Al Pacino as police officer Vincent Hanna …

3 … and Robert De Niro as burglar sit at the same table for the first time.

end of the movie, he is fully conscious of the danger he is in. His main motivation is loyalty.

One of the earliest mentions of the *Heat* project can be found in an interview with Michael Mann (*Film Comment*, 1983) which he gave shortly after the completion of his horror movie *The Keep* (1983). He talks about a screenplay called *Heat* that he wrote and loves, but doesn't want to direct himself. Clearly Mann decided that the project was too important to hand on to someone else and he eventually made two film versions of the same story.

The first work based on the *Heat* screenplay was a television film called *L.A. Takedown* (1989) which was made as a pilot for *Made in L.A.*, a television series which was then never actually made. *L.A. Takedown* is like an early sketch for the feature film as we know it. The basic structure of the movie is already there and many key scenes are already well developed, including the famous cafe scene where Al Pacino meets Robert De Niro. But the earlier version doesn't have the emotional depth of the feature film, nor the uncomfortable feeling that we are watching extraordinary people caught up in an oppressively ordered world. Six years later work on the actual movie started. Spurred on by the worldwide success of his film of James Fenimore Cooper's *The Last of the Mohicans* (1992), Mann began work on his magnum opus.

Mann's production is emotional and dramatic without being exaggerated. The scene where the dying and the living reach out their hands to each other at the end of the movie is one of cinema's truly great moments.

OM

"A guy once told me, don't let yourself get attached to anything you're not willing to walk out on, if you feel the heat around the corner in 30 seconds flat." Neil McCauley in *Heat*

EDWARD BUNKER Author and bit part actor Edward Bunker (1933–2005) first became known to a wider cinema audience as Mr. Blue in Quentin Tarantino's *Reservoir Dogs* (1991). A serious criminal with many convictions to his name, Bunker had been known to crime fiction fans since the publication of his extraordinary debut novel *No Beast so Fierce* in 1973. Bunker was still in prison at the time. When this masterpiece of prison literature was filmed five years later by Ulu Grosbard as *Straight Time* (1978), Bunker not only made his acting debut but was also criminal advisor to the production. This is a role he has played for many prison films since then, including Andrej Kontschalowsky's Oscar-nominated *Runaway Train* (1985), for which Bunker also co-wrote the screenplay. Edward Bunker also worked in an advisory capacity on Martin Bell's *American Heart* (1992) and Michael Mann's *Heat* (1995). His final screen appearance, soon after which he died during a cancer operation, was in *The Longest Yard* (2005) with Adam Sandler.

4 Jon Voight as Nate, the man in the background. The character was designed to pay homage to the writer Edward Bunker, who earned his living in the 1960s by planning break-ins.

5 One of the film's many mirror motifs: the searching look penetrates the inner person.

6 Wherever his gaze turns, it always lights upon himself: Val Kilmer as burglar Chris Shiherlis.

7 The street as battlefield. McCauley and Chris Shiherlis shoot their way to freedom after a holdup.

RUMBLE IN THE BRONX
HUNG FAN KUI

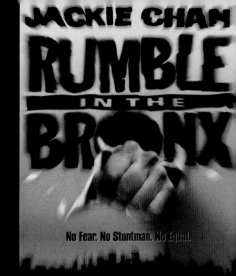

1995 – HONG KONG – 90 MIN. – ACTION FILM, COMEDY, MARTIAL ARTS FILM
DIRECTOR STANLEY TONG (*1960)
SCREENPLAY EDWARD TANG, FIBE MA **DIRECTOR OF PHOTOGRAPHY** JINGLE MA **EDITING** PETER CHEUNG
MUSIC J. PETER ROBINSON, JONATHAN WONG **PRODUCTION** RAYMOND CHOW, LEONHARD HO,
BARBIE TUNG for GOLDEN HARVEST
STARRING JACKIE CHAN (Ah Keung), ANITA MUI (Elaine), FRANÇOISE YIP (Nancy), BILL TUNG
(Uncle Bill), MARC AKERSTREAM (Tony), GARVIN CROSS (Angelo), MORGAN LAM (Danny),
KRIS LORD (White Tiger), AILEN SIT (Gang Member), CHAN MAN SING (Gang Member)

"If you got the guts, drop the gun."

"Something's always happening here, that's New York for you." Keung (Jackie Chan) has just arrived from Hong Kong and he finds the American east coast metropolis run-down and dangerous. At first his uncle's words reassure him, but many adventures await him in the city and they're not all going to be fun.

Keung is a young man who has come over for the wedding of his Uncle Bill (Bill Tung), and on his very first night in America he has to defend the elegant white stretch limousine that Bill has borrowed for the occasion. Bill sells his supermarket in the Bronx and goes off on his honeymoon. Elaine (Anita Mui) buys the store, but still needs Bill's nephew's help and the very next day Keung discovers members of a biker gang raiding the place. He stops them and beats them up. After many chase scenes and fights between the gang and its leader Tony and Keung, the appearance of another gangster mob forces the rivals to pool their forces. Their new mutual enemies are unscrupulous

diamond thieves with automatic rifles who make Tony's boys look like harmless school kids. In the meantime, Keung also makes friends in New York; he meets little Danny (Morgan Lam) who is in a wheelchair and his sister Nancy (Françoise Yip), the girlfriend of gangster leader Tony.

In most Jackie Chan films the story is of secondary importance, but in *Rumble in the Bronx* he gets down to the essentials even faster than normal. The economy of the movie is remarkable. In the space of three minutes Keung is established in New York, he is set up as a loveable character and skilled fighter, and we have also met his uncle and the boy in the wheelchair. Moments later his troubles with the biker gang begins, they get down to business and the carefully choreographed fighting begins. Whether Jackie Chan runs, jumps, climbs over high fences, or water skis in sneakers, whether he fights using refrigerators, shopping carts, or chairs as shields and weapons – his element is still the material world and he moves effortlessly

1

2

"I love action but I hate violence. For this reason, I think this choreographical solution is the best. In Asia I have become the children's idol and I do not want to set a bad example." Jackie Chan in *Abendzeitung*

JACKIE CHAN – ASIA'S SUPERSTAR He does all his stunts himself and during the closing credits shows what went wrong in the process. Unique superstar Jackie Chan was born in 1954. He learned his amazing physical skills at a Peking opera school in Hong Kong, where he was sent at the age of seven. Since his debut in 1971 he has made movie after movie, since 1980 he has also directed films, and the combination of martial arts and comedy is an idea he originally developed himself. Chan's role models are the cinema's great comedians to whom he regularly pays homage, like Harold Lloyd, whose famous clock tower scene he refers to in *Project A* (1983) and Buster Keaton, from whose *Steamboat Bill, Jr.* (1928) he borrows a scene in *Project A, Part 2* (1987). *Rumble in the Bronx* brought the Asian superstar fame and fortune in the USA, as well as an MTV Lifetime Achievement Award. On that occasion Quentin Tarantino said: "If I could choose which actor to be, I would choose Jackie Chan."

1 Keung (Jackie Chan) doesn't use guns, the most he ever uses as a weapon is a ski.

2 Keung dispatches the unscrupulous diamond robbers as promptly …

3 … as the louts from Tony's gangster mob.

4 In 1996 *Rumble in the Bronx* was awarded Best Film at the Hong Kong Film Awards, and Jackie Chan and Stanley Tong Best Action Choreography.

5 In with the wrong crowd: Nancy (Françoise Yip), little Danny's sister.

3

through it. Speed, flexibility, and elegance dominate his films, but the fights are never really brutal and Chan's boyish charm and slapstick humor take away their violent edge. That said, *Rumble in the Bronx* is a movie of unusual extravagance. It rejoices in destructive orgies, like the complete destruction of a supermarket while its owner sits on the toilet. It allows itself the liberty of showing things which have precious little to do with the plot but look good, such as the truck loaded with balls which topples from a multi-story parking garage. And it is full of breathtaking chase scenes, like the one where a hovercraft races through busy streets and over a golf course until the bad guy is finally run over. He survives, if a little shaken.

As in all his films, Jackie Chan does the stunts himself. He broke his ankle jumping onto the moving hovercraft, but then hid the plaster with his trouser leg and carried on. *Rumble in the Bronx* was his breakthrough in America. The movie was made in Vancouver in English, as US audiences don't like dubbed films. The American distributor New Line Cinema shortened the original 105 minute version to 90 minutes by shedding scenes like a wedding duet and a moralizing speech by Chan, and launched the film with a massive advertising campaign. It made $10 million in its first week.

HJK

4

5

MISSION: IMPOSSIBLE

1996 – USA – 110 MIN. – ACTION FILM, THRILLER

DIRECTOR BRIAN DE PALMA (*1940)

SCREENPLAY ROBERT TOWNE, DAVID KOEPP, based on characters from BRUCE GELLER'S TV series of the same name DIRECTOR OF PHOTOGRAPHY STEPHEN H. BURUM EDITING PAUL HIRSCH

MUSIC DANNY ELFMAN, LALO SCHIFRIN (theme tune) PRODUCTION TOM CRUISE, PAULA WAGNER for PARAMOUNT PICTURES

STARRING TOM CRUISE (Ethan Hunt), JON VOIGHT (Jim Phelps), EMMANUELLE BÉART (Claire), KRISTIN SCOTT THOMAS (Sarah Davies), VANESSA REDGRAVE (Max), JEAN RENO (Krieger), VING RHAMES (Luther), HENRY CZERNY (Kittridge), EMILIO ESTEVEZ (Electronics Expert), DALE DYE (Frank Barnes)

"Dear boy, you are a sport."

Jim Phelps (Jon Voight) of the IMF (Impossible Mission Force) is supposed to be neutralizing an enemy agent in Kiev. He succeeds thanks to the help of his wife Claire (Emmanuelle Béart) and his colleague Ethan Hunt (Tom Cruise), who specializes in disguise. He gets home to find the next assignment waiting for him – a traitor called Golitsyn must be found and stopped. Phelps sets a trap for him at the American embassy in Prague: during a reception he gives Golitsyn the opportunity to steal a list of names of double agents. Claire and Ethan also take part along with several other younger agents.

At the beginning it seems as if everything is going to plan and Golitsyn is soon unmasked, but gradually, successive members of the team are put out of action. At first we think only Ethan survives the trap that has been set for him, but later we realize that Claire has also survived. The failed trap

means that Ethan becomes the CIA's prime suspect, and he is accused of being a double agent, especially as the actual aim of the operation was to unmask the traitors in their own ranks.

Ethan is able to escape but knows he will only be able to prove his innocence by finding the real culprit. He searches Jim Phelps's apartment and finds clues to a mysterious contact person called Max. Ethan meets up with Claire again who wants to join in his investigations and find out who murdered her husband. Max turns out to be an elderly lady who deals in top security information and is ready to pay a large sum of money for the real list of double agents' names. That list however only exists in the central CIA computer, and to get the data Ethan has to break in. He is helped by Luther (Ving Rhames), a technical genius and former CIA employee, and Krieger (Jean Reno), an enigmatic killer.

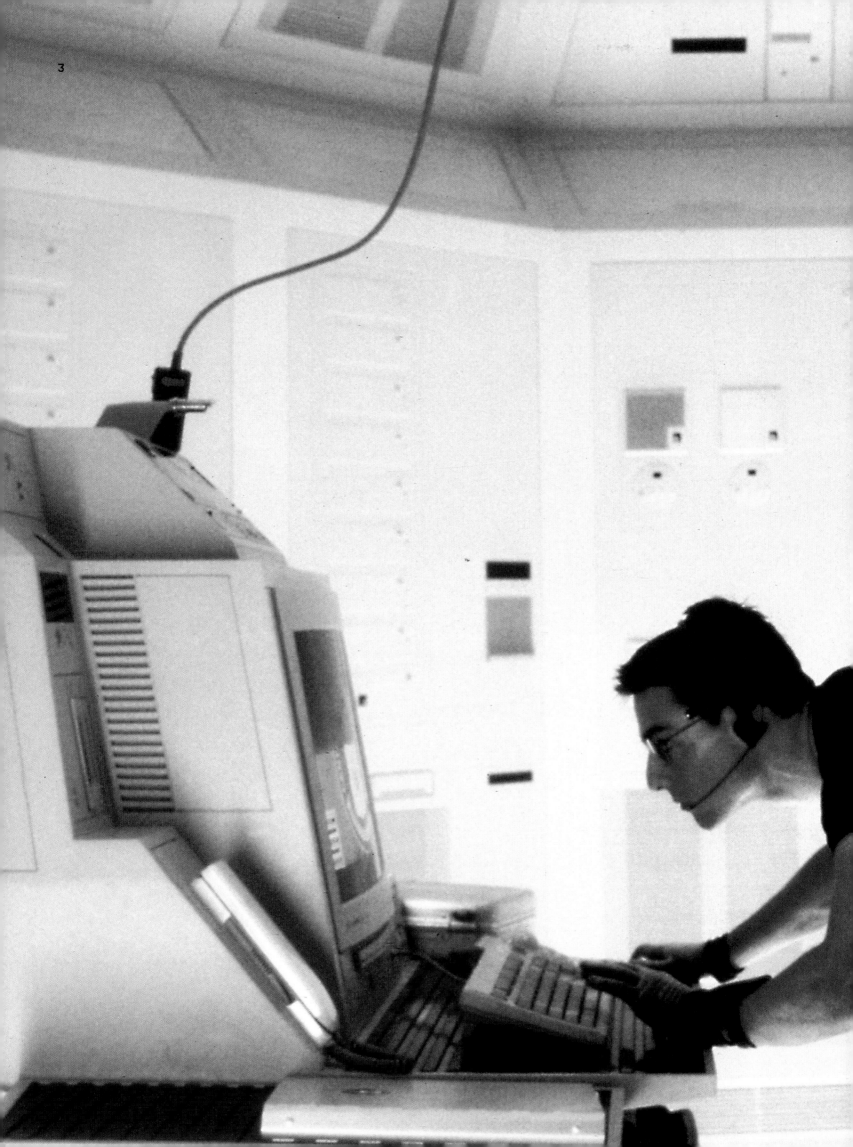

The break-in and data theft are successful. Ethan, Claire, Luther, and Krieger hide in London where Ethan sees his parents being arrested on the television news. To protect them, he leaves his hiding place and turns himself in to the CIA. Jim Phelps, who everyone thought was dead, unexpectedly reappears.

Mission: Impossible is a typically '90s high-concept cinema, with Tom Cruise in some breathtaking action scenes. The opening scene is typical: Cruise blows up a restaurant that has massive aquariums built into its walls. He hangs on a thin line over a floor alarmed with a hypersensitive movement detector. Finally he clings to the roof of a high-speed train which is being followed by a helicopter into a tunnel.

But Brian De Palma's movie is also open to a second interpretation, and the breathless action sequences can also be seen as a meditation on the nature of images and the idea of deception as cinema's main inspiration. Spectators of *Mission: Impossible* are constantly forced to ask themselves what they are really watching, and wonder whether it is simply another trick. De Palma is brilliant at directing scenes where at first we believe what we see and then have to admit that we have been deceived. The central scene of the movie and its decisive moment is the meeting between Ethan Hunt and Jim Phelps – the only two figures who were taken from the TV series. Ethan and Jim discuss the things that have gone wrong, and we see individual moments again in flashback. At first the consequences and events seem clear, but the longer the discussion continues, the more the actual truth emerges: in fact, none of the images are to be trusted. They are all part of a cunningly conceived plot, which is uncovered step-by-step before our very eyes.

OM

JEAN RENO Jean Reno (*1948) made his cinema debut in Raúl Ruiz's *L'Hypothèse du tableau volé* (*The Hypothesis of The Stolen Painting*, 1978) after which he appeared in masterpieces such as Bertrand Blier's *Notre histoire* (*Our Story / Separate Rooms*, 1984). His big breakthrough came in 1987 with *The Big Blue* (*Le Grand Bleu*, 1987) and he went on to collaborate with the director Luc Besson on several occasions. Comedies like *Les Visiteurs* (*The Visitors*, 1993) made Reno a superstar in his home country, while his role as a melancholy hired assassin in Besson's *Leon* (*Léon / The Professional*, 1994) brought him international fame. He has since appeared mainly in thrillers and action movies such as *Mission: Impossible* (1996), *Ronin* (1998), *The Da Vinci Code* (2006), and *22 Bullets* (*L'immortel*, 2010). He enjoyed notable success with the two parts of crime thriller *The Crimson Rivers* (*Les Rivières Pourpres*, 2000 and 2004).

4   5

"Mission: Impossible makes of Brian De Palma the key analyst of the transformation of our society into a civilization of image and technology."

Cahiers du cinéma

6

1 Tom Cruise is Ethan Hunt: a man of many masks, whose true character can't be read in his face.

2 A key scene in the movie: Ethan Hunt blows up the aquariums in a restaurant and saves himself with an almighty leap. The reality behind the reflective surfaces is as misleading as it is hard to grasp – a perfect metaphor for Brian De Palma's amoral universe of betrayal.

3 One of the film's most striking images: Ethan Hunt gains access to the CIA's central computer.

4 Jean Reno plays mercenary agent Krieger.

5 Face to face: it doesn't take long for Hunt and Krieger to stop trusting each other.

6 Emmanuelle Béart plays Claire, wife of Hunt's boss Jim Phelps (Jon Voight).

7 The computer specialist Luther played by Ving Rhames proved to be a key figure in the film: he also plays a decisive role in John Woo's sequel.

7

SHALL WE DANCE?
SHALL WE DANSU?

1996 – JAPAN – 119 MIN. – COMEDY
DIRECTOR MASAYUKI SUO (*1956)
SCREENPLAY MASAYUKI SUO **DIRECTOR OF PHOTOGRAPHY** NAOKI KAYANO **EDITING** JUN'ICHI KIKUCHI
MUSIC YOSHIKAZU SUO **PRODUCTION** SHOJI MASUI, YASUYOSHI TOKUMA, YUJI OGATA for DAIEI,
NIPPON TELEVISION NETWORK
STARRING KOJI YAKUSHO (Shohei Sugiyama), TAMIYO KUSAKARI (Mai Kishikawa),
NAOTO TAKENAKA (Tomio Aoki), ERIKO WATANABE (Toyoko Takahashi), AKIRA EMOTO
(Toru Miwa), YU TOKUI (Tokichi Hattori), HIROMASA TAGUCHI (Masahiro Tanaka),
REIKO KUSAMURA (Tamako Tamura), HIDEKO HARA (Masako Sugiyama),
SHUICHIRO MORIYAMA (Ryo Kishikawa)

"Slow, slow, quick quick slow."

Shohei Sugiyama (Koji Yakusho) leads the sober life of an average Japanese citizen. He is married with a daughter, owns his own home in the suburbs and has an office job in the city. But he still feels unfulfilled. One day on his way home in the train, he happens to see a woman standing at the window in the upper story of a dance studio. The next day he sees her again. and soon he is waiting impatiently every day for the moment when his train will pass her building. One evening he can resist the temptation no longer and he gets out and goes to the studio. The beautiful stranger – whose name is Mai (Tamiyo Kusakari) – is a teacher there. Social dancing is not the done thing in Japan, but Shohei steels himself and puts his name down for a beginners' course. All he really wants is to get to know Mai. However, although his efforts in this direction fail, he begins to make real progress as a dancer after his first clumsy attempts. Gradually he is gripped by dance fever and his whole outlook on life begins to change, so much so that his wife becomes suspicious and engages a private detective to investigate the source of her husband's renewed vigor.

Back in 1937, Mark Sandrich directed *Shall We Dance?*, one of Hollywood's greatest musical successes. Fred Astaire and Ginger Rogers danced their way into the public's heart in the main roles, and for a few moments America could forget that its daily life was still overshadowed by the consequences of the Depression. Masayuki Suo's film of the same name was a smash hit in Japan in 1996 when economic recession hit the country. Decades of economic euphoria had come to an end, and more and more people began to question Japan's legendary work ethos and look instead for ways of satisfying their individual needs. This social change is reflected in Suo's charming comedy. Unlike the Astaire film, Suo's movie does not use professional dancers to distract his audiences from their daily cares. Instead it shows how an ordinary family man in midlife crisis discovers a love of dance that lifts him out of his depression. Shohei Sugiyama is a figure familiar primarily from European and American movies, but with whom many Japanese were able to identify.

The shape and narrative form of Suo's pictures are strongly influenced by the conventions of the Western. His references however are often ironic as he plays on the Americanization of Japanese culture. Shohei is attracted by a woman in a window, a motif which has a long tradition in European and American film and has become something of a stale cliché. The mysterious beauty usually turns out to be a femme fatale, who threatens the man with sexual obsession and almost always with existential ruin, whereas in Suo's comedy, she turns out to be a comparatively harmless dancer who teaches the hero the simple lesson that there is pleasure in life outside work. Shohei's marriage still seems to be in danger, but only because he has to keep his dance course secret from his wife and work colleagues.

The drama and comedy of *Shall We Dance?* come above all from the heightened absurdity of daily routine at a time of national crisis. Despite his frequent ironic asides, Suo never fails to take his characters and their longing seriously – although their lives often seem banal, he gives them a heroic aspect. This opens the way for wonderful things at the movie's end.

JH

FRED ASTAIRE Fred Astaire was born in 1899 in Omaha and died in 1987 in Los Angeles. He appeared on the stage as an actor, dancer, and singer from his earliest youth. His film career began in 1933 during the most glamorous period of the Hollywood musical. Despite his skinny build and unusual looks Fred Astaire became one of Hollywood's most popular stars over the years that followed, with the help of his partner Ginger Rogers. He was famous above all for his extraordinary and incomparable dancing talent, which was a combination of precision, versatility, and elegance. He was also very popular as a singer. Astaire made his last appearance as a singer and dancer in Francis Ford Coppola's *Finian's Rainbow* (1968) but continued acting to a ripe old age. His most famous musicals include *Top Hawt* (1935), *Shall We Dance?* (1937), *Easter Parade* (1948), and *Daddy Long Legs* (1955).

1 And all your dreams will come true: Shohei and Mai (Koji Yakusho and Tamiyo Kusakari) find common ground in dancing.

2 The beautiful dance teacher shows the way.

3 Carried away by the music: at Mai's side Shohei really flies across the dance floor.

4 Beautiful and unattainable: the mysterious Mai arouses Shohei's passion.

5 Shohei is transformed from a run-of-the-mill pencil pusher into an elegant dancer.

6 Laborious first steps: at the beginners' course Shohei and his fellows are treading on unfamiliar ground.

"The movie has a great deal of zest and charm, and Yakusho gets so exactly that crest of melancholy that is a man's early 40s, until he decides to go for another kind of life, that the movie is infinitely touching." *The Washington Post*

7   Gripped by dance fever, Shohei adds unexpected élan to a normal day at the office.

8   The Japanese reveal their individual needs: spellbound, Shohei watches the dance teacher's demonstration with his comrades-in-arms.

WHEN WE WERE KINGS

1974/1996 – USA – 87 MIN. – DOCUMENTARY
DIRECTOR LEON GAST (*1936)
SCREENPLAY LEON GAST DIRECTOR OF PHOTOGRAPHY MARYSE ALBERTI, PAUL GOLDSMITH,
KEVIN KEATIN, ALBERT MAYSLES, RODERICK YOUNG EDITING LEON GAST,
TAYLOR HACKFORD, JEFFREY LEVY-HINTE, KEITH ROBINSON MUSIC WAYNE HENDERSON,
TABU LEY PRODUCTION DAVID SONNENBERG, LEON GAST, TAYLOR HACKFORD,
VIKRAM JAYANTI, KEITH ROBINSON for UFA NON FICTION
STARRING MUHAMMAD ALI, GEORGE FOREMAN, DON KING, JAMES BROWN, B. B. KING,
MIRIAM MAKEBA, MOBUTU SESE SEKO, SPIKE LEE, NORMAN MAILER,
GEORGE PLIMPTON
ACADEMY AWARDS 1997 OSCAR for BEST DOCUMENTARY

"Say it loud, I'm black and proud."

Muhammad Ali was a rapper. His speech is poetic, melodic, full of images and rhymes. He insulted his opponents, humiliated them, and predicted their downfall in the ring ("dissing" as this is known among rappers today). His charisma attracted people who went away inspired – that would be enough for any rap musician.

Documentary maker Leon Gast shows Ali as a rapper, he lets him do the talking and puts a drumbeat under his words at the beginning of the movie; he also shows sport and the music of artists like James Brown and B. B. King as part of the Black Consciousness Movement. Gast documents the legendary fight between Ali and the then world champion George Foreman in Kinshasa, Zaire, today's Congo.

As a result of his refusal to fight in the Vietnam War, Ali received a five-year prison term in 1967 and lost the world champion title of the World Boxing Association (WBA). In 1970 his sentence was lifted and Ali set about trying to win back the title. The decisive fight between the 32-year-old and Foreman, who was six years younger, was a huge event, not just because Foreman had a unique record to defend (37 KO victories and no defeats since he turned professional) and Ali was considered an aging sportsman in comparison. The circumstances were also spectacular: the boxing promoter Don King offered both Ali and Foreman five million dollars. He cast around for the total of ten million that he needed and finally received it from Mobutu Sese Seko,

military dictator of Zaire. The great fight, which quickly became known as "the rumble in the jungle," was supposed to take place on September 25, 1974, in the capital Kinshasa. The three days preceding the fight were reserved for a big music festival with James Brown, B. B. King, Miriam Makeba, and The Spinners. The festival took place but the fight had to be postponed by six weeks as Foreman injured his eye during training and had to wait until it healed. In this six weeks, most of the documentary recordings that Gast filmed with Muhammad Ali were made.

Gast's Ali is a fascinating figure, and the director gives him plenty of opportunity to play up to the camera. What jumps out to the eye is Ali's tremendous musicality, which is made all the clearer by the way Gast sandwiches the Ali scenes between montages of the music festival. His speech, his movements, and his fighting are filled with rhythm, and as Ali keeps repeating himself, he's going to dance, dance, dance, so that Foreman won't even be able to find him in the ring. That was pure bluff, as the pictures of the fight prove. In interviews with the writer Norman Mailer and George Plimpton, who were there at the time, the situation before and during the fight is analysed over and over, and Ali's obvious fear of the giant Foreman is compared to his fighting strategy.

Gast finds wonderful rhythm for his images and the film is just as musical as its protagonist. Eyewitness statements, interviews from the time,

"This film is more besides being a successful movie about Muhammad Ali – it is a film about Ali's skill at combining sport and politics and in so doing becoming the epitome of a people's hero."

Frankfurter Allgemeine Zeitung

2

3

BOXING AT THE MOVIES Boxing has often been used as a film subject over the years, both in documentaries and feature films. In the early days of cinema, boxing was ideal for the static cameras used at the time, as it offered lots of movement in an enclosed space. It is a sport that has remained popular with cinema audiences, giving scope for rags to riches stories about people who box their way to the top, like John Garfield as the Jewish boy in *Body and Soul* (1947) and Sylvester Stallone as a gangster's small-time hired fighter in *Rocky* (1977). *Rocky* and its five sequels have remained the prototype of the boxer who loses in the ring but comes out on top, finding himself instead. Many biopics have made boxing idols into screen heroes: the American middle weight champion Jake La Motta played by Robert De Niro in *Raging Bull* (1980); Muhammad Ali, memorialized by Michael Mann in *Ali* (2001); and Max Schmeling in the movie of the same name in 2010. There have also been many documentaries, including *Muhammad Ali, The Greatest* (1964–1974) and *Klitschko* (2010).

1   Did he always believe he would win? In the ring, Ali seemed to have occasional doubts about himself.

2   Two icons of black culture: Muhammad Ali and soul star James Brown.

3   Ali won the Zairians' hearts with elaborate descriptions of his preparations, loud-mouthed threats against Foreman – and by kissing babies, just like a politician.

4   "Ali Bomaye!" – "Ali, kill him!" A thousand voices spur Muhammad Ali on.

5   Advance announcements that he would dance in the ring were a ruse – Ali let Foreman box himself into exhaustion.

archive material, and music scenes are bound together in a harmonious whole – and the result is a gripping portrait of a genuine idol.

The film took decades to take on its finished form. Gast had already made several music movies (including *The Dead*, 1977, on The Grateful Dead) and originally was only supposed to document the music festival. When the fight was canceled, he decided to stay on in Zaire and film. He used 100,000 meters of film, and needed nearly 15 years to get the money together to develop it all. The editing took another couple of years. His filmmaker friend Taylor Hackford filmed the additional interviews with Mailer, Plimpton, and the Black Cinema director Spike Lee, to complete Gast's material. Almost 22 years after the filming began, *When We Were Kings* was given its first showing at the Sundance Film Festival. HJK

FARGO ♟♟

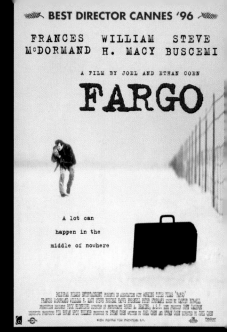

1996 – USA – 98 MIN. – CRIME FILM

DIRECTOR JOEL COEN (*1954)

SCREENPLAY JOEL COEN, ETHAN COEN **DIRECTOR OF PHOTOGRAPHY** ROGER DEAKINS **EDITING** ETHAN COEN, JOEL COEN (AS RODERICK JAYNES) **MUSIC** CARTER BURWELL **PRODUCTION** ETHAN COEN for WORKING TITLE FILMS

STARRING FRANCES MCDORMAND (Marge Gunderson), STEVE BUSCEMI (Carl Showalter), PETER STORMARE (Gaear Grimsrud), WILLIAM H. MACY (Jerry Lundegaard), HARVE PRESNELL (Wade Gustafson), KRISTIN RUDRÜD (Jean Lundegaard), JOHN CARROLL LYNCH (Norm Gunderson), TONY DENMAN (Scotty Lundegaard), LARRY BRANDENBURG (Stan Grossman), BRUCE BOHNE (Lou)

IFF CANNES 1996 BEST DIRECTOR (Joel Coen)

ACADEMY AWARDS 1997 OSCARS for BEST ACTRESS (Frances McDormand) and BEST ORIGINAL SCREENPLAY (Joel Coen, Ethan Coen)

"Jean and Scotty never have to worry about money."

Minnesota, 1987. Two tiny lights appear in the distance, vanish suddenly, and return somewhat larger. They are the headlights of a car in a hilly landscape. Winter, the movie seems to suggest, is the only possible season in Minnesota. The Coen brothers have a nasty story to tell. Car salesman Jerry Lundegaard (William H. Macy) is heavily in debt and has come up with a cunning plan to solve his problem: he's going to have his wife Jean (Kristin Rudrüd) kidnapped and demand a ransom from his father-in-law. Carl Showalter (Steve Buscemi) and Gaear Grimsrud (Peter Stormare) are to do the dirty work for him, and he'll pocket the one million dollars ransom money that he wants his rich father-in-law Wade Gustafson (Harve Presnell) to pay. He tells his accomplices that it's only a matter of 80,000 dollars, of which they'll get half for their pains. The two henchmen are total caricatures, Gaear in particular coming across as a complete fool. Their stupidity means that the abduction scene, where they snatch Jean from the shower, is a combination of the comic and

the macabre, and cinema connoisseurs can hardly fail to recognize a parody of Hitchcock's *Psycho* (1960). Subsequently however the plan goes badly awry and the story becomes both brutal and grisly. When Carl and Gaear try to take Jean to the hiding place in one of Jerry's cars and are held up close to Brainerd by a police patrol, they kill a policeman and two tourists. Gaear seems devoid of any feeling, first killing Jean and then disposing of Carl.

Since it's one of her officers who has been murdered, the heavily pregnant police chief of Brainerd Marge Gunderson (Frances McDormand) decides to get personally involved in the hunt for the killers. Her husband Norm meanwhile paints nature pictures for a postage stamp picture competition. When Marge finds the remaining killer he is busy stuffing the corpse of his partner in crime through a woodchip shredder. He tries to run away and Marge shoots him dead. One of Norm's pictures is selected to go on a postage stamp – the three-cent stamp – which is only needed when postage rates are raised

Fargo is a hard movie to categorize. It is grotesque and definitely absurd, but above all it is eerie. Cruelty and brutality become forces in their own right, and the story ends in an unexpected bloodbath because the protagonists have so little control over the situation. In *Fargo* everything moves a little more slowly. Not just because the world is deep in snow and each movement requires three times the usual effort, but also because the people of Minnesota, largely descendants of Scandinavian immigrants, are generally slower. Slow in the sense of speaking in a strange provincial drawl, and slow on the uptake. All of which has a role to play in this story about the reality of crime and the ability of evil to assert itself. It is a movie which aims infallibly for the worst-case scenario with pessimistic Protestant determinism. The criminals are greedy, stupid, and nervous, the police are powerless to do anything but trudge after them and pick up the pieces, counting the corpses and finally making a useless arrest.

Fargo is the Coen brothers' coolest, most reserved movie to date, partly because it is so unspectacular optically. The colors are simple, almost monochrome, the music is practically minimalist, and the dialogues are uncommunicative poetry intensified by the grinding singsong of the local dialect. The Coen brothers were born in Minnesota and *Fargo* is a grotesque and gruesome homage to their homeland. OM

WILLIAM H. MACY A character actor and one of the most interesting faces since the '90s, Macy is particularly convincing as a small-town character whose livelihood is in danger, like the desperate car salesman who turns criminal in *Fargo* (1996). His excellent performance as the model family man who discovers the Nazi within him in *Pleasantville* (1998) is as memorable as his role in *Magnolia* (1999) as a former quiz show child prodigy who feels unloved. Macy's brilliance lies above all in his capacity to dignify even the most ridiculous figures. An excellent example is his role in *The Cooler* (2003) as a casino worker whose job is to bring bad luck to the gamblers.

1 Dim petty criminals with a tendency to overreact: Steve Buscemi as Carl Showalter and Peter Stormare as Gaear Grimsrud.

2 The facial expression of the film: grim determination bordering on the grotesque.

3 After a meal like that the day can only turn out well: one of the many Minnesotan-cum-Scandinavian idiosyncrasies that turn the film into a parody of a sentimental regional film.

3

"Fargo is undoubtedly our most traditional film. It's also the first time that we've used a news story."

Ethan Coen in *Cahiers du cinéma*

4 A sticky end: stupidity and greed cause events to escalate.

FROM DUSK TILL DAWN

1996 – USA – 108 MIN. – HORROR FILM, COMEDY
DIRECTOR ROBERT RODRIGUEZ (*1968)
SCREENPLAY QUENTIN TARANTINO, based on an idea by ROBERT KURTZMAN
DIRECTOR OF PHOTOGRAPHY GUILLERMO NAVARRO EDITING ROBERT RODRIGUEZ MUSIC GRAEME REVELL
PRODUCTION GIANNI NUNNARI, MEIR TEPER for A BAND APART, MIRAMAX, LOS HOOLIGANS
PRODUCTIONS
STARRING HARVEY KEITEL (Jacob Fuller), GEORGE CLOONEY (Seth Gecko),
QUENTIN TARANTINO (Richard Gecko), JULIETTE LEWIS (Kate Fuller), ERNEST LIU
(Scott Fuller), SALMA HAYEK (Santanico Pandemonium), CHEECH MARIN (Border Guard /
Chet Pussy / Carlos), DANNY TREJO (Razor Charlie), TOM SAVINI (Sex Machine),
FRED WILLIAMSON (Frost)

"All right, vampire killers – let's kill some fucking vampires!"

Mexico is so near and yet so far... The Gecko brothers are on the run, and Mexico is their only hope. The border is swarming with Texan policemen who close off every possible route into the promised land, but cool gangsters like the Geckos (George Clooney and Quentin Tarantino) shoot first and ask questions later: they currently have 16 dead men, a bank robbery, and a bombed-out store on their conscience. Jacob (Harvey Keitel), a former pastor, happens to cross their path, on holiday with his kids in a camper van. With his unwilling help the brothers smuggle themselves over the border by hiding inside the bodywork of the camper. The Geckos promise that they will set their hostages free as soon as they find Carlos, their Mexican contact man. They drink to their freedom with the family in an exotic, eccentric trucker bar called "Titty Twister." Too late, they realize that all five of them have landed in the pit of hell: the barman and the snake dancers suddenly turn into bloodthirsty vampires before their very eyes.

From Dusk Till Dawn is a double feature, a double whammy combining two completely different movies in one show. It begins like a gangster film and then completely out of the blue is transformed into a comic-like splatter

film where blood hits the screen in bucketfuls and all kinds of limbs fly through the air. While director Robert Rodriguez (*Desperado*, 1995) is allowed to spread gore to his heart's content in the fight scene in the "Titty Twister" bar, the first half of the movie is clearly the work of Quentin Tarantino. Screenwriter and main actor, Mr. "Pulp Fiction" himself clearly had a strong influence on the look and the tone of the movie, from the gangsters' laid-back remarks ("Fight now, cry later") to insane dialogue like "Where are we going?" – "Mexico." – "What's in Mexico?" – "Mexicans."

Both Rodriguez and Tarantino love quotations and constantly refer to their cinematic models, so the characters eat "Kahuna Burger" and smoke the "Red Apple" cigarettes that we already know from *Pulp Fiction* (1994). "Precinct 13," written on a T-shirt, refers to John Carpenter's film *Assault on Precinct 13* (1976), from which the directors also steal one dialogue word for word. They play this self-reflexive game so comprehensively that *From Dusk Till Dawn* is like a patchwork movie cobbled together from bits of other films.

It takes an especially bizarre twist when the figures begin to question their own roles. In a short break in the action, everyone who hasn't been

5

6

1 Wherever the Gecko brothers show up, there's sure to be blood. To prepare themselves for their roles as brothers, George Clooney and Quentin Tarantino spent whole nights wandering the clubs of Los Angeles.

2 The Titty Twister, the wildest dive this side of the Rio Grande. What the Gecko brothers do not know is that the truckers and bikers bar is located right on top of an enormous vampires grave.

3 Bar customer Sex Machine shows what's hiding in his trousers. Tom Savini is an expert in bloodthirsty films: he has written books on the art of makeup in horror movies, and even produced a few such films himself, as well as taking part now and then as an actor. He can be found, for instance, in *Martin* (1977) by George A. Romero.

QUENTIN TARANTINO Tarantino had just turned 31 when he won the most important trophies in the movie business for *Pulp Fiction* (1994): the Golden Palm at Cannes and an Oscar for the screenplay. The movie where killers shoot people as casually as they eat hamburgers caused a veritable outbreak of "Tarantinomania," with several directors trying to copy that special Tarantino touch. There was a sudden rash of gangsters dropping cool wisecracks against a backdrop of as much bloodshed as possible and a shameless parade of quotations from other films. Tarantino's formidable knowledge of films didn't come from any university, but from his job in a video shop in Los Angeles. To pass the time, he wrote film scripts. After the unexpected success of his first movie *Reservoir Dogs* (1991), a gangster story about a bungled bank robbery, the scripts he had in his bottom drawer suddenly became very desirable: Oliver Stone bought the rights to *Natural Born Killers* (1994) and Tony Scott filmed *True Romance* (1993). After writing and starring in *From Dusk Till Dawn* (1996) Tarantino made the surprisingly calm *Jackie Brown* (1997), paying homage to the Blaxploitation cinema of the '70s. Things became crazier again with the two parts of *Kill Bill* (2003, 2004), doffing his cap to '70s kung fu movies among others, and the Nazi satire *Inglourious Basterds* (2009), which brought Christoph Waltz the Oscar for Best Supporting Actor.

chomped gets together to consider how to defend themselves against the monstrous vampires. Someone suggests crossing two sticks, as that was how Peter Cushing always defeated Dracula alias Christopher Lee. Jacob the ex-pastor doesn't think much of this idea: "Has anybody here read a real book about vampires, or are we just remembering what some movie said?" What makes this scene so comical is that the film figures find themselves in a grotesque nightmare situation and yet they consider their options and come up with rational arguments. Jacob talks with contempt about "some movie" – and is himself part of one.

Unfortunately most critics didn't think this far, however. They weren't happy with *From Dusk Till Dawn* at all, and it was almost universally written off as too bloody and too self-satisfied. They only thing about the movie was George Clooney. The role of the gangster Seth, who has to deal not only with the vampires but also with his sex-obsessed younger brother Richard (Quentin Tarantino) liberated Clooney from the operating theater of the TV series *ER* and smoothed his path to stardom on the silver screen.

NM

7

4 Santanico Pandemonium (Salma Hayek) bewitches the Titty Twister clientele with her erotic snake dance. To the horror of the Gecko brothers, she too turns into a bloodthirsty monster when the first drops of blood appear.

5 The vampires in the Titty Twister have little in common with Dracula-style bloodsuckers. Roberto Rodriguez based them on models from the mythological culture of the Aztecs.

6 George Clooney's screen career began with the role of Seth Gecko. Juliette Lewis plays Kate, daughter of Jacob the pastor, who is taken hostage by the Geckos along with her brother and father.

"Those who think that *From Dusk Till Dawn* is a fake horror movie, be warned. Rodriguez gives the viewer the real thing: the high art of tastelessness, pure unadulterated Punch and Judy." *epd Film*

7 The monsters in the Titty Twister come straight from the underworld. Tarantino originally wrote the screenplay for a special effects company, who give ample demonstration of their talents in the second half of the movie.

8 Seth pleads with the pastor Jacob Fuller (Harvey Keitel) to find his faith again, since the preacher had turned his back on God after the agonizing death of his wife. Now he is the final weapon in the battle against evil.

KOLYA 🏆

1996 – CZECH REPUBLIC / GREAT BRITAIN – 105 MIN. – TRAGICOMEDY
DIRECTOR JAN SVERAK (*1965)
SCREENPLAY ZDENEK SVERAK, based on an idea by PAVEL TAUSSIG; DIRECTOR OF PHOTOGRAPHY; VLADIMIR SMUTNY **EDITING** ALOIS FISÁREK **MUSIC** ONDREJ SOUKUP
PRODUCTION ERIC ABRAHAM, JAN SVERAK for PORTOBELLO PICTURES, BIOGRAF JAN SVERAK, PANDORA CINEMA, CESKA TELEVIZE, CINEMART
STARRING ZDENEK SVERAK (Frantisek Louka), ANDREJ CHALIMON (Kolya), LIBUSE SAFRANKOVA (Klara), STELLA ZAZVORKOVA (Frantisek's Mother), ONDREJ VETCHY (Mr. Broz), LADISLAV SMOLJAK (Mr. Houdek), IRENA LIVANOVA (Nadeshda), LILIYA MALKINA (Tamara), PETRA SPALKOVA (Pasa), NELLA BOUDOVA (Brozova)
ACADEMY AWARDS 1997 OSCAR for BEST FOREIGN LANGUAGE FILM

"You filthy little rascal, when are you going to grow up?"

A reverent string quartet fills the chapel, and the camera swings up over the musicians. Now we see a foot tapping in time to the beat, a sock full of holes, a beer bottle standing on the floor and a kettle that starts to boil. Louka (Zdenek Sverak), a cellist from Prague, and his three musician colleagues play funerals with singer Klara (Libuse Safrankova) to make ends meet. Louka once played in the Philharmonic Orchestra, but he was fired after he wrote obscenities in a survey conducted by the state security forces. Now he has given up any idea of political protest and as far as he's concerned, the country can go to the dogs in its own sweet time.

Louka lives from day to day, plays the occasional gig between funerals and works as a mason restoring inscriptions on gravestones. He is 55 years old, single, flirts with virtually every woman he meets, and is in debt to the funeral director Broz (Ondrej Vetchy). One day, Broz suggests an unusual deal:

Louka should marry his Russian niece Nadeshda (Irena Livanova) – in a marriage of convenience so that she gets a Czech passport. His reward: 40,000 Krone. Marriage, family, and above all children terrify the philanderer Louka, and he refuses in horror. But slowly the idea starts to grow on him. With 40,000 Krone, he could finally buy himself a car, replace the drainpipes at his mother's house, and still pay off most of his debts. Louka, the inveterate bachelor, finally gets hitched, and so begin the developments that plunge him into a series of catastrophes. Nadeshda immediately disappears to West Germany, leaving her son Kolya (Andrej Chalimon) with his grandmother who lives in Prague. The grandmother has a stroke and then dies in hospital, and suddenly Louka has to take care of his "stepson." The combination of the aging womanizer who only speaks Czech and the shy lonely five-year-old who only speaks Russian, both under the same roof looks like a recipe for

"Kolya and Louka. Two lonely souls, from two different generations, two races in a love-hate relationship, with two languages that refuse to understand one another despite being related, are suddenly forced to share life." *Zoom*

4

CZECH FILM AND THE WEST If Klara's face seems familiar to some viewers, that may be because Libuse Safrankova appeared in the classical fairy-tale movie *Three Nuts for Cinderella* (*Tři oříšky pro popelku*) way back in 1973. The West often thinks of Czech film primarily in terms of children's movies. Pan Tau, the innumerable fairy-tale adaptations, are well known all over the world but Czech cinema has a lot more than that to offer. *Kolya* was not the first Czech movie to win the foreign-language Oscar: in 1967, Jiri Menzel carried off the prize with *Closely Watched Trains* (*Ostře sledované vlaky*). Together with directors such as Vera Chytilova, Menzel symbolizes a Nouvelle Vague in Czech cinema. Milos Forman can also be included in this group – he is still the most famous Czech director, although he emigrated to Hollywood after making his first three films in his native land.

1 It's a long hard road before philandering bachelor Louka (Zdenek Sverak) and timid Kolya (Andrej Chalimon) finally come to trust each other.

2 "It's not hard to become a father: the only woman with whom Louka spends the night without their sleeping together leaves him a son." *Frankfurter Allgemeine Zeitung*

3 The age of Communism is over: Louka and Kolya at a demonstration during the Velvet Revolution.

4 Zdenek Sverak, who plays Louka, has been appearing on stage since the 1960s; he has acted in various films and written plays and filmscripts.

5 "Children rank among the oldest tricks in the book. They transform embittered loners into warmhearted family types, and even convicted atheists start to hope that something like mercy exists." *Süddeutsche Zeitung*

TRAINSPOTTING

Trainspotting

1996 – GREAT BRITAIN – 93 MIN. – DRAMA
DIRECTOR DANNY BOYLE (*1956)
SCREENPLAY JOHN HODGE, based on the novel of the same name by IRVINE WELSH
DIRECTOR OF PHOTOGRAPHY BRIAN TUFANO **EDITING** MASAHIRO HIRAKUBO **MUSIC** Various, including
IGGY POP, LOU REED, LEFTFIELD, NEW ORDER, BRIAN ENO, BLUR, UNDERWORLD
PRODUCTION ANDREW MACDONALD for FIGMENT FILM
STARRING EWAN MCGREGOR (Renton), EWEN BREMNER (Spud), JONNY LEE MILLER
(Sick Boy), ROBERT CARLYLE (Begbie), PETER MULLAN (Swanney), KELLY MACDONALD
(Diane), SUSAN VIDLER (Alison), KEVIN MCKIDD (Tommy), PAULINE LYNCH (Lizzy),
IRVINE WELSH (Mikey)

"And the reasons? There are no reasons, who needs reasons when you've got heroin."

Two youths run through the streets, the police hot on their heels. Offscreen, the voice of the protagonist debates the consequences of saying yes to "normal" life and concludes that heroin is a way of escaping from convention and banality. Danny Boyle's *Trainspotting* is one of the fastest-moving films of the 90s. To the sound of Iggy Pop's "Lust for Life," we see a rapid overview of the highlights of the lives of a group of youngsters. Mark Renton (Ewan McGregor), "Sick Boy" Simon (Jonny Lee Miller), "Spud" Daniel (Ewen Bremner), and Alison (Susan Vidler) – together with Dawn, the baby she has from one of the other three – all live together in a filthy, dilapidated apartment in a shabby neighborhood of Edinburgh. The main thing they have in common is their drug addiction. The course of their daily lives revolves solely around the quickest possible way of getting a fix of drugs, preferably without ever having to take on gainful employment.

From time to time almost all of them try to kick the habit and begin a normal life. Their other interests are not so different from those of other young people: football, the pub, sex. Sick Boy is a snobby James Bond fan who holds forth about Ursula Andress and considers her to be the definitive Bond girl. Robert Carlyle gives an astonishing performance as the universally feared psychopath Begbie and Ewan McGregor appears in one of his best roles to date.

The movie may be gruesome, but above all, it is funny. At its best, *Trainspotting* is reminiscent of the British films of Swinging London, where social reality was dosed with a generous dollop of surrealism. Renton, for example, dives into the lavatory in search of his drugs and finds them at the bottom of the sea. Instead of moralizing about the dangers of drug abuse, we are shown pictures of the joys of drug taking – and the price that has to be paid.

The friends' situation escalates when Dawn's baby dies as a result of drug-induced neglect. Renton and Spud are caught shoplifting and Spud goes to prison; Renton is allowed out on parole, takes one of his many guarantee

"Mainly due to the ambivalence in McGregor's face, you get the feeling that Mark wouldn't say no to a bit of feeling. But he's numb – he can't say yes and he can't say no." *Sight and Sound*

"last ever" shots and overdoses. At the hospital they just manage to save him, but his parents have had enough and they lock him up in his bedroom and force him to go cold turkey. Once he is clean he moves down to London and reinvents himself as a real estate agent. But his past catches up with him when Sick Boy and Begbie turn up. To get away from his friends for good, Renton eventually has to betray them.

Irvine Welsh's novel *Trainspotting* came out in 1992 and quickly became a runaway cult success. The English edition quoted the self-confident comment "Deserves to sell more copies than the Bible," by *Rebel Inc.*

The novel was crying out to be made into a movie – and that cry was heard by a team with a sure instinct for works with cult status: Danny Boyle (director), John Hodge (screenplay), Andrew Macdonald (production), and Brian Tufano (director of photography), who had had a global success with their black comedy *Shallow Grave* (1994) and were able to go one better with *Trainspotting*. The movie became the cinema event of 1996, the first Britpop film with a promotion campaign using posters designed to look like concert publicity.

OM

1 An antihero for the 1990s: The only thing Renton (Ewan McGregor) cares about is where his next fix is coming from.

2 The working classes run amok: Begbie (Robert Carlyle) is the psychopath of the group. He embodies everything that goes wrong in all the pubs on the island every Friday and Saturday night.

3 Renton is swallowed up by the primeval sludge of his fears and dreams. This is one of the most frequently referred to scenes in the film, and became a commonplace among cinema images of the 1990s.

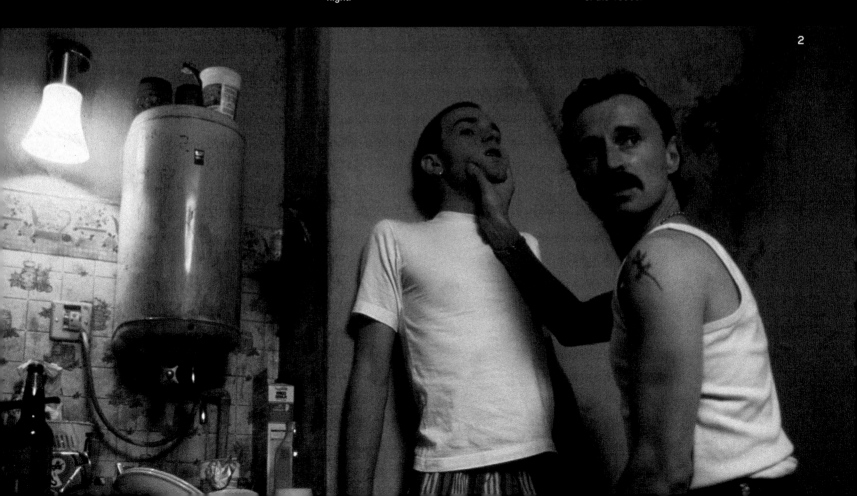

2

3

"[Sick Boy is] the chief trainspotter, with his encyclopedic riffs on the career and charisma of Sean Connery. Connery being Scotland's only superstar, what more apt than a Glasgow junkie high on movie junk to get off on earnest comparisons between *Dr. No* and *Thunderball*. This is siege-warfare iconolatry." *Film Comment*

"The book is exciting, funny and dangerous in a way that a severe heroin addict's life isn't. The book has the vibrancy which connects with why people take drugs. It blazes away with this sense of experiment and risk." Danny Boyle in *Sight and Sound*

DANNY BOYLE The English director (*1956) made his first films with his friends, scriptwriter John Hodge and producer Andrew Macdonald. Their debut *Shallow Grave* (1994) was an immediate success, followed by *Trainspotting* (1996), the black comedy *A Life Less Ordinary* (1998), and the adaptation of the bestselling novel *The Beach* (2000) starring Leonardo DiCaprio. After the horror movie *28 Days Later* (2002), Boyle again tackled a literary adaptation, which has proved his biggest hit to date: *Slumdog Millionaire* (2008), about the Indian version of the TV show *Who Wants to Be a Millionaire?* It won eight Oscars, one of which was Best Director for Boyle.

4 Renton at work: rarely has drug use been so casually portrayed as by Danny Boyle, who briefly became a superstar of European cinema thanks to this film.

5 Air of defiance: Renton is not only sickened by consumer society, but also by the status of his native country as a supposed colony of England.

6 Time for a change: Renton and his mates (Jonny Lee Miller, Kevin McKidd) take a trip to the country.

MARS ATTACKS!

996 – USA – 106 MIN. – SCIENCE FICTION, COMEDY
DIRECTOR TIM BURTON (*1958)
SCREENPLAY JONATHAN GEMS based on the TOPPS COMIC COLLECTOR'S CARDS 'MARS ATTACKS!" DIRECTOR OF PHOTOGRAPHY PETER SUSCHITZKY EDITING CHRIS LEBENZON
MUSIC DANNY ELFMAN PRODUCTION TIM BURTON, LARRY FRANCO for WARNER BROS.
STARRING JACK NICHOLSON (President James Dale / Art Land), GLENN CLOSE
(Marsha Dale), ANNETTE BENING (Barbara Land), PIERCE BROSNAN (Donald Kessler),
DANNY DEVITO (Gambler), MARTIN SHORT (Jerry Ross), NATALIE PORTMAN (Taffy),
ROD STEIGER (General Decker), SARAH JESSICA PARKER (Nathalie West), MICHAEL J. FOX
(Jason Stone), LUKAS HAAS (Richie Norris), SYLVIA SIDNEY (Grandmother)

"Nice Planet. We'll take it!"

A white dove of peace flies up into the air and is accidentally roasted by a stray shot from a laser gun. The Martians have landed! Unfortunately, things don't quite go the way earthlings had imagined. An enormous military contingent has traveled to the desert of Nevada, accompanied by hordes of media people, curious spectators, New Age disciples, and alien fans. It's a warm welcome from the blue planet to the little green men, who must have come in peace as they come from a more highly developed culture. But things don't quite work out as planned. The huge-brained creatures babble "dagg dagg dagg," open fire, and shoot wildly all around them. They take the reporter Nathalie (Sarah Jessica Parker) on board their spaceship and subject her to useless medical experiments. They then leave a path of destruction in their wake as they rampage through the world – Big Ben is reduced to rubble, the faces of the presidents on Mount Rushmore are shot off, and the sculptures on Easter Island tipped over.

For generations it was automatically assumed that beings from outer space would be belligerent warriors. At some point however, doubtless

inspired by the television series *Star Trek – The Next Generation* and its message of tolerance, we moved away from such one-sided images, and started believing that aliens would have peaceful intentions. Director Tim Burton laughs openly in the face of such intergalactic political correctness. His aliens were moved to undertake the long journey from Mars by their most base instincts. For them the Earth is just one big galactic fairground shooting range, they fire at everything that moves and have a great time in the process. At the same time, they cunningly stress their peaceful intentions.

The people they meet are however not necessarily loveable and well meaning either. The powerless president James Dale (Jack Nicholson) is desperate for some kind of success in foreign affairs and wants to take up diplomatic relations with the Martians – even after their first attacks. Dodgy property speculator Art Land (Nicholson again) scents new – green! – clients for his casinos. A white trash family who live in a trailer park only have one thought when the Martian invaders arrive: "They're not getting the TV!" Journalists want a sensation to sell, and the mad scientist Kessler (Pierce

MARTIAN ANATOMY

1 "Lisa Marie as a seven-foot-tall, blankly gum-chewing, bubble-coiffed, hip-swivelling, torpedo-breasted, alien-designed sex doll."
Sight and Sound

2 With true British style and without the faintest idea of what he's talking about, Dr. Kessler (Pierce Brosnan) explains all there is to know about the Martians.

3 "I'm not allowing that thing in my house." – The world is coming to an end, and the First Lady (Glenn Close, second from right) is worried about the carpet.

"The Martians gabble like geese, and the President is a lame duck, yet they still fail to find

"*Mars Attacks!* in particular arose from the certainty that it is itself an alien."

Tim Burton in *Süddeutsche Zeitung*

4 In keeping with the trash aesthetic of *Mars Attacks!*
   the Martians weapons look like toys. They're deadly
   all the same.

Brosnan) wants to show off his knowledge and skill although he hasn't a clue about the Martians or their motives. Ross (Martin Short), the president's spokesman is overcome by his animal instincts, and he allows a big-bosomed beauty into the White House (Lisa Marie, Vampira from *Ed Wood*) out of sheer lust, and thus opens the door for the invaders to the center of American power.

Burton only permits a tiny number of earthlings to come out of it with any credit: soul legend Tom Jones plays himself, a cool and stylish singer who directly after the end of the Martian invasion is allowed to sing "It's Not Unusual." Jim Brown plays the black boxer Byron Williams, who works in Las Vegas in a pharaoh costume. And last but not least, there is the deaf grandmother (Sylvia Sidney), who saves the world with appalling folk music, the yodel blues by Slim Whitman.

Once again, Burton gives us a loving adaptation of popular culture: *Mars Attacks!* is based on collector's cards from the chewing gum brand Topps. The original cards numbered 55 and went on the market in 1962 although they were withdrawn soon afterwards. Card titles such as "Crushed to Death" or "Destroying a Dog" make it easy to understand why.   HJK

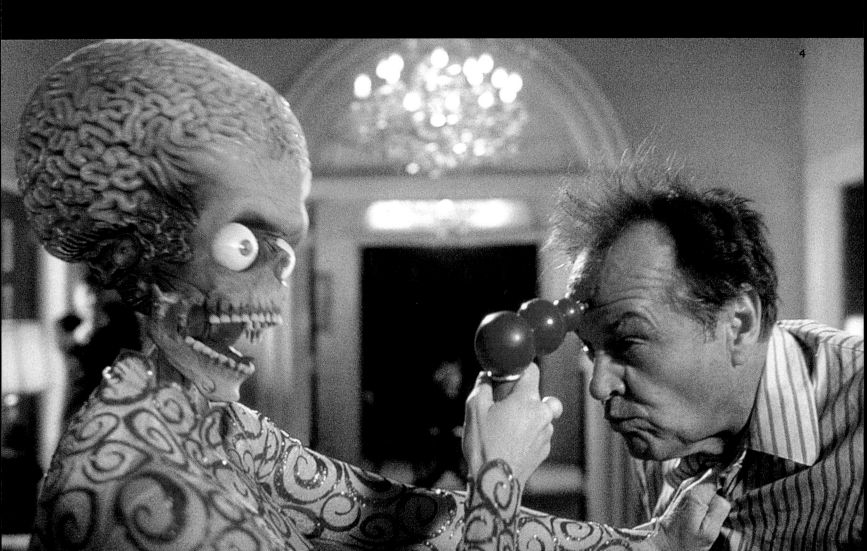

> **"Burton tells of a world that it no longer sure of itself and that therefore looks for meaning in the most stupid of things. However, 'daggdagg dag' simply means 'daggdagg dag.'"** *Süddeutsche Zeitung*

5 "Although *Mars Attacks!* often seems to parody *Independence Day*, it was actually longer in the production pipeline." *Sight and Sound*

6 The Martians not only use X-ray weapons, they can also see right through people's selfishness and delusions of grandeur (Danny DeVito).

TIM BURTON: FILMMAKER AND FILM CONNOISSEUR Journalist Nathalie's head, transplanted onto the body of her own Chihuahua, and the free-floating head of the scientist Kessler declare their undying love for each other – a moment that is pure Tim Burton. His films, from *Beetlejuice* (1988) and *Edward Scissorhands* (1990) to *Ed Wood* (1994) and *Big Fish* (2003), are fairy tales – mythical stories that show his love of fantastic genres (science fiction, classic horror movies) and the B movies of the '50s. Even the musical *Sweeney Todd: The Demon Barber of Fleet Street* (2007) is first and foremost a romantic Gothic chiller. Tim Burton cites as one of his role models the cartoonist Ray Harryhausen, who brings fencing skeletons and mythological creatures to life in single image animation. This stop-motion technique was actually what Burton wanted to use for the little green men in *Mars Attacks!* (1996). The process would have been too expensive, however, so he decided on computer animation instead. In 2010, Burton released his first 3D movie *Alice in Wonderland*, although it was "converted" in post-production rather than shot using 3D cameras. In the meantime, Burton's bizarre and ingenious fantasies have taken their place in the art world, as the MoMA in New York presented his work in 2009–10 in a major exhibition, including an extensive collection of drawings.

7   Highly advanced, particularly in the military domain: no terrestrial tank can withstand the Martians' "plastic weapons."

8   Voyeurs, hooligans, murderers – it was the Martians' baser instincts that brought them to Earth.

IMPRINT

Endpapers / Pages 1, 748–749 **LOST HIGHWAY** / David Lynch / SENATOR FILM / OCTOBER FILM; Pages 2–3, 6–17, 386–387 **THE SILENCE OF THE LAMBS** Jonathan Demme / COLUMBIA / TRI-STAR / ORION PICTURES.

Photographs: Filmbild Fundus Robert Fischer, München
ddp images, Hamburg (Pages 81–85, 511–515, 581–587, 741–747)
Heritage Auctions/HA.com (Pages 22, 30, 42, 46, 56, 62, 66, 76, 80, 92, 98, 110, 120, 124, 132, 138, 146, 150, 162, 168, 172, 176, 188, 192, 214, 218, 222, 228, 234, 254, 262, 268, 278, 284, 288, 292, 296, 304, 308, 316, 320, 324, 330, 334, 344, 354, 362, 372, 378, 394, 398, 402, 408, 414, 418, 424, 436, 448, 454, 458, 482, 490, 496, 506, 510, 526, 532, 538, 550, 562, 566, 582, 588, 594, 624, 630, 634, 644, 652, 666, 672, 680, 692, 702, 718, 722, 726, 730, 736)
The Kobal Collection, London/New York (Page 182)

Editorial Coordination: Martin Holz and Florian Kobler, Cologne
Technical Editing: Malte Hagener and Heinz-Jürgen Köhler, Hamburg
English Translation: Deborah Caroline Holmes, Vienna (Texts), Harriet Horsfield in association with First Edition Translations Ltd, Cambridge (Introduction), Katharine Hughes, Oxford (Captions)
Production: Ute Wachendorf, Cologne
Design: Sense/Net, Andy Disl und Birgit Eichwede, Cologne
www.sense-net.net

Texts: Ulrich von Berg (UB), Philipp Bühler (PB), Malte Hagener (MH), Steffen Haubner (SH), Jörn Hetebrügge (JH), Annette Kilzer (AK), Heinz-Jürgen Köhler (HJK), Steffen Lückehe (SL), Nils Meyer (NM), Olaf Möller (OM), Anne Pohl (APO), Burkhard Röwekamp (BR), Markus Stauff (MS), Rainer Vowe (RV), Christoph Ziener (CZ)

To stay informed about upcoming TASCHEN titles, please request our magazine at www.taschen.com/magazine or write to TASCHEN America, 6671 Sunset Boulevard, Los Angeles, CA 90028, USA; contact-us@taschen.com; Fax: +1-323-463-4442. We will be happy to send you a free copy of our magazine, which is filled with information about all of our books.

© 2012 TASCHEN GmbH
Hohenzollernring 53, D–50672 Köln
www.taschen.com

Printed in South Korea
ISBN 978-3-8365-3263-1